Palgrave Studies in Compromise after Conflict

Series Editor
John D. Brewer
Queen's University Belfast
Belfast, UK

This series aims to bring together in one series scholars from around the world who are researching the dynamics of post-conflict transformation in societies emerging from communal conflict and collective violence. The series welcomes studies of particular transitional societies emerging from conflict, comparative work that is cross-national, and theoretical and conceptual contributions that focus on some of the key processes in post-conflict transformation. The series is purposely interdisciplinary and addresses the range of issues involved in compromise, reconciliation and societal healing. It focuses on interpersonal and institutional questions, and the connections between them.

More information about this series at
http://www.palgrave.com/gp/series/14641

Cathy Bollaert

Reconciliation and Building a Sustainable Peace

Competing Worldviews in South Africa and Beyond

palgrave
macmillan

Cathy Bollaert
Ulster University
Belfast, UK

Palgrave Studies in Compromise after Conflict
ISBN 978-3-030-03654-6 ISBN 978-3-030-03655-3 (eBook)
https://doi.org/10.1007/978-3-030-03655-3

Library of Congress Control Number: 2018960497

Cover illustration: Greatstock/Alamy Stock Photo

This Palgrave Macmillan imprint is published by the registered company Springer Nature Switzerland AG
The registered company address is: Gewerbestrasse 11, 6330 Cham, Switzerland

To my parents

Acknowledgements

The seeds of this book were sown many years ago through countless stimulating discussions and debates with my family as we sought to make sense of the realities we lived and continue to live in. It is dedicated to my parents who provided endless support and keenly engaged me on various issues presented throughout the book.

I would like to thank all the participants in the study and those who opened doors for me making it possible to carry out the research. My special thanks go to Professor John Brewer (the editor of the book series) and Josephine Taylor from Palgrave Macmillan who made publishing this book possible. The content of this book was informed by my Ph.D. research with the Transitional Justice Institute, Ulster University. I will always remain indebted to my supervisors: Professor Brandon Hamber, Dr. Kris Brown and Professor Fionnuala Ni Aolain for their guidance, engagement and support throughout the research process. I want to give special thanks to Stanley McDowell for his help in proofreading the original script.

To my all family and friends living in Northern Ireland/the North of Ireland, England, Canada, Angola, Nigeria, Ghana, Switzerland, South Africa and other parts of the world whose friendship and love gave me the energy to keep going—a very special thank you (you know who you are)! I would especially like to thank James; your love, craic and continued presence keep me sane! I will always be grateful for the ways you have all stood by me.

Contents

Abbreviations

ANC	African National Congress
ANCWL	African National Congress Women's League
BEE	Black Economic Empowerment
COSATU	Congress of South African Trade Unions
CVE	Combatting Violent Extremism
DA	Democratic Alliance
EFF	Economic Freedom Fighters
GEAR	Growth, Employment and Redistribution strategy
ICC	International Criminal Court
ICTJ	International Center for Transitional Justice
IFP	Inkatha Freedom Party
KZN	KwaZulu-Natal
NDP	National Development Plan
NP	National Party
NUMSA	National Union of Metalworkers of South Africa
PSC	Protracted Social Conflict
SACP	South African Communist Party
TMT	Terror Management Theory
TRC	Truth and Reconciliation Commission

UDF	United Democratic Front
UK	United Kingdom
UN	United Nations

List of Figures

List of Tables

Series Editor's Introduction

Compromise is a much used but little understood term. There is a sense in which it describes a set of feelings (the so-called spirit of compromise) that involve reciprocity, representing the agreement to make mutual concessions towards each other from now on: no matter what we did to each other in the past, we will act towards each other in the future differently as set out in the agreement between us. The compromise settlement can be a spit and a handshake, much beloved in folklore, or a legally binding statute with hundreds of clauses.

As such, it is clear that compromise enters into conflict transformation at two distinct phases. The first is during the conflict resolution process itself, where compromise represents a willingness among parties to negotiate a peace agreement that represents a second-best preference in which they give up their first preference (victory) in order to cut a deal. A great deal of literature has been produced in Peace Studies and International Relations on the dynamics of the negotiation process and the institutional and governance structures necessary to consolidate the agreement afterwards. Just as important, however, is compromise in the second phase, when compromise is part of post-conflict reconstruction, in which protagonists come to learn to live together despite their former enmity and in face of the atrocities perpetrated during the conflict itself.

In the first phase, compromise describes reciprocal agreements between parties to the negotiations in order to make political concessions sufficient to end conflict; in the second phase, compromise involves victims and perpetrators developing ways of living together in which concessions are made as part of shared social life. The first is about compromises between political groups and the state in the process of statebuilding (or rebuilding) after the political upheavals of communal conflict; the second is about compromises between individuals and communities in the process of social healing after the cultural trauma provoked by the conflict.

This book series primarily concerns itself with the second process, the often messy and difficult job of reconciliation, restoration and repair in social and cultural relations following communal conflict. Communal conflicts and civil wars tend to suffer from the narcissism of minor differences, to coin Freud's phrase, leaving little to be split halfway and compromise on, and thus are usually especially bitter. The series therefore addresses itself to the meaning, manufacture and management of compromise in one of its most difficult settings. The book series is cross-national and cross-disciplinary, with attention paid to interpersonal reconciliation at the level of everyday life, as well as culturally between social groups, and the many sorts of institutional, interpersonal, psychological, sociological, anthropological and cultural factors that assist and inhibit societal healing in all post-conflict societies, historically and in the present. It focuses on what compromise means when people have to come to terms with past enmity and the memories of the conflict itself, and relate to former protagonists in ways that consolidate the wider political agreement.

This sort of focus has special resonance and significance for peace agreements are usually very fragile. Societies emerging out of conflict are subject to ongoing violence from spoiler groups who are reluctant to give up on first preferences, constant threats from the outbreak of renewed violence, institutional instability, weakened economies and a wealth of problems around transitional justice, memory, truth recovery and victimhood, among others. Not surprisingly therefore, reconciliation and healing in social and cultural relations are difficult to achieve, not least because interpersonal compromise between erstwhile enemies is difficult.

Lay discourse picks up on the ambivalent nature of compromise after conflict. It is talked about in common sense in one of two ways, in which compromise is either a virtue or a vice, taking its place among the angels or in Hades. One form of lay discourse likens concessions to former protagonists with the idea of restoration of broken relationships and societal and cultural reconciliation, in which there is a sense of becoming (or returning) to wholeness and completeness. The other form of lay discourse invokes ideas of appeasement, of being *compromised* by the concessions, which constitute a form of surrender and reproduce (or disguise) continued brokenness and division. People feel they continue to be beaten by the sticks which the concessions have allowed others to keep; with restoration, however, weapons are turned truly in ploughshares. Lay discourse suggests, therefore, that these are issues that the Palgrave Studies in Compromise after Conflict series must begin to problematise, so that the process of societal healing is better understood and can be assisted and facilitated by public policy and intervention.

This latest book in the series is by a young author and researcher who grapples with some of the key issues affecting peace, compromise and reconciliation, namely culture, identity and belief. It is a challenging and provocative book and takes its inspiration from this series as a whole, in the way the series seeks to rethink compromise and peace-building. The book throws out a challenge also to the way apartheid should be understood, which has profound implications for how we need to rethink intergroup relations in post-apartheid South Africa.

South Africa is an iconic case in the study of conflict transformation. The saintly figure of Mandela, the rhetoric of the 'rainbow nation' and its well-known Truth and Reconciliation Commission have combined with other events to almost universalise the mechanisms of its peace process. It is a society, however, where very little social transformation has accompanied its conflict transformation, and it is noteworthy now also for a whole series of travails and problems, from corruption, continued structural violence, widening inequality, high levels of anger and disillusion in second and third generation victims, and growing political instability. The attention Bollaert gives to South Africa's peace-building is thus timely.

The book isolates another critical aspect relevant to the series. Culture and identity are vitally important to the post-conflict process of learning to live together, and there are many examples of fragile peace processes that highlight how difficult it is to resolve differences in culture and identity. This difficulty is understandable in those cases of conflict where it was about culture and identity, where conflict was understood and experienced in terms of culture and identity or where intercultural and multi-identity formations constitute the chief forms of reconciliation.

The first provocative challenge that emerges from this volume is thus the attempt to assert the importance of what the author calls 'world-view' in mediating culture and identity. This is more than ideology and belief, for the notion of worldview is portrayed as more deep-seated and ontological—something rooted in culture and identity but going beyond them. In applying this to South Africa, the author formulates her second challenge. The interpretative framework of 'race' and class through which people have commonly understood apartheid and the problems it has left for post-apartheid South Africa is tested by using differences in people's worldview as the organising principle.

Three questions emerge from these challenges, and they help to define the distinctiveness of this volume. First, Bollaert asks whether differences in people's worldview shape and influence how they understand peace in South Africa. Second, she asks how deeply embedded are the new intergroup relations in post-apartheid South Africa, looking at whether peace has eroded old apartheid culture and identities. Third, Bollaert asks about the implications of this focus on worldview for our understanding of peace-building theory and practice.

These are interesting, challenging and important questions. The answers will be provocative but in as much as they do cause us to confront taken-for-granted ideas, the volume admirably suits the purposes of the series in encouraging us to rethink what peace means. This volume makes a valuable addition to the series, and as Series Editor, I warmly welcome it.

Belfast, UK
August 2018

John D. Brewer

1

Introduction: The Significance of Cultural Diversity on Peace-Building in Divided Societies

This book raises the question of identity and how different social groups make sense of the world around them. It is concerned with the implications that culture and competing interpretations of reality (worldviews) have on intergroup relations and building sustainable peace in deeply divided societies. The significance of this is well illustrated by the furore that erupted across South Africa following the public exhibition of a painting by a 'white' South African artist, Brett Murray in an art gallery in 2012. Expressing a strand of public perception relating to the numerous scandals surrounding Jacob Zuma, the former president of South Africa, it depicts the president in a Lenin-like posture with his genitals exposed. As well as the painting being vandalised shortly after it was displayed, strong opinions both for and against it were expressed in the media as per the following examples:

> It is a sad day for South Africa when creative production is being threatened with censorship from our ruling party…we support our artists' *freedom of speech and expression* and encourage them to show work that challenges the status quo, ignites dialogue and shifts consciousness. (emphasis mine, Burbidge 2012)

C. Bollaert, *Reconciliation and Building a Sustainable Peace*,
Palgrave Studies in Compromise after Conflict,
https://doi.org/10.1007/978-3-030-03655-3_1

> This man has insulted the entire nation and he deserves to be stoned to death. (May and Nagel 2012)

This was a fascinating debate to follow as it raised the question of why something one might have thought as an acceptable form of public commentary within the context of a democracy could provoke such an impassioned response. Due to the artist being 'white', and bearing in mind South Africa's racist past, many have interpreted this painting through a racial lens. However, to interpret it in this way is insufficient as it does not account for the way in which the conflicting views crossed racial boundaries, as indeed many 'whites' also took exception to it. Pointing to different systems of meaning-making (worldviews) at play, I would argue the furore was the result of an unintended but volatile clash of values: freedom of speech versus dignity and respect, fuelled by an unresolved Apartheid past.

In the Western worldview, there is a growing sense that talking about culture is politically incorrect. Indeed, the extremes to which British society avoids deeper engagement with the complexities surrounding culture is inferred in a list of 'racial micro-aggressions' that was disseminated by Oxford University's Equality and Diversity Unit (University of Oxford 2017). For example, it suggested that avoiding eye contact with someone was a form of racism. Not only does this trivialise a very serious and deep-rooted issue but it shows a complete lack of cultural understanding (in some cultures avoiding eye contact is a sign of respect) and is contributing to a social fear that by talking about culture one may be accused of racism, Islamophobia, xenophobia or perhaps even sectarianism. In a society that is driven by values of equality, the consequence is that the issue of culture has become the proverbial elephant in the room. Yet, the growing tensions and violence surrounding what has been dubbed the 'European migration crisis' underscores the fact that culture and worldview matters in fostering positive intergroup relations.

These illustrations raise a number of deeper questions that need to be probed. For example, it raises the question of identity and how different groups interpret and make sense of the world around them. It raises the question of social values and how groups prioritise certain values over others. It requires asking what happens when competing values and ways of interpreting reality collide and investigating what this means for reconciliation and social healing in societies emerging from conflict and violence. It also requires asking how one's process of meaning-making influences one's interpretation of peace and how cultural pluralism, and potentially competing worldviews, impact on building a lasting peace. Perhaps more importantly, what does this mean for how we undertake peace-building in deeply divided, multicultural societies? It is to this issue of intergroup communication in divided and culturally diverse transitional societies emerging from conflict this book seeks to contribute.

1.1 Book Rationale

In South Africa, the Truth and Reconciliation Commission (TRC) marked the country's transition from a long history of inequality and racism that reached its zenith during Apartheid, to a state of democracy in which majority rule and equal rights for all were recognised (Terreblanche 2002).[1] As embodied in Desmond Tutu's symbol of the Rainbow Nation, this was accompanied with the hope of national unity, social reconstruction, peace and reconciliation (Truth and Reconciliation Commission of South Africa 1998: vol. 1). However, since then, persistent economic inequality, intergroup conflict, racial and ethnic divisions, xenophobic violence and disputes around land redistribution are impeding national stability and the building of a sustainable peace. More recently this has been exacerbated by public displays of police brutality, such as the events that took place at Marikana,[2] bringing into question the full impact of police reform (Dixon 2013).

---

[1]The post-amble to South Africa's Interim Constitution [See Appendix 1] and the Promotion of National Unity and Reconciliation Act No. 34 of 1995 (Department of Justice and Constitutional Development 1995) provide the framework in which to understand the mandate and work of the TRC (Truth and Reconciliation Commission of South Africa 1998: vol. 1).

[2]In August 2012, 34 miners were killed when police opened fire during a strike at the Lonmin mine in Marikana. It was seen to be one of the worst incidents of police use of force since Apartheid (Amnesty International 2015; Davies 2015; South African History Online, n.d.).

Since the TRC, a number of policies (referred to as transitional policies) were implemented through which to facilitate the country's transition to democracy. These include, among others, affirmative action policies which were implemented to promote employment equity; Broad-Based Black Economic Empowerment which was developed as strategy to assist with the economic transformation of the country (from here on it shall be referred to simply as Black Economic Empowerment [BEE]); land reform processes aimed at increasing land ownership among 'black' South Africans; and other policies relating to housing, education, social welfare and health that were developed under the Reconstruction and Development Programme.[3] However, despite these efforts at redressing the wrongs of the past, almost 25 years since the birth of its democracy South Africa remains a deeply divided society largely on the basis of race.

The study is anchored in three interconnected concepts namely: identity, culture and worldview. Located within the constructivist school of thought identity is understood as the unit of survival that speaks to one's sense of survival, safety and belonging in the world (Arthur 2011a; Northrup 1989).

Culture is often understood by scholars as a shared system of meaning-making for making sense of the world and through which the behaviour and actions of others are interpreted (Geertz 1973; Ross 2007, 2009). However, this is sometimes referred to as a 'worldview' which underscores the complexity and the lack of conceptual clarity around these concepts. To distinguish between the notion of culture and worldview, in this book culture is understood as that which gives expression to a society's worldview which is embodied, among others, in its social institutions, organisations, social rules, values, symbols and rituals (Ross 2007, 2009; Avruch 1998). Worldview refers to the ontology and epistemology informing how one interprets one's social reality and 'truth' (Berger and Luckmann 1966; Goffman 1986;

[3]The RDP framework was later replaced by the Growth, Employment and Redistribution (GEAR) strategy, followed by the Accelerated and Shared Growth Initiative for South Africa, and most recently the National Development Plan (NDP). Nonetheless, many of the policies developed under the RDP framework are still relevant today.

Koltko-Rivera 2004). Moreover, it is what provides the social rules for how one engages with the world and it gives order to social priorities and values (Ross 2007, 2009; Clark 1989; Schwartz 1999; Atran 2010). Recognising that one's identity and process of meaning-making (worldview) are interconnected, this study seeks to apply a worldview lens to interpreting South Africa's intergroup conflict and understanding what is required for building a sustainable peace. Sustainable peace is understood to be concerned with the question of transforming conflicts to ensure a peace that will be both resilient and lasting (United Nations Security Council 2001). (These definitions are taken up again in Chapter 3.)

Against this backdrop, the book invites the reader to look beyond the normative interpretative frameworks of race and class for analysing intergroup conflict in South Africa. The difficulty with these interpretative frameworks is they are often based on fixed or primordial understandings of identity which act to reproduce race-based solutions to the conflict and reinforce a society that is divided along racial (and racist) lines. The book argues that worldview has a deeper reach than such normative interpretations and can provide a more nuanced analysis that opens the space to understand the values that are being defended and find new solutions that move beyond the traditional lines of the conflict. In so doing, more contextually and culturally appropriate peace-building interventions can be developed. However, by exploring the component of culture and worldview in intergroup conflict this book could be accused of cultural relativism or of justifying racist attitudes. However, to do so is to miss the point of applying a worldview lens to intergroup conflict and peace-building. Indeed, failing to acknowledge another way of being in the world could be considered another form of racism as it serves to reinforce the dominant 'white' and Western discourses.

To understand the significance of worldview on intergroup relations in South Africa one must recognise that for more than 300 years the social, economic and political life of South Africans developed in a context of escalating levels of segregation, inequality and racism and around disparate group identities, including the Dutch, British and indigenous populations, in conflict with one another.

This meant that until 1994 most South Africans would have had little or no contact and interaction with the 'other' except in the context of highly powered relations in which 'whites' were regarded as superior and 'blacks' inferior. Accepting that democracy can force one to encounter the 'other' as equals, with the transition to democracy South Africans were suddenly faced with negotiating new identities and new ways of relating to each other. Adding to the challenge of negotiating new identities is the emergence of new migrant communities. As the victims of xenophobic violence (BBC News 2015; Wicks 2015; News24.com 2015) this has also brought new challenges and dynamics to intergroup conflict. Nonetheless, with each group being informed by a different history, environment and set of experiences groups would have encountered the 'other' with different ways of perceiving and interpreting the world around them. The implications of encountering cultural diversity, complicated by the history of Apartheid, were not fully anticipated by the architects of the transition (Krog 2008a, b).

The South African case study points to the significance of identity and worldview in peace-building and transitional justice. To understand its significance it is important to define what is meant by peace-building and transitional justice. Broadly speaking, peace-building aims to prevent the occurrence, protraction or return to violence (UN 2001). As one of the pillars of peace-building, transitional justice 'seeks recognition for victims and promotion of possibilities for peace, reconciliation and democracy' (International Center for Transitional Justice 2009: 1).[4] Encompassing structural and relational approaches, both are concerned with the transformation of conflicts and reconciliation to ensure a peace that will be both resilient and lasting. However, within this discipline there is growing criticism for the tendency of Western approaches to peace-building and transitional justice to be reproduced and imposed into non-Western

[4]It should be noted that not all scholars agree to the inclusion of reconciliation into the goals of transitional justice arguing that it renders it too broad and diminishes its effectiveness (Roht-Arriaza and Mariezcurrena 2006: 2; Weinstein 2011; Olsen et al. 2010).

contexts (Huyse and Salter 2008; Palmer et al. 2015; Merry 2006; Sriram 2007, 2012; Kelsall 2009; Doe 2009). For example, Merry (2006) explains how concepts such as gender, violence and justice are deeply embedded in a societies system of beliefs (worldview) which, to be meaningful, she argues, need to be translated into the vernacular of the local context. This has led to increasing recognition by scholars that for peace-building initiatives to be sustainable they need to be tied into local values and take local sociocultural norms and practices into consideration (McEvoy 2007; McEvoy and McGregor 2008; Shaw and Waldorf 2010; Lundy and McGovern 2008; Mac Ginty 2014). These scholars are pointing to a lacuna within the field of peace-building and transitional justice relating to the nexus between identity, culture and worldview and the impact this has on intergroup relations and building a lasting peace in culturally diverse and divided societies (Arthur 2011b; Hamber 2012).

Recognising a myriad of factors, notwithstanding histories of oppression, power and persisting inequality and poverty, which all converge in acts of violence, this book is concerned with the cultural dimension in peace-building and reconciliation. It provides a valuable and needed contribution to how peace-building interventions can become more sustainable if tied into local values and embedded in a society's system of meaning-making. The book engages with questions relating to the extent to which transitional policies speak to individualist societies and the implications this might have for how they are implemented in collective societies with different values and forms of social organisation. It raises the question of cultural equality and transformation and whether or not this is something that needs to be addressed within peace-building theory. It argues that inculcating worldview into peace-building theory and practice is a vital part of restoring dignity and promoting healing among victims and formerly oppressed groups. This book, therefore, makes an important contribution to what is at best a partially researched topic by providing a deeper understanding of how worldview intersects with peace-building when seeking to build a sustainable peace in societies emerging from conflict.

1.2 Notes on Methodology

The research underpinning this book is located within a constructivist methodological paradigm which employed grounded theory as its strategy of inquiry (Charmaz 2008a, b). Using semi-structured interviews respondents were selected according to the following three key criteria:

1. Leaders (defined as an individual who, within their respective organisation, is managing others) between the ages of 30–45 years. This age bracket was selected on that the basis that they constitute South Africa's so-called transitional generation.[5]
2. Racial identity ('black', 'white', 'Indian' or 'coloured') in conjunction with one's ethnic group (Zulu, Xhosa, English-speaking white or Afrikaans) and/or national identity (migrants from other African countries).
3. The professional sector of the respondent work namely: business, political or religious.

Adding to the uniqueness of this study is the inclusion of migrant identities. Historically, South African studies have tended to research Apartheid related identities and migrant identities within two separate discourses. It is only more recently that they are being included within the South African identity discourse (Pattman and Khan 2007; Palmery et al. 2015). With the recent rise in xenophobic violence, this adds an additional identity dimension to the conflict and tensions in the country (Amisi et al. 2011).

[5]The term 'transitional generation' is based on Robert Mattes (2011) delineation of South African political generations; the premise being that one's politically formative years begin around the age of 16 years. From this, it was deduced that at the peak of the political violence when, in 1985, a state of emergency was declared, everybody within this age bracket would have been younger than 16 years of age. This means that while those at the upper end of the age spectrum would have had more awareness and memory of this period compared to those at the lower end, nobody would have reached their politically formative years. Consequently, persons within this age group would have experienced Apartheid only as children or young adults. Moreover, compared to the generation before them, they would have had limited experience of the struggle against Apartheid.

The constructivist paradigm underpinning this research recognises the researcher is a socially constructed being within a broader political and social context (Guba and Lincoln 1998). Even if unintended, this risks the researcher imposing their own worldview and beliefs about the nature of reality onto an inquiry which, in turn, risks compromising the credibility and trustworthiness of the research. Reflexive engagement provides a useful technique through which these risks can be mitigated (Smyth and Robinson 2001; Mruck and Mey 2007; Alvesson and Sköldberg 2009). Accepting the importance of reflexivity in researching divided societies, I will now provide a more detailed background into my own identity construction:

I come from a mixed heritage in which my father is third-generation South African but has ancestry in England and Belgium, and my mother is French speaking Swiss but grew up in Angola. After marrying they decided to settle in South Africa where I was born and completed my schooling and Bachelor of Science degree. However, despite this mixed heritage, by virtue of being 'white', attending English-speaking schools (as opposed to Afrikaans medium schools), and attending a 'white' Methodist church, socially I was seen as an English-speaking 'white' South African. It meant that I grew up in an environment protected by a sophisticated Apartheid architecture that controlled almost every aspect of life including the media, education, where we lived, and the standard of our living. While it meant that I enjoyed a relatively comfortable and privileged childhood it also meant being strongly influenced by 'white' thought. This is not what I chose or with which I necessarily identify but one that I must navigate nonetheless.

Although I grew up in a largely 'white' world, my upbringing was not typical of my 'white' peers. Due to my father's active engagement in the anti-Apartheid struggle this meant that as a child I had regular contact with 'black' South Africans. At the time I had no cognisance of the impact this would have in shaping my life choices and relations with the 'other'. Later, as I became more politically aware and cognisant of what my 'white' identity represented it became something I increasingly rejected and with which I have continued to grapple. Moreover, I became extremely disillusioned and critical of the 'white' (my) worldview for the way it taught us to interpret our reality. As an adult I have had multiple opportunities to live abroad in societies such as Northern Ireland, Sri Lanka, Ghana and England. As well as providing useful experiences through which to engage with my racial identity they also made me more aware of my gender identity. In the non-Western countries my gender, more than my race, seemed to define my professional experience.

Furthermore, with 'white' South Africa drawing its culture from Europe I would have been strongly influenced by a scientific and objectivist view of reality—this would have been entrenched by my scientific background. However, this training and upbringing was useful for understanding the worldview in which most 'whites' were raised. Together with my cross-cultural experience, which was useful for understanding a non-Western worldview, it has provided a strong background for analysing the findings produced in this book.

Finally, it is significant to note the research underpinning this book took place during the country's fifth democratic elections in 2014. There were a whole array of circumstances that contributed to the significance and expectancy surrounding this vote. Firstly, it was the first election following Mandela's death which created a sense of insecurity and uncertainty about the future of the country, particularly among 'white' South Africans. Secondly, it was the first election in which the 'born free' generation (people born after the end of Apartheid), as it is referred to locally, were eligible to vote. This created a high level of expectancy and hope surrounding the potential of these elections to bring much needed change to the country seen to be failing under the leadership of the ruling African National Congress (ANC). Unfortunately, the anticipated buy-in to the elections from the 'born-frees' proved disappointing as only 33% registered to vote (Schulz-Herzenburg 2014; Essa 2014). Thirdly, the announcement of Dr. Mamphele Ramphele being put forward as the Democratic Alliance's (DA)[6] presidential candidate had sparked a great sense of hope for the future of the country. The hope lay in the fact that she was a 'black' woman, extremely well educated with a remarkable history of business and leadership and opposed to the power bloc of the ANC. Giving her further credibility was her former relationship with

[6]Historically, the DA was a party for 'white' voters. Today it is the official opposition party. Despite its large 'black' voter base is still perceived to be the party for 'whites'.

Steve Biko and the Black Conscious Movement. Consequently, her candidacy was a symbol of transformation 'whites' could support and, based on anecdotal evidence, would support. However, within a week of the appointment she relinquished her position (Underhill 2014) which for many appeared to lead to a greater sense of hopelessness.

This sense of hopelessness and exasperation with the ANC was not limited to 'white' quarters as many 'black' South Africans were faced with the dilemma of whether they should continue voting for the party who had brought them liberation or if they should now place their vote elsewhere (McKaiser 2014). Elucidating on this McKaiser explains these dilemmas included, on the one hand, the growth of corruption under the ANC, the failure of the ANC to deliver services, the continued marginalisation of a large majority of the population, and the leadership crisis the ANC was facing. On the other hand, although the DA seemed effective in their running of municipalities, crucially, they did not appear to have a deep understanding of the past and the impact Apartheid had (and continues to have) on people. Furthermore, in the years preceding the elections fracture lines within the ANC were increasingly visible. In conjunction with the multiple corruption scandals surrounding the then president, Jacob Zuma and the ANC, and the rise of the Economic Freedom Fighters (EFF) lead by Julius Malema, there was a growing speculation surrounding the life expectancy of the ANC and the need for political change (Mashele and Qobo 2014). Together this indicates that South Africa's political landscape continues to be in a state of transition in which the dynamics of shifting identities need to be understood.

1.3 Terminology Employed

There are several points of clarification surrounding various terms that have been used in this book.

Firstly, this study has deliberately chosen to use the terms that were used to class ify each 'race' group during the Apartheid regime namely: 'black', 'white', 'Indian' and 'coloured'. Significantly, these are the terms that continue to be used officially in South Africa and which continue to shape much of the society. Further to this, the term 'black' usually refers to indigenous populations of African descent, such as the Zulu and Xhosa ethnic groups. However, it can also be used to encompass all the 'non-white' groups that were subjugated and disadvantaged under Apartheid among which there is a sense of solidarity. This definition was popularised with the anti-Apartheid movement for political reasons, however in reality many divisions exist. The usage of the term 'black' is usually determined by the context in which it is used. In this book, it will refer to indigenous populations, unless otherwise stated.

Secondly, it should be noted that there is shift taking place relating to how these terms are employed. Increasingly 'black' South Africans are being referred to as 'Africans' while the remaining 'race' identity groups continue to be referred to by their former Apartheid constructs. Subsequently, this has become a contested term reflecting the debates surrounding the question of who is an African or South African. The implications these terms have on the society are significant as inclusion in the 'African' group has greater benefit in the context of current policies aimed at economic redress, i.e. BEE and affirmative action policies. This has had strong implications on one's sense of belonging and participation in the country. For migrants coming from other African countries their exclusion from this term has contributed to their sense of marginalisation and to being victims of heinous acts of xenophobic violence. Due to its deeply contested nature, in this book I have refrained from referring to 'black' indigenous South Africans as 'Africans'.

Thirdly, the use of the term 'migrants' is used to denote those groups who have come from other African countries to South Africa as refugees, asylum seekers and/or for better economic opportunities. In the light of the xenophobic violence in South Africa, the term 'migrant' is a more inclusive term than the terms 'foreigner' or 'non-South African' depicts within the South African context. Although migrants to South Africa come from all parts of the world, in this book I am talking about migrants from the African continent.

Lastly, this leads to me to use of inverted commas when referring to the various race groups in South Africa. The reason is to acknowledge the delineation of humanity into separate 'races' as social constructs. With the 'white race' being constructed as the most superior and the 'black race' as the most inferior these constructs were used to justify the power hierarchies within the colonial conquest and the Apartheid system. Although these terms have become a deeply entrenched marker of identity, the purpose of using inverted commas throughout the book is to maintain cognisance of racial identities as socially engineered.

1.4 Structure of Book

Using South Africa as a case study, this book is concerned with the question of how culture and worldview shape one's interpretation of peace and the impact this has on sustainable peace and reconciliation in culturally diverse societies. It is structured around the argument that unless peace-building processes take worldview into consideration they risk contributing to the hardening of intergroup boundaries which can potentially lead to the use of lethal violence undermining the goal of building sustainable peace. The book is structured into seven additional chapters.

Chapter 2 contextualises the study within South Africa's identity landscape. While not dismissing the agency of racism in shaping contemporary South Africa, it interprets the rise of Apartheid through a worldview lens. This opens the analysis to move beyond race-based interpretations of the society, which are insufficient to account for much of the violence taking place in the society today. The chapter concludes by reviewing the current nature of intergroup relations in the society which continue to be interpreted using racial categories.

Chapter 3 deconstructs the anchoring concepts underpinning this research, namely sustainable peace, identity, culture and worldview, and examines how they intersect and relate to intergroup conflict. This forms the framework for interpreting different notions of peace in South Africa and understanding how worldview shapes intergroup relations.

Chapter 4 builds on the worldview framework developed in Chapter 3 by deconstructing the idealised forms of a Western liberal, nationalist and interconnected worldview (specifically the *ubuntu* worldview) that have shaped South African society. It demonstrates how different processes of meaning-making led to competing interpretations of South Africa's truth recovery process highlighting the inherent assumptions worldview brings to how peace-building and reconciliation is approached.

Chapter 5 is the first of three chapters based on the empirical research informing this book. By uncovering the dominant worldviews held by the respondents in the study, it develops a worldview lens through which the relationship between worldview and building a sustainable peace can be explored. This chapter raises questions about what worldview diversity means for how peace-building interventions are contextualised and the impact that different social values have on reconciliation.

Chapter 6 employs a worldview lens for exploring how peace is interpreted across the diverse groups in South Africa. Eleven core themes emerged which reflect the structural and relational components of building sustainable peace and which resonated with the different worldview attributes. The chapter shows that when a person's own interpretation of peace was not seen in the 'other' it reinforced existing stereotypes and contributed to the hardening of intergroup boundaries. Moreover, the chapter underscores the need for peace-building to accommodate different systems of meaning-making.

Chapter 7 engages with how transitional policies in the 'new' South Africa are shaping group identity. As a means of past redress, they were designed to promote equality across race, class and gender lines. However, what may be described as an unintended consequence, they also introduced new forms of inequality into the society. With South Africa continuing to be a landscape in a struggle over identity and belonging the chapter demonstrates the need for a deeper and more complex understanding of identity and culture to accompany the implementation of transitional policies in culturally diverse societies emerging from conflict.

Chapter 8 reviews the contributions and recommendations that the worldview model developed throughout the book makes to peace-building theory and practice. Using the insights gained from the South African case study, the chapter explores how worldview matters in other protracted conflicts and culturally diverse and divided societies.

References

Alvesson, Mats, and Kaj Skoldberg. 2009. *Reflexive methodology: New vistas for qualitiative research*. Thousand Oaks, CA, London, New Delhi, and Singapore: Sage.

Amisi, Baruti, Patrick Bond, Nokuthula Cele, and Trevor Ngwane. 2011. Xenophobia and civil society: Durban's structured social divisions. *Politikon: South African Journal of Political Studies* 38 (1): 59–83.

Amnesty International. 2015. South Africa: Suspend those behind the Marikana killings and subsequent cover-up. https://www.amnesty.org/en/latest/news/2015/08/south-africa-suspend-those-behind-the-marikana-killings-and-subsequent-cover-up/. Accessed 23 August 2018.

Arthur, Paige. 2011a. Introduction: Identities in transition. In *Identities in transition: Challenges for transitional justice in divided societies*, ed. Paige Arthur, 1–16. New York: Cambridge University Press.

Arthur, Paige. 2011b. *Identities in transition: Challenges for transitional justice in divided societies*. New York: Cambridge University Press.

Atran, Scott. 2010. *Talking to the enemy: Violent extremism, sacred values, and what it means to be human*. Bristol and New York: Allen Lane and HarperCollins.

Avruch, Kevin. 1998. *Culture and conflict resolution*. Washington, DC: United States Institute of Peace Press.

BBC News. 2015. Xenophobic violence: South Africa's identity crisis. *BBC*, May 7. http://www.bbc.co.uk/news/world-africa-32580807. Accessed 23 August 2018.

Berger, Peter L., and Thomas Luckmann. 1966. *The social construction of reality: A treatise in the sociology of knowledge*. London: Allen Lane.

Burbidge, Matthew. 2012. Gallery refuses to remove 'spear of the nation' artwork. *Mail & Guardian Online*, May 17. http://mg.co.za/article/2012-05-17-anc-irate-over-spear-of-the-nation-artwork. Accessed 23 August 2018.

Charmaz, Kathy. 2008a. Grounded theory. In *Qualitative psychology: A practical guide to research methods*, ed. Jonathan A. Smith, 81–110. London and Thousand Oaks: Sage.

Charmaz, Kathy. 2008b. Grounded theory in the 21st century: Applications for advancing social justice studies. In *Strategies of qualitative inquiry*, 3rd ed., ed. Norman K. Denzin and Yvonna S. Lincoln, 203–241. Thousand Oaks, CA: Sage.

Clark, Mary E. 1989. *Ariandne's thread: The search for new modes of thinking*. Hampshire and London: Macmillan.

Davies, Nick. 2015. The savage truth behind the Marikana massacre. *Mail & Guardian Online*, May 22. http://www.sahistory.org.za/article/marikana-massacre-16-august-2012. Accessed 23 August 2018.

Department of Justice and Constitutional Development. 1995. Promotion of National Unity and Reconciliation Act 34 of 1995. http://www.justice.gov.za/legislation/acts/1995-034.pdf. Accessed 23 August 2018.

Dixon, Bill. 2013. Marikana, social inequality and the relative autonomy of the police. *SA Crime Quarterly* 46: 5–11.

Doe, Samuel Gbaydee. 2009. Indigenizing post-conflict state reconstruction in Africa: A conceptual framework. *Africa Peace and Conflict Journal* 2 (1): 1–16.

Essa, Azad. 2014. Why aren't South Africa's born frees voting? *Al Jazeera*, May 7. http://www.aljazeera.com/indepth/features/2014/05/why-aren-south-africa-born-frees-voting-20145617536762389.html. Accessed 26 August 2018.

Geertz, Clifford. 1973. *The interpretation of cultures: Selected essays*. New York: Fontana Press.

Goffman, Erving. 1986. *Frame analysis: An essay on the organization of experience*. Boston: North Eastern University Press.

Guba, Egon G., and Yvonna S. Lincoln. 1998. Competing paradigms in qualitative research. In *The landscape of qualitative research: Theories and issues*, ed. Norman K. Denzin and Yvonna S. Lincoln, 195–220. Thousand Oaks, London, and New Delhi: Sage.

Hamber, Brandon. 2012. Transitional justice and intergroup conflict. In *Oxford handbook of intergroup conflict*, ed. Linda Tropp, 328–343. New York: Oxford University Press.

Huyse, Luc, and Mark Salter. 2008. *Traditional justice and reconciliation after violent conflict: Learning from African experiences*. Stockholm: International IDEA.

International Center for Transitional Justice. 2009. What is transitional justice? https://www.ictj.org/sites/default/files/ICTJ-Global-Transitional-Justice-2009-English.pdf. Accessed 23 August 2018.

Kelsall, Tim. 2009. *Culture under cross-examination: International justice and the special court for Sierra Leone*. New York: Cambridge University Press.

Koltko-Rivera, Mark E. 2004. The psychology of worldviews. *Review of General Psychology* 8 (1): 3–58.

Krog, Antjie. 2008a. '…if it means he gets his humanity back…': The worldview underpinning the South African Truth and Reconciliation Commission. *Journal of Multicultural Discourses* 3 (3): 204–220.

Krog, Antjie. 2008b. 'My heart is on my tongue': The untranslated self in a translated world. *Journal of Analytical Psychology* 53: 225–239.

Lundy, Patricia, and Mark Mcgovern. 2008. Whose justice? Rethinking transitional justice from the bottom up. *Journal of Law and Society* 35 (2): 265–292.

Mac Ginty, Roger. 2014. Everyday peace: Bottom-up and local agency in conflict-affected societies. *Security Dialogue* 45 (6): 548–564.

Mashele, Prince, and Mzukisi Qobo. 2014. *The fall of the ANC: What next?* Johannesburg: Picador Africa.

Mattes, Robert. 2011. The 'born frees': The prospects for generational change in post-Apartheid South Africa. Working Paper No. 131. Afrobarometer.

May, Jackie, and Andrea Nagel. 2012. Ban the spear, stone its maker. *Times Live*, May 22. http://www.timeslive.co.za/politics/2012/05/22/ban-the-spear-stone-its-maker. Accessed 23 August 2018.

McEvoy, Kieran. 2007. Beyond legalism: Towards a thicker understanding of transitional justice. *Journal of Law and Society* 4 (4): 411–440.

McEvoy, Kieran, and Lorna McGregor. 2008. *Transitional justice from below: Grassroots activism and the struggle for change*. Portland, OR: Hart.

McKaiser, Eusebius. 2014. *Could I vote DA?: A voter's dilemma*. Johannesburg: Bookstorm.

Merry, Sally Engle. 2006. *Human rights and gender violence: Translating international law into local justice*. Chicago and London: University of Chicago Press.

Mruck, Katja, and Gunter Mey. 2007. Grounded theory and reflexivity. In *The SAGE handbook of grounded theory*, ed. Antony Bryant and Kathy Charmaz, 515–538. Thousand Oaks, London, New Delhi, and Singapore: Sage.

News24.com. 2015. Thousands mob KwaMashu police as xenophobic attacks continue. *Mail & Guardian Online*, April 13. http://mg.co.za/article/2015-04-13-thousands-mob-kwamashu-police-as-xenophobic-attacks-continue. Accessed 23 August 2018.

Northrup, Terrell A. 1989. The dynamic of identity in personal and social conflict. In *Intractable conflicts and their transformation*, ed. Louis Kriesberg, Terrell A. Northrup, and Stuart J. Thorson, 68–76. New York: Syracuse University Press.

Olsen, Tricia D., Leigh A. Payne, and Andrew G. Reiter. 2010. *Transitional justice in the balance: Comparing processes, weighing efficacy*. Washington, DC: United Institute of Peace Press.

Palmer, Nicola, Briony Jones, and Julia Viebach. 2015. Introduction: Ways of knowing atrocity: A methodological enquiry into the formulation, implementation, and assessment of transitional justice. *Canadian Journal of Law and Society* 30 (2): 173–182.

Palmery, Ingrid, Brandon Hamber, and Lorena Núñez. 2015. *Healing and change in the city of gold: Case studies of coping and support in Johannesburg*. Switzerland: Springer.
Pattman, Rob, and Sultan Khan. 2007. *Undressing Durban: Beyond the tourist gaze*. Durban: Madiba Publishers.
Roht-Arriaza, Naomi, and Javier Mariezcurrena. 2006. *Transitional justice in the twenty-first century*. Cambridge: Cambridge University Press.
Ross, Marc Howard. 2007. *Cultural contestation in ethnic conflict*. Cambridge: Cambridge University Press.
Ross, Marc Howard. 2009. Cultural contestation and the symbolic landscape: Politics by other means? In *Culture and belonging in societies: Contestation and symbolic landscapes*, ed. Marc Howard Ross, 1–23. Philadelphia: University of Pennsylvania Press.
Schulz-Herzenberg, Collette. 2014. The influence of the social context on South African voters. *Journal of Southern African Studies* 40 (4): 839–859.
Schwartz, Shalom H. 1999. A theory of cultural values and some implications for work. *Applied Psychology* 48 (1): 23–47.
Shaw, Rosalind, and Lars Waldorf. 2010. Introduction: Localizing transitional justice. In *Localizing transitional justice: Interventions and priorities after mass violence*, ed. Rosalind Shaw and Lars Waldorf with Pierre Hazan, 3–26. Stanford: Stanford University Press.
Smyth, Marie, and Gillian Robinson. 2001. *Researching violently divided societies: Ethical and methodological issues*. New York: United Nations University Press.
Sriram, Chandra Lekha. 2007. Justice as peace? Liberal peacebuilding and strategies of transitional justice. *Global Society* 21 (4): 579–591.
Sriram, Chandra Lekha. 2012. Post-conflict justice and hybridity in peace-building: Resistance or cooptation? In *Hybrid forms of peace: From everyday agency to post-liberalism*, ed. Oliver P. Richmond and Audra Mitchell, 58–72. Basingstoke: Palgrave Macmillan.
Terreblanche, Sampie. 2002. *A history of inequality in South Africa: 1652–2002*. Pietermaritzburg: University of Natal Press.
Truth and Reconciliation Commission of South Africa. 1998. *Truth and Reconciliation Commission of South Africa Report, volume 1*. Cape Town: Juta.
Underhill, Glynnis. 2014. Ramphele and Zille's brief DA marriage over. *Mail & Guardian Online*, February 2. http://mg.co.za/article/2014-02-02-ramphele-and-zilles-da-marriage-over. Accessed 26 August 2018.
United Nations Security Council. 2001. *Statement by the President of the Security Council: Peace-building: Towards a comprehensive approach*. S/PRST/2001/5.

University of Oxford. 2017. Newsletter. http://www.admin.ox.ac.uk/media/global/wwwadminoxacuk/localsites/equalityanddiversity/documents/newsletter/Equality_&_Diversity_Newsletter_trinity17_web.pdf. Accessed 23 August 2018.

Weinstein, Harvey M. 2011. The myth of closure, the illusion of reconciliation: Final thoughts on five years as co-editor-in-chief. *International Journal of Transitional Justice* 5: 1–10.

Wicks, Jeff. 2015. Several dead as xenophobic violence boils over in Durban. *Mail & Guardian Online*, April 14. http://mg.co.za/article/2015-04-14-several-dead-as-xenophobic-violence-boils-over-in-durban. Accessed 23 August 2018.

2

The Rainbow Nation: Identity, Intergroup Relations and Worldviews in South Africa

This chapter explores the relationship between identity, worldview and interpretations of intergroup relations in South Africa. Accepting that one cannot interpret the nature of the conflict (and its solution) without talking about race, class and inequality, the chapter argues that these interpretations alone are insufficient and invites the reader to look deeper into the beliefs and worldviews that informed the policies that led to the system of Apartheid and that continue to shape the society today. The chapter begins by mapping out the influence that worldview and the belief systems in nineteenth-century Europe which acted as the power base in the formation of Apartheid and the entrenching of race-based identities. It then provides a brief overview of South Africa's transition to democracy and the formation of the new South Africa's 'Rainbow Nation' which includes a snapshot of the different identity groups represented in the book, namely 'black', 'white', 'Indian', 'coloured' and migrants. The chapter gives definition to key policies that were implemented to facilitate the transition including the Truth and Reconciliation Commission (TRC) and policies, such as Broad-Based Black Economic Empowerment (B-BBEE) aimed at economic redistribution. It concludes by reviewing the nature of intergroup relations

C. Bollaert, *Reconciliation and Building a Sustainable Peace*,
Palgrave Studies in Compromise after Conflict,
https://doi.org/10.1007/978-3-030-03655-3_2

in post-Apartheid South Africa which continue to be interpreted using racial categories; this is insufficient for understanding the dynamics at play.

2.1 Interpreting Apartheid

Apartheid was a system of governance introduced in South Africa in 1948 by the then ruling National Party (NP) which called for the separate development of people on the basis of race. It is generally interpreted from the perspective of race, class and inequality (referred to as normative interpretations of Apartheid). These normative interpretations led to the 'race-clas debate' which focused on the primacy of race or class in shaping Apartheid (Posel 1983; Louw 2004). Central to the debate was the question of how Apartheid and capitalist interests were related (Truth and Reconciliation Commission 1998b: vol. 4). Those who emphasised race argued that they were mutually incompatible and that Apartheid was primarily driven by racial prejudice (Dubow 1987, 1992; Van Zyl Slabbert 1975). Those emphasising class argued that Apartheid was primarily driven by economic interest which led to a racially based form of capitalism (Wolpe 1972, 1990; Legassick 1974; O'Meara 1975). Despite the binary nature of these debates, race and class are deeply intertwined and continue to be the dominant lens through which Apartheid and its impact on the society are interpreted.

There are also interpretations that emphasise the influence of the Cold War narrative on shaping Apartheid (Van der Merwe 1989; Du Toit 2000; Truth and Reconciliation Commission 1998a: vol. 1). During that period (1950s–1980s) Russian Communism was seen as a serious threat to Western democracy leading to nations aligning themselves accordingly. In South Africa, this translated into liberation movements, such as the African National Congress (ANC), colluding with Russia, and 'white' South Africa with the West. From this perspective, the fear of Communism controlling Southern Africa in conjunction with escalating violence from the ANC in the 1960s onwards is seen to have fuelled the large-scale military action by the 'white' Apartheid government on 'black' South Africans.

While these interpretations offer important insights into understanding Apartheid and cannot be ignored, they alone are insufficient. The influence of worldview in shaping Apartheid and, in particular, Afrikaans nationalism needs to be considered (Dubow 1987, 1992; Louw 2004; Giliomee 2003; Moodie 1975). To understand this interpretation, it is useful to refer to the three paradigm shifts which, Terreblanche (2002) explains, led to the hardening of intergroup boundaries and eventually to the policy of Apartheid. Within these shifts, one can also identify the influence of identity on Apartheid and on defining race-based identities that continue to shape South Africa's sociopolitical landscape.

The evolution of racism in South Africa began with the arrival of the Dutch at the Cape in 1652 (from which Afrikaans identity is largely derived). The colonisation of the Cape by the Dutch lasted about 150 years, after which it was conquered by the British (from which English-speaking 'white' identity originates). Significantly, this marked the start of the first paradigm shift which Terreblanche explains led to the first version of 'black' labour repression (1841–1874) and introduced a racially based form of capitalism in the agricultural sector. Integral to this was the creation of a 'black' working class which was achieved through strategies of direct rule that stripped 'black' Africans of their identity and way of life. In addition, to help meet the growing agricultural demands in the KwaZulu-Natal province, Indians (from which 'Indian' identity in South Africa can be traced) were shipped in as indentured labour (Ebrahim-Vally 2001).

It is important to understand that these events (and colonialism more broadly) did not just simply occur. They were shaped by the worldview and discourses taking placing in nineteenth-century Europe. One of these, on scientific racism, justified the deeply held belief that the 'white race' was superior to the 'black race' and supported the belief that 'black' African's were uncivilised barbarians. This narrative was used to defend the use of Africans as cheap, subservient labour, which was integral to sustaining the British capitalist agenda. Another discourse was the ideology of Social Darwinism which was used to justify the military conquest and economic exploitation by strong nations over weaker ones. Christian injunctions were also used to support beliefs in racial purity and fuel the fear of sexual relations between people from different race groups (Terreblanche 2002; Dubow 1987, 1992).[1] However, due to the shortage of European women at the time, allowances were made as it was cheaper than sending women aboard the ships (Hendricks 2001). It is from here the origins of 'coloured' identity are derived. Together, this complex system of beliefs and view of the world acted as the power base driving the formation of what ultimately became the Apartheid state.

The significance of one's belief system is also seen in the second paradigm shift towards the hardening of racial attitudes. This commenced with the abolishment of slavery by the British in 1833 which was deeply resented by the Dutch as, for them, it was ideologically and theologically impossible to place slaves on an equal footing as themselves. An extract from the diary of a Dutch women, Anna Steenkamp, reveals how it was 'contrary to the laws of God and natural distinctions of race and religion, so that it was intolerable for any decent Christian to bow down beneath such a yoke; wherefore we withdrew in order thus to preserve our doctrines in purity' (Bunting 1972: 35). Determined to restore right relations between the 'white' master and the 'black' servant, the Dutch began what is today known as the Great Trek in a quest to establish a territory independent of British rule. This was an important event as it entrenched in the minds of both the Africans and the Europeans the inferiority of the 'black' slave, and later all people of colour, and the superiority of the 'whites'. Furthermore, it resulted in the discovery of gold and diamonds, which Terreblanche explains onset a more aggressive form of 'black' labour repression, this time within the mining industry (1894–1972).

To give meaning to their experiences, De Gruchy and De Gruchy (2004) explain the Dutch (from which Afrikaans identity is derived) needed to transform their history into a sacred narrative that identified with the Biblical narrative of Israel and their liberation from Egypt and entry into the Promised Land. Such an interpretation of the world was fundamental to Afrikaans identity and self-understanding

[1]For a more in-depth discussion on Social Darwinism, refer to: Dickens (2000) and Jones (1980).

(Van Jaarsveld 1964). Indeed, De Klerk (1975) explains how the NP's rise to power in 1948 was rooted in this theological interpretation and how there was growing impetus to reconstruct South Africa within this Afrikaans worldview.

This system of meaning-making supported the growth of an aggressive Afrikaans Christian Nationalism and the third paradigm shift in the hardening of racial attitudes. This was fuelled by the fear of 'black' Africans becoming increasingly active in the political and economic life of the country. In what was seen as an effort to protect 'white' superiority and purity, several policies were adopted. Among these was the 1913 Land Act, which prohibited 'black' Africans from owning or renting land outside their designated reserves, and the policy of Apartheid which stated:

> That a policy of apartheid should be adopted in the mutual interests of the white and non-white population of South Africa...that it was the Christian duty of whites to act as guardians over the non-white races until such a time as they reached the level necessary to decide their own concerns; that in the interests of all races no further blood-mixture should take place; that the calling and duty of the white race in South Africa was to ensure that full control over all aspects of government in white areas should be retained in white hands. (Dubow 1987: 256–257)

The above excerpt shows how deeply Afrikaans Nationalism was infused with a complex system of beliefs associated with racism and Christian theological discourses relating to racial purity, superiority and the separation of nations (Moodie 1975; Dubow 1987, 1992; Terreblanche 2002). Through a massive social engineering project to protect the purity and supremacy of 'whites', the 1950 Population Registration Act was implemented. This consolidated South African identities classifying them along racial lines, namely 'white', 'black', 'coloured' and 'Indian'. Figure 2.1 is an extract of the classification certificate I (the author) was issued. Significantly, this strengthened the foundations for the justification of oppression, exploitation and humiliation of 'non-white' people (La Guma 1972). This act was further supported by the 1950 Group

REPUBLIEK VAN SUID-AFRIKA
REPUBLIC OF SOUTH AFRICA

Neem asseblief kennis dat –
Please note that –

VAN
SURNAME BOLLAERT

VOORNAME
FIRST NAMES CATHERINE ELIZABETH

IDENTITEITSNOMMER
IDENTITY NUMBER

gekassifiseer is
has been classified

AS A WHITE PERSON

vir die doeleindes van die Bevolkingsregistrasiewet, 1950
for the purposes of the Population Registration Act, 1950

OP LAS VAN DIE SEKRETARIS VAN BINNELANDSE SAKE
BY ORDER OF THE SECRETARY FOR THE INTERIOR

Fig. 2.1 Excerpt of the classification certificate issued to the author

Areas Act which designated separate land to the different racial groups.[2] For many, this meant being forcibly removed from their homes, families being broken up and bearing the associated trauma. Ultimately, one's racial category determined everything about an individual's life as one did not exist outside of it. It determined where and with whom one could live, work, own land, worship, marry, attend school and play sport. It also determined the quality of one's education, health care, access to water and electricity, and general standard of living. Further to this, Afrikaans was positioned as the language of superiority and power, English was considered a neutral language, and indigenous languages

[2] For a full list of the policies that were implemented, see Truth and Reconciliation Commission Report (1998a: vol. 1, 448–477).

were viewed as symbols of ignorance and illiteracy (Dlamini 2001). Overall, South Africa's long history of inequality and racism leads to race-based inequalities perceived as 'normal' within the society.

South Africa's project in social engineering resulted in 'white' South African identity being constructed on the basis of privilege, superiority and economic hegemony within the constructs of racially based power relations (Steyn 2001; Steyn and Foster 2008; Verwey and Quayle 2012). Afrikaner identity was largely constructed on the basis of language and ethnicity (Southern 2008; Verwey and Quayle 2012) and religion (Bornman and Appelgryn 1997). In conjunction with the ethnic nationalism it promoted and the collective identity it fostered, this distinguishes it from English-speaking 'white' identity which tends to prioritise the interests of the individual rather than the collective (Southern 2008; Lambert 2009). Significantly, individualism and collectivism are also attributes of worldview which will be further defined in Chapter 3. Further, distinguishing the two groups is their relationship to land. For Afrikaners, the possession of land provided the space in which an ethno-nationalist sense of belonging could be fostered and was deeply intertwined with sacred narratives that were used to make sense of their history of defeat under the British (Akenson 1992). For English-speaking 'whites', land ownership did not carry with it a sense of the scared but was associated more with the colonial conquest and serving the capitalist agenda (Lambert 2009). Both these interpretations of land differ from the way the ANC interpreted it under their policy of non-racialism, which embraced a more shared understanding of property ownership (ANC, n.d.). Due to beliefs in racial purity, for 'coloured' South Africans, the nation's history led to an identity associated with shame, rejection, marginalisation and hybridity (Adhikari 2004, 2006a, b; Petrus and Isaacs-Martin 2012). Finally, the way in which Western interpretations of reality and what it means to be fully human were imposed stripped 'black' South Africans of their dignity and constructed an identity on the basis of inferiority.

While one cannot interpret Apartheid (and its solution) without talking about race and class, this discussion underscores the significance of worldview and deeper systems of meaning-making in its formation. The discussion also points to a bias in the literature in terms of how Apartheid has been interpreted which emphasises European and Afrikaans Nationalist discourses but fails to bring into account African and indigenous interpretations on issues such as land, identity and religion. In doing so, these interpretative frameworks continue to promote mainstream Western thought at the same time marginalising the voice of the 'other'. While the scope of this book does not permit incorporating African and indigenous interpretations of Apartheid, the significance of these voices for peace-building in culturally plural societies in transition is, nonetheless, recognised.

2.2 The Rainbow Nation: South Africa's Transition to Democracy

Following a series of negotiations in the early 1990s, Apartheid was formerly dismantled. This was marked by the first democratic elections held in 1994 in which the ANC came into power supported by its alliance with the Congress of South African Trade Unions (COSATU) and the South African Communist Party (SACP). Central to South Africa's transition was a range of policies aimed at promoting reconciliation and building a new and democratic society. The most prominent of these was the establishment of the TRC as mandated by the Government of National Unity and set out within the Promotion of National Unity and Reconciliation Act, No. 34 of 1995 (Department of Justice and Constitutional Development 1995).

Supporting South Africa's transition was the ideal of 'non-racialism' which meant that citizenship would no longer be tied to race (Du Toit 2000). However, within this nation-building discourse there were two competing schools of thought. The first, which defined ANC politics during the time of the transition, was the most prominent. It supported a non-racial South African nationalism that would unite the country under a common South African identity rather than a racial or ethnic identity (Adam 1994; Isaacs-Martin 2012; Ramsamy 2007). It was believed that this was what was required to overcome racism and build a non-racial and democratic society. However, the second, whose supporters were known as 'ethnic realists', argued against this position stating that non-racialism was unrealistic as it would not be able to deal with historic injustices (Horowitz 1991; O'Malley 1994). Furthermore, such an ideal leaves little room for competing values which, from a worldview perspective, is significant. For example, while national pride is important for all groups, research shows it is experienced differently across the social groups; 'black' groups expressed the highest level of national pride and placed the greatest importance on national symbols while 'white' groups placed the least importance on them (Bornman 2006). Chapters 5–7 show how differences in the way values are prioritised across groups can contribute to hardening intergroup boundaries.

Later, locating itself within the ethnic realist school of thought, the ANC shifted its position from non-racialism to multiculturalism under the imagery of the 'Rainbow Nation'; a term coined by Desmond Tutu (1999). It served as a vision for national identity that united South Africans under one rubric while at the same time recognising the racial diversity of the nation (Wilson 2001; Bornman 2006; Ramsamy 2007). In the early years of South Africa's transition, the Rainbow Nation became a strong symbol of national pride which was seen as integral to the stability of the nation (Isaacs-Martin 2012). Indeed, the 'proudly South African' narrative captured the imagination and inspired hope in the future of the country.

While Tutu's image of the rainbow supports the arguments made by the ethnic realists, it also espouses many of the ideals of unity and equality that are captured within the objectives of non-racialism. This makes it worth considering why the ANC shifted its position and embraced the metaphor of the Rainbow Nation. An ideal of non-racialism makes it impossible to have any distinction between races which, as the ethnic realists point out, is unrealistic. However, multiculturalism opens the door to racial differences. From a positive perspective, it is more accommodating of diverse identities which Ramsamy (2007) argues was instrumental in making outside groups, such as 'Indians' and 'coloureds', more secure in the new dispensation. In addition, it provides the space for race-based, affirmative action policies to be introduced as a means of addressing past wrongs. However, these policies have become extremely controversial as they are seen to be discriminatory and only benefitting a 'black' minority (Ansell 2004; Gilroy 2000; Durrheim et al. 2011). Thus, interpreting multiculturalism from a more negative perspective brings into question the ANC's loyalties and commitment to nation-building.

The way in which the TRC interpreted the metaphor of the Rainbow Nation has been criticised by several scholars on the basis that it sought to create a new identity using the language of the nation as body in need of healing (Wilson 2001). Whether or not nations can be healed in the same way individuals can be has been the subject of strong critique (Ignatieff 1998; Hamber 2002). In doing so, critics argue that it created a victim identity that both failed to hold perpetrators and beneficiaries accountable for the wrongs of the past and failed to engage with the issue of race (Valji 2004; Mamdani 2000). Significantly, it also points to competing visions of what was meant by reconciliation (Wilson 2001; Hamber 2002). The metaphor of the Rainbow tended to support the cathartic and more inter-relational aspects of reconciliation whereas critics of this position tended to interpret the proceedings from a more legal perspective which prioritised the protection of human rights as basis on which to build a new society. These tensions have led to vast body of literature critiquing the proceedings and outcomes of the TRC (Asmal et al. 1996; Asmal 2000; Norval 1998; Boraine 2000; Borer 2004; Gibson 2004; Hay 1999; Hayner 2001; Mamdani 2000; Van Zyl 1999; Hamber 2002). However, the extent to which these competing views relate to worldview and one's interpretation of reality remains largely unexplored. Recognising the implications this on how peace-building is approached, Chapter 4 will further examine the relationship between worldview and how the TRC was interpreted.

Further to this, several symbolic actions directed towards building a non-racial and inclusive nation with a new identity were also implemented (Du Toit 2000; Mac Ginty 2001). Among these were the inauguration of a new South African flag and national anthem, and the decision that statues representing Apartheid and the colonial past would be allowed to remain. The renaming of airports, sports stadiums and other public spaces also formed part of this agenda and has largely been accepted by the society. However, the renaming of the cities and, in particular, roads has been far more contested.

A number of policies aimed at improving socio-economic opportunities for the previously disadvantaged groups were also implemented. Among these were:

- The Reconstruction and Development Plan (RDP) which was implemented during Mandela's term as president. This was a strategy aimed at alleviating poverty and promoting economic growth and development. With a strong social focus, it included addressing issues such as the lack of housing, access to electricity and clean water, land reform and health care. It also established a strong welfare system.
- The Growth, Employment and Redistribution strategy (GEAR) which was a macroeconomic strategy aimed at stimulating economic growth replaced the RDP, although some of the social aspects (such as the housing development programme) remained. GEAR was implemented under the Mbeki administration in 1996 and included initiatives aimed at job creation and private investment. The policy generated widespread criticism and debate as to why the ANC was shifting from its socialist agenda to neoliberal policies (Marais 2001).
- The National Development Plan (NDP), which was most recently adopted (2013) under the Zuma administration, is a long-term socio-economic strategy which sets out a roadmap for alleviating poverty and reducing unemployment and inequality by 2030.
- Affirmative action policies which were implemented as a means of preventing discrimination and promoting equal opportunities in education, employment, as well as in the sports sector.
- B-BBEE policies were implemented as an additional mechanism through which to prevent discrimination and to redistribute wealth. Commonly referred to as Black Economic Empowerment (BEE), it requires businesses to obtain a BEE score that assesses the extent to which a company has contributed to integrating previously disadvantaged groups into the economy. It carries with it incentives for trade.
- Policies that relate to land restitution and land redistribution which are aimed at increasing the area of land owned by 'blacks' were also implemented.

These policies, among others, were implemented with the intention of facilitating South Africa's transition to democracy and promoting reconciliation under the policy of non-racialism and later the rubric of the Rainbow Nation. However, despite the unifying narratives birthed within South Africa's transitional period, the country continues to be characterised by its Apartheid-based identities and competing claims to identity.

Among 'whites' the political and social changes in South Africa have resulted in a variety of responses seeking to interpret and make sense of their new reality. While these have been generally positive, transformative and anti-racist, others have been extremely reactionary and resistant (Steyn 2001). However, studies indicate that racial prejudices are often couched in the language of class and culture (Durrheim and Dixon 2005; Bhana and Pattman 2010). This is contributing to a growing understanding of 'white' identity more as a cultural construct than a racial one (Seekings 2008; Steingo 2005). The political changes also led to the mass emigration of 'white' South Africans, known as the 'brain drain', which resulted in a 16% decrease in the country's 'white' population (Andrucki 2010). This illustrates the way in which 'white' South Africans, and, in particular, English-speaking 'whites' have maintained links and a cultural affinity to their Western countries of origin (Lambert 2009; Bornman 2010, 2011; Andrucki 2010). Lambert (2009) argues this is one of the features that distinguish English-speaking 'whites' from Afrikaners. The latter had cut all ties with Europe and interpreted being a real South African within the constructs of Afrikaner nationalism. Thus, implied within this association with Britain and Europe more generally is disloyalty to South Africa. For Afrikaners, the failure and collapse of Apartheid resulted in a crisis of identity and what it means to be Afrikaans and African (Steyn 2004; Verwey and Quayle 2012). Nonetheless, being reminded that South Africa's Apartheid past left the majority of 'blacks' formally undereducated, while most 'whites' received a superior education, the sudden 'white flight' meant a loss of skills for the country and a vacuum which needs to be filled.

These responses have largely been interpreted through the lens of hegemonic race and class relations, and the loss of exclusive power. However, Andrucki (2010: 360) offers a slightly different interpretation when he argues that 'white' identity is constructed along the lines of 'material accomplishment'. This would help account for the way in which many 'whites' have withdrawn from mainstream society and immersed themselves in the world of business and sporting success (Lambert 2009). With 'material accomplishment' defined as an attribute of worldview (see Chapter 3), this interpretation extends beyond race and class for interpreting 'white' identity and opens the door to interpreting identity through the deeper structures of meaning-making.

For 'black' South Africans, the transition has meant gaining political power. Significantly, it has also contributed to asserting an African identity (in contrast to a Western identity) which was first driven by Mbeki's re-imagining of the African renaissance (Mpama 2007; Bornman 2010). In addition, the establishment of ethnic identity, which is linked to language, culture, history and place of birth, has also become an integral component of 'black' identity (Dlamini 1998, 2005). However, the transition has also led to some complex changes within 'black' identity including the growth of a 'black' middle class alongside a persistently impoverished 'black' majority and an internal struggle within 'black' identity as its members negotiate their new reality. It has introduced new fracture lines between 'blacks' seen to be privileged and 'blacks' who continue to live in poverty (Mpama 2007). Moreover, it has introduced a new intergroup dynamic to the extent that 'whites' are used by 'blacks' as a benchmark against which to measure themselves and 'whites' who delineated between what they refer to as westernised 'blacks' who are more fluent in English (and likely to speak in an English accent) and more traditional blacks (Durrheim and Mtose 2006). This has led to these groups being labelled 'white-blacks' and 'black-blacks', respectively, with the former perceived as more acceptable to 'whites' and more prestigious for 'blacks' (Durrheim and Mtose 2006; Mckinney 2007). It has also contributed to divisions within 'black' identity where 'white-blacks' and those who adopt English as their primary language are no longer perceived to be real Africans. The emergence of these hybrid identities and changes in identity from traditional to Western is significant. As well as pointing to the shifting and constructed nature of identities, it also challenges the way in which identity is often depicted in binary terms when seeking solutions to conflict.

Since the transition, 'Indian' identity continues to be strongly linked to India, as well as Sri Lanka. This is largely achieved by integrating aspects of Bollywood into 'Indian' arts and culture (Boshoff 2011). This affiliation to their country of origin, while resembling that of English-speaking 'whites', is different in that many 'whites' maintain their bond to the UK through a British citizenship. However, 'Indian' identity is also strongly driven by a need to assert a South African identity and gain a sense of belonging in the country. Scholars argue that this has been strongly influenced by the economic exclusion experienced by members of this group as a result of the country's BEE and affirmative action policies which threaten the 'Indian' sense of belonging (Vahed and Desai 2010; Radhakrishnan 2005). Despite these policies being aimed at all 'non-white' groups who were previously disadvantaged under the old regime, increasing emphasis is being given to 'blacks' as indigenous African groups and not as the broader construct of all previously subjugated groups (Ramsamy 2007; Moodley and Adam 2000). This raises the hotly contested question of identity and belonging in South Africa. Consequently, one of the key identity challenges for Indians in the new South Africa is to be recognised as equal participants and citizens (Radhakrishnan 2005).

As with the 'Indian' group, there is also a general sense among 'coloureds' of not being any better off in the new political dispensation (Adhikari 2006a; Petrus and Isaacs-Martin 2012). Similarly, this is attributed largely to the effect of affirmative action and BEE policies which has led to a common expression among 'coloureds' of previously not being 'white' enough and now not 'black' enough (Erasmus 2001; Hammett 2010; Adhikari 2004). This underpins a dichotomy within 'coloured' identity which is divided between 'blackness' and 'whiteness'. Some 'coloured' groups tend to associate more with 'black' South African culture and speak local indigenous languages such as isiZulu and isiXhosa, but the majority associate more closely with 'white' culture and mostly speak Afrikaans and to a lesser extent English. Thus, while 'coloured' identity continues to be associated with confusion and controversy as to what it means, it is increasingly being associated as a symbol of freedom and choice in terms of how and with whom the identity is expressed (Petrus and Isaacs-Martin 2012; Adhikari 2006a, b; Hammett 2010).

Referred to as new communities, African migrants to South Africa come from many different countries including Angola, Burundi, Cameroon, Republic of the Congo, Democratic Republic of the Congo, Ethiopia, Ghana, Kenya, Lesotho, Malawi, Nigeria, Somalia, Zambia and Zimbabwe. Despite this diversity, they are increasingly being combined by South Africans into one generic group. Notwithstanding, the experience of migrant groups in South Africa is decidedly different from that of the other South African identities. Excluded from any of the affirmative action policies, with limited access to government support, and faced with the real threat of xenophobic violence they are in many regards the new victims within South African society. Furthermore, pointing to South African notions of superiority over other Africans, migrants are often referred to as '*makwerekwere*' which is a slang and derogatory term for foreigners, specifically those of African origin (Matsinhe 2011).

This snapshot on identities in South Africa highlights the failures of non-racialism and nation-building to do away with the socially constructed nature of identity. Pointing to a tension in relation to the goals of transitional justice, reconciliation and nation-building, it could be argued that a policy of multiculturalism has served to entrench Apartheid-based identities. It also raises the question of how transitional justice and policies implemented to address the past impact on identity, belonging and nation-building more generally. Taking this further, Chapter 7 investigates how transitional policies have shaped identity in South Africa and, in turn, one's interpretation of peace.

2.3 The End of the Rainbow? Intergroup Relations in the 'New' South Africa

Despite the way in which the metaphor of the Rainbow Nation inspired South Africa towards a non-racial citizenship while recognising the early emergence of a class-based society, 'race' continues to be a salient marker of identity (Pattman 2007; Seekings 2008; Hammett 2010;

Bornman 2011; Isaacs-Martin 2012). Contributing to this was a shift that took place from the Mandela administration in which non-racialism, unity and reconciliation were promoted, to the Mbeki administration which saw a return to a more race-based rhetoric and understanding of nation-building in the new South Africa. In a speech delivered to Parliament, Mbeki refers to South Africa as:

> [A] country of two nations...One...is white, relatively prosperous, regardless of gender or geographic dispersal...The second and larger nation of South Africa is black and poor. (Mbeki 1998)

In doing so, Louw (2004) argues that Mbeki reduced the problem in South Africa to a problem of 'race' and 'white' greed. Furthermore, he asserts this served a number of interests including those of the 'black' elite and its 'white' big business allies; being able to use 'race' as a means of protection against criticisms that are levelled against the ANC by 'white' opposition parties and feeding the hope for access to wealth among 'black' South Africans who continue to live in relative poverty.

Policies aimed at economic redress have also had an influence on intergroup relations. Firstly, they have been linked to the issue of participation and inclusion in the country and the question of who is an African (Verwey and Quayle 2012). Initially, they were structured around the former Apartheid-based categories, i.e. 'black' 'coloured', 'Indian' and 'white'. However, more recently the 'black' category was substituted for the term 'African'. As Verwey and Quayle (2012: 555–556) assert, this defines 'who belongs, who deserves access to resources, and the fairness of structural redress such as affirmative action'. Despite the 'black', 'Indian' and 'coloured' groups all being disadvantaged under Apartheid, these policies are seen to be making 'African' a privileged class (Seekings 2008). However, this construct only refers to 'black' South African and excludes Africans from other African countries. Consequently, not only are these policies entrenching race-based identities, they are also contributing to a feeling of continued marginalisation among the 'Indian' and 'coloured' population and hostilities between these groups and 'black' South Africans. Coupled with the failure of the current government to redistribute wealth, alleviate poverty and reduce inequality, it has also resulted in resentment being expressed towards migrants and the escalation of xenophobic violence (Reilly 2001).

Secondly, these policies are seen to be contributing to new subtle forms of racism (Durrheim and Mtose 2006; Bornman 2011; Durrheim et al. 2011). The theory of 'subtle racism' argues that as 'blacks' are no longer being discriminated against, their lack of progress can be accounted for by their personal incompetence and weakness (Bornman 2011: 731). Those in opposition to the policies see them as promoting the employment of less competent personnel and, thereby, causing a drop in standards across the nation. Moreover, they see them as discriminating against 'whites' and promoting a reverse form of racism which supports a growing victim identity among the 'white' population.

Overall, these policies are contributing to making South Africans more 'race' conscious. At every level of opportunity, be it in relation to admission into education or sports teams, or in gaining access to social allowances or employment opportunities, one is required to identify with a particular race category (Maré 2001). Although public and social spaces such as restaurants, nightclubs and beaches are no longer designated as such by law, they have, however, assumed racial identities (Durrheim and Dixon 2005; Misgun and Oakes 2007; Moodley 2007). Often racist stereotypes are based on issues such as cleanliness and security or in both examples the lack of it (Pattman and Khan 2007). For example, among 'whites' going to a 'white' beach is justified on the basis of being cleaner and safer. Although there are some studies to suggest intergroup relations and attitudes towards the 'other' in the new South Africa are improving, contact between groups remains limited with mistrust, suspicion and tensions between groups persisting (Bornman 2011; Durrheim et al. 2011; Gibson and Claassen 2010). In conjunction with persisting levels of poverty, inequality, growing incidences of crime and violence, and endemic corruption, the stability of the country is being eroded (Boraine 2014; Mashele and Qobo 2014).

2.4 Conclusion

South Africa is experiencing a number of key socio-economic challenges including poverty, unemployment and inequality which are referred to as the 'triple challenge' (National Planning Commission 2012). In terms of income inequality, South Africa ranks 116 out of 186 countries and has a Gini coefficient of 65 (United Nations Development Programme 2015: 217). This makes it one of the most economically unequal societies in which to live. It also has a high unemployment rate of almost 27% (Statistics South Africa 2018). Competition for resources, including competition for power and material resources, fuelled by histories of racism, oppression and inequality, have contributed to intergroup conflict in South Africa. Indeed, these are crucial factors that cannot be ignored when considering approaches to conflict transformation and building a sustainable peace.

However, as this chapter seeks to show, competing worldviews played a significant role in South Africa's history inequality which reached its zenith through Apartheid. Indeed, these worldviews were inextricably linked to identity and competition for resources. Despite this, normative interpretative frameworks, which exclude engaging with the deeper systems of meaning-making, continue to be applied to intergroup conflict in the society. Alone, these are insufficient and arguably contribute to reinforcing race-based approaches to peace-building and addressing the legacy of the past. While not the only cause of conflict, competing worldviews remain an under-valued cause of conflict and a barrier to their successful resolution. This prompts an enquiry into understanding worldviews, how they operate in society and their relationship to intergroup conflict and building a sustainable peace in culturally diverse societies. These questions are taken up in the following chapter which explores and gives definition to the relationship between sustainable peace, worldview and conflict and introduces a 'worldview lens' for interpreting identity-based conflicts.

References

Adam, Heribert. 1994. Nationalism, nation-building, and non-racialism. In *Democratic nation-building in South Africa*, ed. Nic Rhoodie and Ian Liebenberg, 37–51. Pretoria: HSRC.

Adhikari, Mohamed. 2004. 'Not black enough': Changing expressions of coloured identity in post-Apartheid South Africa. *South African Historical Journal* 51: 167–178.

Adhikari, Mohamed. 2006a. Hope, fear, shame, frustration: Continuity and change in the expression of coloured identity in white supremacist South Africa, 1910–1994. *Journal of Southern African Studies* 32 (3): 467–487.

Adhikari, Mohamed. 2006b. 'God made the white man, God made the black man: Popular racial stereotyping of coloured people in Apartheid South Africa. *South African Historical Journal* 55 (1): 142–164.

Akenson, Donald Harman. 1992. *God's peoples: Covenant and land in South Africa, Israel and Ulster*. New York: Cornell University Press.

ANC. n.d. The Freedom Charter. http://www.anc.org.za/content/freedom-charter. Accessed 26 August 2018.

Andrucki, Max J. 2010. The visa whiteness machine: Transnational motility in post-Apartheid South Africa. *Ethnicities* 10 (3): 358–370.

Ansell, Amy. 2004. Two nations of discourse: Mapping racial ideologies in post-Apartheid South Africa. *Politikon* 31 (1): 3–26.

Asmal, Kader. 2000. Truth, reconciliation and justice: The South African experience in perspective. *The Modern Law Review* 63 (1): 1–24.

Asmal, Kader, Louise Asmal, and Suresh Roberts. 1996. *Reconciliation through truth: A reckoning of Apartheid's criminal governance*. Claremont: David Philip Publishers.

Bhana, Deevia, and Rob Pattman. 2010. White South African school girls and their accounts of black girls at school and cross-racial heterosexual relations outside school. *Ethnicities* 10 (3): 371–386.

Boraine, Alex. 2000. *A country unmasked: Inside South Africa's Truth and Reconciliation Commission*. Oxford: Oxford University Press.

Boraine, Alex. 2014. *What's gone wrong? On the brink of a failed state*. Johannesburg and Cape Town: Jonathan Ball Publishers.

Borer, Tristan Anne. 2004. Reconciling South Africa or South Africans? Cautionary notes from the TRC. *African Studies Quarterly* 8 (1): 23–26.

Bornman, Elirea. 2006. National symbols and national-building in the post-Apartheid South Africa. *International Journal of Intercultural Relations* 30: 383–399.

Bornman, Elirea. 2010. Emerging patterns of social identification in post-Apartheid South Africa. *Journal of Social Issues* 66 (2): 237–254.

Bornman, Elirea. 2011. Patterns of intergroup attitudes in South Africa after 1994. *International Journal of Intercultural Relations* 35: 729–748.

Bornman, Elirea, and Ans Appelgryn. 1997. Ethnolinguistic vitality under a new political dispensation in South Africa. *The Journal of Social Psychology* 137 (6): 690–707.

Boshoff, Priscilla. 2011. Bollywood nights: Indian youth and the creation of diasporic identity in South Africa. *Topia* 26: 29–46.

Bunting, Brian. 1972. The origins of Apartheid. In *Apartheid: A collection of writings on South African racism by South Africans*, ed. Alex La Guma, 19–36. London: Lawrence and Wishart.

De Gruchy, W. John, and Stephen De Gruchy. 2004. *The church struggle in South Africa*. London: SCM Press.

De Klerk, William Abraham. 1975. *The Puritans in Africa: A story of Afrikanerdom*. London: Rex Collings.

Department of Justice and Constitutional Development. 1995. *Promotion of National Unity and Reconciliation Act 34 of 1995*. http://www.justice.gov.za/legislation/acts/1995-034.pdf. Accessed 23 August 2018.

Dickens, Peter. 2000. *Social Darwinism: Linking evolutionary thought to social theory*. Buckingham: Open University Press.

Dlamini, Sibusisiwe Nombuso. 1998. The construction, meaning and negotiation of ethnic identities in KwaZulu Natal. *Social Identities* 4 (3): 473–497.

Dlamini, Sibusisiwe Nombuso. 2001. The construction, meaning and negotiation of ethnic identities in Kwa-Zulu Natal. In *Social identities in the new South Africa*, ed. Abebe Zegeye, 195–221. Cape Town: Kwela Books.

Dlamini, Sibusisiwe Nombuso. 2005. *Youth and identity politics in South Africa, 1990–1994*. Toronto: University of Toronto Press.

Dubow, Saul. 1987. Race, civilization and culture: The elaboration of segregationist discourse in the inter-war years. In *The politics of race, class and nationalism in twentieth century South Africa*, ed. Shula Marks and Stanley Trapido, 71–94. Essex: Longman.

Dubow, Saul. 1992. Afrikaner nationalism, Apartheid and the conceptualization of 'race'. *The Journal of African History* 33: 209–237.

Durrheim, Kevin, and John Dixon. 2005. *Racial encounter: The social psychology of contact and desegregation*. London: Routledge.

Durrheim, Kevin, and Xoliswa Mtose. 2006. Being black in the new South Africa. In *Psychology and the challenges of deracialization in South Africa*, ed. G. Stevens, V. Franchi, and T. Swart, 153–169. Pretoria: University of South Africa Press.

Durrheim, Kevin, John Dixon, Colin Tredoux, Liberty Eaton, Michael Quayle, and Beverley Clack. 2011. Predicting support for racial transformation policies: Intergroup threat, racial prejudice, sense of group entitlement and strength of identification. *European Journal of Social Psychology* 41 (12-08): 23–41.

Du Toit, Pierre. 2000. In search of post-settlement peace. In *The management of peace processes*, ed. John Darby and Roger Mac Ginty, 16–60. Basingstoke, London, and New York: Macmillan Press.

Ebrahim-Vally, Rehana. 2001. *Kala pani: Caste and colour in South Africa*. Colorado Springs: International Publishers.

Erasmus, Zimitri. 2001. *Coloured by history, shaped by place: New perspectives on coloured identities in Cape Town*. Cape Town: Kwela Books.

Gibson, James L. 2004. *Overcoming Apartheid: Can truth reconcile a divided nation?* New York: Russel Sage Foundation.

Gibson, James L., and Christopher Claassen. 2010. Racial reconciliation in South Africa: Interracial contact and changes over time. *Journal of Social Issues* 66 (2): 255–272.

Giliomee, H. 2003. *The Afrikaners: Biography of a people*. London: Hurst & Company.

Gilroy, Paul. 2000. *Against race: Imagining political culture beyond the colour line*. Cambridge, MA: Harvard University Press.

Hamber, Brandon. 2002. 'Ere their story die': Truth, justice and reconciliation in South Africa. *Race & Class* 44 (1): 61–79.

Hammett, Daniel. 2010. Ongoing contestations: The use of racial signifiers in post-Apartheid South Africa. *Social Identities* 16 (2): 247–260.

Hay, Mark. 1999. Grappling with the past: The Truth and Reconciliation Commission of South Africa. *African Journal on Conflict Resolution* 1 (1): 29–51.

Hayner, Priscilla B. 2001. *Unspeakable truths: Confronting state terror and atrocity*. New York: Routledge.

Hendricks, Cheryl. 2001. 'Ominous' liaisons: Tracing the interface between 'race' and sex at the Cape. In *Coloured by history, shaped by place: New perspectives on coloured identities in Cape Town*, ed. Zimitri Erasmus, 29–44. Cape Town: Kwela Books.

Horowitz, Donald L. 1991. *A democratic South Africa? Constitutional engineering in a divided society, perspectives on Southern Africa*. Berkeley: University of California Press.

Ignatieff, Michael. 1998. *The Warrior's honour: Ethnic war and the modern conscience*. London: Chatto & Windus.

Isaacs-Martin, Wendy. 2012. National identity and distinctiveness: Developing a common identity in a nation state (with reference to South Africa). *Africa Insight* 42 (2): 169–170.

Jones, Greta. 1980. *Social Darwinism and English thought: The interaction between biological and social theory*. Brighton: Harvester Press.

La Guma, Alex. 1972. *Apartheid: A collection of writings on South African racism by South Africans*. London: Lawrence and Wishart.

Lambert, John. 2009. 'An unknown people': Reconstructing British South African identity. *The Journal of Imperial and Commonwealth History* 37 (4): 599–617.

Legassick, Martin. 1974. South Africa: Capital accumulation and violence. *Economy and Society* 3 (3): 253–291.

Louw, Eric. 2004. *The rise, fall, and legacy of Apartheid*. Westport, CT and London: Praeger Publishers.

Mac Ginty, R. 2001. The political use of symbols of accord and discord: Northern Ireland and South Africa. *Civil Wars* 4 (1): 1–21.

Mamdani, Mahmood. 2000. The truth according to the TRC. In *The politics of memory: Truth, healing and social justice*, ed. Ifi Amadiume and Abdullahi An-Na'im, 177–190. London and New York: Zed Books.

Marais, Hein. 2001. *South Africa limits to change: The political economy of transition*. Kenwyn: UCT Press; London: Zed Books.

Maré, Gerhard. 2001. Race counts in contemporary South Africa: 'An illusion of ordinariness'. *Transformation* 47: 75–93.

Mashele, Prince, and Mzukisi Qobo. 2014. *The fall of the ANC: What next?* Johannesburg: Picador Africa.

Matsinhe, David Mario. 2011. Africa's fear of itself: The ideology of *Makwerekwere* in South Africa. *Third World Quarterly* 32 (2): 295–313.

Mbeki, Thabo. 1998. Statement of Deputy President Thabo Mbeki at the Opening of the Debate in the National Assembly. *Reconciliation and Nation Building*, May 29. Department of International Relations and Cooperation.

McKinney, Carolyn. 2007. 'If I speak English, does it make me less black anyway?': Race and English in South African desegregated schools. *English Academy Review* 24 (2): 6–24.

Misgun, Biniam, and Wesley Oakes. 2007. The white and black sands of the Durban beachfront. In *Undressing Durban: Behind the tourist gaze*, ed. Rob Pattman and Sultan Khan, 118–125. Durban: Madiba Publishers.

Moodie, Dunbar. 1975. *The rise of Afrikanerdom: Power, Apartheid and Afrikaner civil religion*. Berkeley: University of California Press.

Moodley, Shabashni. 2007. Nightlife in Durban and 'racial' divisions. In *Undressing Durban: Behind the tourist gaze*, ed. Rob Pattman and Sultan Khan, 126–131. Durban: Madiba Publishers.

Moodley, Kogila, and Heribert Adam. 2000. Race and nation in post-Apartheid South Africa. *Current Sociology* 48: 51–69.

Mpama, Sibusiso. 2007. Black solidarity and black divisions. In *Undressing Durban: Behind the tourist gaze*, ed. Rob Pattman and Sultan Khan, 332–333. Durban: Madiba Publishers.

National Planning Commission. 2012. *Our future—Make it work: National Development Plan 2030*. Republic of South Africa: The Presidency.

Norval, Aletta J. 1998. Memory, identity and the (im)possibility of reconciliation: The work of the Truth and Reconciliation Commission in South Africa. *Constellations* 5 (2): 250–265.

O'Malley, Kieran. 1994. A neglected dimension of nation-building in South Africa. In *A democratic nation-building in South Africa*, ed. Nic Rhoodie and Ian Liebenberg, 77–103. Pretoria: HSRC.

O'Meara, Dan. 1975. The 1946 African mineworkers strike and the political economy of South Africa. *Journal of Commonwealth and Comparative Politics* 13 (2): 146–173.

Pattman, Rob. 2007. The significance students attach to 'race' at the University of KwaZulu-Natal. In *Undressing Durban: Behind the tourist gaze*, ed. Rob Pattman and Sultan Khan, 390–404. Durban: Madiba Publishers.

Petrus, Theodore, and Wendy Isaacs-Martin. 2012. The multiple meanings of coloured identity in South Africa. *Africa Insight* 41 (1): 87–102.

Posel, Deborah. 1983. Rethinking the 'race-class debate' in South African historiography. *Social Dynamics* 9 (1): 50–66.

Radhakrishnan, Smitha. 2005. 'Time to show our true colors': The gendered politics of 'Indianness' in post-Apartheid South Africa. *Gender & Society* 19 (2): 262–281.

Ramsamy, Edward. 2007. Between non-racialism and multiculturalism: Indian identity and nation building in South Africa. *Tijdschrift Voor Economische en Sociale Geografie* 98 (4): 468–481.

Reilly, Janet E. 2001. Nation building and the construction of identity: Xenophobia in South Africa. *Refuge* 19 (6): 4–11.

Seekings, Jeremy. 2008. The continuing saliency of race: Discrimination and diversity in South Africa. *Journal of Contemporary African Studies* 26 (1): 1–25.

Southern, Neil. 2008. The freedom front plus: An analysis of Afrikaner politics and ethnic identity in the new South Africa. *Contemporary Politics* 14 (4): 463–478.

Statistics South Africa. 2018. Quarterly Labour Force Survey—QLFS Q2:2018. http://www.statssa.gov.za/?p=11361. Accessed 26 August 2018.

Steingo, Gavin. 2005. 'I am proud to be South African because I am South African': Reflections on 'white pride' in post-Apartheid South Africa. *African Identities* 3 (2): 195–210.

Steyn, Melissa. 2001. *'Whiteness just isn't what it used to be': White identity in a changing South Africa*. Albany, NY: State University of New York Press.

Steyn, Melissa. 2004. Rehabilitating a whiteness disgraced: Afrikaner white talk in post-Apartheid South Africa. *Communication Quarterly* 52 (2): 143–169.

Steyn, Melissa, and Don Foster. 2008. Repertoires for talking white: Resistant whiteness in post-Apartheid South Africa. *Ethnic and Racial Studies* 31 (1): 25–51.

Terreblanche, Sampie. 2002. *A history of inequality in South Africa: 1652–2002*. Pietermaritzburg: University of Natal Press.

Truth and Reconciliation Commission of South Africa. 1998a. *Truth and Reconciliation Commission of South Africa Report*, vol. 1. Cape Town: Juta.

Truth and Reconciliation Commission of South Africa. 1998b. *Truth and Reconciliation Commission of South Africa Report*, vol. 4. Cape Town: Juta.

Tutu, Desmond M. 1999. *No future without forgiveness*. London: Rider.

United Nations Development Programme. 2015. *Human development report 2015: Work for human development*. New York: United Nations Development Programme.

Vahed, Goolam, and Ashwin Desai. 2010. Identity and belonging in post-Apartheid South Africa: The case of Indian South Africans. *Journal of Social Science* 25 (1–3): 1–12.

Valji, Nahla. 2004. Race and reconciliation in a post-TRC South Africa. *Ten years of democracy in Southern Africa*. Johannesburg: Centre for the Study of Violence and Reconciliation.

Van der Merwe, Hendrick. 1989. *Pursuing justice and peace in South Africa.* London and New York: Routledge.

Van Jaarsveld, Floris Albertus. 1964. *The Afrikaners' interpretation of South African history.* Cape Town: Simondium.

Van Zyl, Paul. 1999. Dilemmas of transitional justice: The case of South Africa's Truth and Reconciliation Commission. *Journal of International Affairs* 52 (2): 647–668.

Van Zyl Slabbert, F. 1975. Afrikaner nationalism, white politics, and political change in South Africa. In *Change in contemporary South Africa*, ed. Leonard Thompson and Jeffrey Butler, 3–18. Berkeley and Los Angeles: University of California Press.

Verwey, Cornel, and Michael Quayle. 2012. Whiteness, racism, and Afrikaner identity in post-Apartheid South Africa. *African Affairs* 111 (445): 551–575.

Wilson, Richard A. 2001. *The politics of truth and reconciliation in South Africa: Legitimizing the post-Apartheid state.* Cambridge: Cambridge University Press.

Wolpe, Harold. 1972. Capitalism and cheap labour power in South Africa: From segregation to Apartheid. *Economy and Society* 1 (4): 425–456.

Wolpe, Harold. 1990. *Race, class and the Apartheid state.* Trenton: Africa World Press.

3

Anchoring Concepts: Sustainable Peace, Identity, Culture and Worldview

Worldview as a lens for interpreting intergroup conflict is underdeveloped within the literature as Western academia tends to focus on the structural and developmental aspects of peace-building, and not the relational ones. Bearing this in mind, the aim of this chapter is to understand the significance worldview has on intergroup relations and building a sustainable peace. To do so, it deconstructs the anchoring concepts underpinning this research, namely sustainable peace, identity, culture and worldview, and examines how they intersect and relate to intergroup conflict. Together, this forms the framework for interpreting different notions of peace in South Africa and understanding how worldview shapes intergroup relations. To deal with this, it is necessary to draw on literature from disciplines outside transitional justice and peace-building including the fields of social psychology and anthropology.

C. Bollaert, *Reconciliation and Building a Sustainable Peace*,
Palgrave Studies in Compromise after Conflict,
https://doi.org/10.1007/978-3-030-03655-3_3

3.1 Sustainable Peace

Central to peace-building and transitional justice is the question, 'what comprises sustainable peace and how best can it be achieved?'. Without a single definition of 'sustainable peace', scholars and practitioners within the field peace-building and transitional justice tend to select which aspects of it they emphasise, of which there are a wide range. A review of the literature suggests these can be divided into structural and relational pillars. The structural pillars tend to emphasise the institutional and policy aspects of building a sustainable peace including:

- Peace agreements and accords (Darby and Mac Ginty 2003; Bell 2000);
- Institutional reform including military, security, political and legal reform (Oberschall 2007; Bryden and Hänggi 2005);
- Justice, accountability and maintaining the rule of law (Oberschall 2007; Gross and Ní Aoláin 2006; Schabas 2011);
- Protecting and promoting a culture of human rights (Mallinder 2008; Buchanan and Zumbansen 2014; Borer 2003; Sarkin 1998);
- Development and socio-economic transformation that promotes equality, reduces poverty and addresses issues relating to human security such as health, education and employment (Oberschall 2007; Laplante 2008; Mani 2008; Aiken 2010; Miller 2008; Muvingi 2009); and
- Victim redress and reparations (De Greiff 2006; Torpey 2003; Parmentier et al. 2006; Laplante 2014).

Significantly, these pillars also reflect Western liberal approaches to peace-building (Richmond 2011). In contrast, the relational pillars tend to emphasise the interpersonal aspects of building a lasting peace including:

- Social rehabilitation and reconciliation (Jeong 2005; Lederach 1997; Mani 2005; Hamber 2009; Lambourne 2009; Aiken 2013; Bar-Siman-Tov 2004; Bloomfield et al. 2003);
- The need for truth and acknowledgement (Lederach 1997; Hamber and Kelly 2009; Hayner 2001);

- The need for healing and addressing the trauma and psychological impact of conflict (Lambourne 2009; Hamber 2009; Krog 2008b);
- Apology, forgiveness and dealing with emotions (Shriver 2001; Moon 2004; Chapman and van der Merwe 2008; Thomas 2009; Long and Brecke 2003; Cohen 2004; Auerbach 2004; David and Choi 2006);
- Rebuilding positive relationships and creating a culture of trust. This includes breaking down negative perceptions of the 'other' through contact, dialogue and encounter (Lederach 1997; Hamber and Kelly 2009);
- Developing a shared vision of the future (Lederach 1997; Hamber and Kelly 2009); and
- The need to develop one's spiritual resources without which Curle (1999) argues violence will continue to reinvent and transform itself no matter what efforts are used to root it out.

Recognising that the pillars are intertwined, grouping the pillars in this way is useful for analysing the relationship between identity, worldview and peace-building. As Chapters 5 and 6 will show, different pillars tend to resonate more with certain identity groups and worldview attributes than others. Significantly, these differences have a strong bearing on intergroup dynamics. Arguably, further research is needed on how intergroup conflict and building a sustainable peace are affected by variables such as identity, culture and worldview, which this book seeks to address (Hamber 2012; Arthur 2011b; Aiken 2013; Mac Ginty 2008, 2010, 2013; Brigg 2010).

The most appropriate approaches and mechanisms on how to deal with the legacy of the past, while at the same time working to build a peaceful and sustainable future, is the subject of extensive debate. Reflecting the 'structural' and 'relational' pillars for building a sustainable peace, the first debate surrounds the different approaches to justice and the value of criminal prosecutions versus non-judicial mechanisms, such as truth commissions, for dealing with the past (Hayner 2001; Orentlicher 2007; Hazan 2006; Drumbl 2007; Kritz 1995; Rotberg and Thompson 2000; Roht-Arriaza and Marriezcurrena 2006; Schabas and Darcy 2004; Gibson 2004).[1] Those who favour a retributive approach to justice tend to emphasise the legal aspects and the necessity of maintaining and establishing the rule of law while those who favour a restorative approach to justice tend to emphasise the relational aspects. It was the latter, a restorative approach to justice that formed one of the distinguishing, albeit controversial features of South Africa's transitional process. Significantly, Desmond Tutu (1999), the chairman of the South African Truth and Reconciliation Commission (TRC), argues that criminal prosecutions represent a more Western approach to justice which is not suited to the traditional African approach.

This leads to a second debate surrounding Western and non-Western approaches to peace-building and transitional justice (Huyse and Salter 2008; Babo-Soares 2004; Kent 2011; Clark 2007; Quinn 2007, 2009; Mac Ginty 2008, 2010, 2011, 2013; Richmond 2011; Brown 2013; Sriram 2007; Kelsall 2009; Merry 2006; Palmer et al. 2015). Founded on values such as individualism, reason, progress and improvement which are rooted in the Enlightenment, Western approaches to peace-building tend to function within the liberal peace agenda and emphasise the structural and institutional aspects (institutional reform, security, democracy, the rule of law and human rights among others) of building a sustainable peace. However, due to their top-down approach to peace-building they are criticised for their lack of community recognition and failure to bring in local and less powerful voices (McEvoy and McGregor 2008; Lundy and McGovern 2008). This contrasts with non-Western, bottom-up approaches to peace-building which emphasises participation, local agency and ownership, and the relational pillars of sustainable peace.

Integral to this debate are the different cultural interpretations given to key concepts within transitional justice (such as truth, responsibility, justice, forgiveness, accountability and human rights) and the incumbent challenge of translating Western approaches to peace-building into

[1]Another component of this debate relates to whether the goals of peace and reconciliation are mutually compatible with justice (Teitel 2000; Fletcher and Weinstein 2002). Integral to this is the debate surrounding amnesties and whether they are a necessary part of promoting a lasting peace or rather if they serve to entrench a culture of impunity (Mallinder 2007; Mallinder and McEvoy 2011; Hamber 2009; Robinson 2003).

non-Western contexts (Kelsall 2009; Merry 2006; Krog 2008a, 2015; Sriram 2007). As these concepts are deeply rooted in a society's system of meaning-making, to become meaningful they need to be translated into the vernacular of the local context (Merry 2006). However, pointing to the importance of worldview in building a sustainable peace Sriram (2007) cautions that efforts to implement Western approaches into non-Western contexts could in fact act to destabilise the fragile peace in post-conflict societies.

The difficulty with the Western versus non-Western debate is it can lead to binary approaches to peace-building (Richmond 2011; Brown 2013). On the one hand, the international Western community has romanticised its own values and capacity to implement institutions that promote peace while denigrating the agency of local actors to contribute to such processes as local culture is seen to be in opposition to international peace-building mechanisms. On the other hand, critics of the Western approach tend to perceive local and indigenous approaches to building peace as more authentic and sustainable. The danger is that those aspects of indigenous culture that promote conflict can be overlooked (Mac Ginty 2011). This is well illustrated in the case of South Africa and the way in which the African indigenous philosophy of *ubuntu* was popularised. As Wilson (2001) contends, although *ubuntu* was equated with the African sense of restoration, forgiveness and non-retribution, there was (and remains) a widespread practice of revenge.

In response to this binary approach to peace-building, the concept of a hybrid peace that integrates Western liberal and local approaches to peace-building is gaining currency (Mac Ginty 2008, 2010, 2013; Lidén et al. 2009; Richmond 2010, 2011). The benefit of promoting a hybrid peace is the potential it has for offering a more complex approach to peace-building. In this way, the hybrid peace model can serve as a transformative and emancipatory framework for peace which considers the local context and is representative of both the local and international actors (Richmond 2011). Moreover, because hybrid peace inherently challenges Western superiority and the location of power in peace-building it also has the capacity to break down historic colonial power constructs (Mac Ginty 2011; Bhabha 1994).

Despite hybrid peace trying to move away from the binary approach to peace-building it still appears to interpret non-Western societies as culturally homogenous when in fact they are more complex. While grass-roots, bottom-up approaches to peace-building recognise the need to take cultural views and local agency into consideration, it is not clear if either models fully take into account the plurality of approaches to peace-building within societies, as in the case of a culturally diverse South Africa.

South Africa's peace process did not follow the normative liberal model in that it did not involve international actors such as the United Nations. If anything, one might argue that it was an indigenous process as all the primary actors were South African. However, as depicted in Chapter 2, South African identities are historically derived from both Western and non-Western cultures which largely developed separately within the power constructs of segregation and Apartheid. Reflecting the hybrid peace framework these divided identities existed within a global and local context where different influences and approaches came to bear on the South African social landscape. The principles raised within hybrid peace offer a framework in which to interpret the nexus between peace-building, transitional justice and identity in South Africa that can also challenge the power and superiority of 'white' ontologies and epistemologies.

3.2 Identity

Reflecting the complexity and challenges surrounding the concept of identity, there are three core theoretical and competing paradigms through which identity is interpreted namely: primordialism, instrumentalism and constructivism (Arthur 2011a). The primordial school of thought interprets identity as a fixed and unchanging entity that is passed down the generations through the pertaining cultural traditions. While within the social sciences this view does not hold much currency, it is popular among politicians and the wider society in general and is often used to design policies and peace-building interventions around managing group differences (Arthur 2011a). For example, the speech made by Thabo Mbeki (1998), former President of South Africa, in which he defined South Africa in terms of two nations, i.e. 'black' and 'white' is illustrative of a primordial interpretation of identity. By keeping groups separated, primordialism tends to be associated with racism, nationalism and xenophobia (Balcomb 2014). Furthermore, referring to different communities within a post-conflict society in binary terms such as Catholic/Protestant also reflects a primordial interpretation of identity. While such language not only excludes new communities being able to participate in the society, it also entrenches fixed, essentialised notions of identity into one's psyche as was evidenced among persons interviewed in the research that contributed to this book:

> I am a white South African. That's who I am. That informs, that does inform you. You can't, I don't know that in South Africa we can let go of that yet. It would be like; it would like letting go of the fact that I'm female. It's who I am. It doesn't make it wrong. (Respondent 5)

> They [whites] can be South Africans; I think when we're referring to Africans we're referring to blacks. (Respondents 17)

Despite primordialism being disregarded by social scientists it is, nonetheless, a widely held view, as the rise in right-wing nationalism in Europe and America suggests.

The second paradigm relates to instrumentalism in which identities are seen as strategically 'chosen' by an individual on the basis of incentives that serve to advance their interests (Arthur 2011a). This view of identity is exemplified in a 2008 South African court ruling which won the right for Chinese, who had been classified as 'coloured' during Apartheid but were later regarded as 'honorary whites', to be classified as 'previously disadvantaged' so as to benefit from the Black Economic Empowerment (BEE) system (Centre for Chinese Studies 2008). It is also seen among 'black' South Africans who sought to change their identity to 'coloured' to gain slightly improved living conditions within the Apartheid system.

Constructivism is the third paradigm for understanding identity and the one in which the research in this book is located. It argues that identity is not something that is chosen or innate but is nurtured and constructed through 'the social relationships, the everyday practice of perceiving and treating others, and the institutions in which they are embedded' (Arthur 2011a: 5). Identities within this school of thought are understood to be flexible, emerging and continually shifting as the context in which they are embedded changes (Arthur 2011a; Weedon 2004; Eriksen 2001). It argues that as one encounters a new reality or a changed environment, one's interpretation of reality can develop and be reconstructed to become more sophisticated and accommodating of the changing environment (Guba and Lincoln 2008). This underscores the importance of the social, economic and political context in shaping identity. It also leads to the concept of hybridity which recognises that as cultures interact they become mixed and influence each other (Bhabha 1994; Cohen and Kennedy 2000).[2] For example, hybrid identities are evidenced among 'black' South Africans who have integrated both traditional and Western ways of being in the world. However, while identities may be seen to shift and change, in the context of deeply divided societies their flexibility may be more rigid and complex than constructivism suggests, especially when policies (including community relations policies) based on primordial interpretations of identity continue to be implemented.

It is important to note that although one can refer to an individual having a certain identity at a point in time; this does not suggest they are fixed. It is expected that as South Africa's social and political landscape continues to shift, so will identity. However, this needs to be held in tension with the centuries of separated history and memory which raises the question of whether identities are able to shift at the same pace as political and social environments and the implications this might have on intergroup boundaries.

Notwithstanding these schools of thought, identity is a system of beliefs for making sense of one's reality that is essential for one's sense of survival, well-being, and physical, psychological, social and spiritual safety (Maslow 1954; Northrup 1989). It is produced and constructed

[2]Bhabha used the concept of hybridity to challenge the discourse on identity that had become fixed under colonial rule and to challenge the use of exclusionary and essentialised notions of 'race' (Bhabha 1994; Yazdiha 2010; Easthope 1998).

through the narratives that people use to interpret their lived reality (Lawler 2008). Moreover, in the interests of protecting one's sense of self, individuals tend to coalesce into groups organised around subscription to certain group rules and behaviours relating to, among other things, physical attributes, beliefs or even ethical commitments (Abrams and Hogg 1998). This sense of self or identity that is derived from membership of a social group is what is referred to as 'social identity' to which is usually attached a sense of importance, pride and superiority over other groups (Tajfel 1981).

3.3 Culture

Integral to understanding identity is the culture in which it is embedded. However, talking about culture is complex and fraught with difficulties, especially given the way it has been used to reinforce theories of difference based on race (such as Gobineau's hierarchy of race and other forms of scientific racism). Such interpretations worked to reduce culture to a defined set of characteristics that could be used to differentiate one group from another. Moreover, it supported the view that one's behaviour and interaction with the world were informed by one's biology and race, and not by culture. This led to the word 'culture' being used as a euphemism for talking about racial difference which accounts for some of the sensitivities when talking about culture. Supporting a more primordial understanding of identity the difficulty with such an interpretation of culture is that it acts to essentialise and fix identities according to defined group characteristics that neglect their flexibility and ability to shift (Weedon 2004). For example, in the South African context such an understanding of culture was used to justify the development of Apartheid and continues to reinforce race-based identities and persisting negative (and often racist) stereotypes of the 'other'. In doing so, it disregards the common humanity and similarities that are shared across groups. This raises the question as to whether one can talk about different cultures or rather about cultural differences. To refer to different cultures may be interpreted as connoting fixed and essentialised identities.

In deconstructing the concept of culture, this book draws on the definition developed by the widely acclaimed anthropologist Clifford Geertz who defines culture as:

> [An] historically transmitted pattern of meanings embodied in symbols, a system of inherited conceptions expressed in symbolic forms by means of which [people] communicate, perpetuate, and develop their knowledge about and attitudes towards life. (Geertz 1973: 89)

In other words, culture is 'a shared system of meaning that helps people make sense of the world in which they live and interpret the actions of others' (Ross 2009: 3). Speaking to a broad interpretation of culture, it is everything that makes us human beings and includes shared meanings of how the self and one's reality are interpreted, shared religious and spiritual beliefs, group values, and shared social rules of conduct (Staub 1996: 117). It can be derived from kinship groups such as tribe, ethnic group and nation, as well as from one's profession, social class, religion or region (Avruch 1998). It is expressed through a range of rituals, symbols, language, emotions and customs; and is embodied in social institutions such as religious, educational, legal and security systems (Staub 1996; Eriksen 2010; Schweder and LeVine 1984; Hendry 2008; Hicks and Gwynne 1996; Ross 2007, 2009). As exemplified by Apartheid, these systems of organisation can, for example, be built around interpretations of race and class and used to inform and justify racist behaviours, attitudes and interpretations of the 'other'.

Furthermore, culture is integral to maintaining the coherency and ability of a group or society to function and survive and can contribute to exacerbating conflict (Bryan and McIntosh 2005; Ross 2007, 2009; Atran 2010). This is well illustrated in the intensity of violence that ensued following the printing of cartoons of the Prophet Mohammed by the French magazine, Charlie Hebdo (Kirby 2015); the furore and threat of violence that followed the painting of Zuma (see Chapter 1); and the hostility and sometimes violent confrontation in Northern Ireland over the meaning and practice of certain symbols and traditions (Bryan 2000). Integral to such conflicts are a society's or group's sacred values which Atran (2010: xiv) defines as those 'deeper cultural values that are bound up with people's identity which often trump other values, particularly economic ones'. Citing the example of Islamic suicide bombers, he argues sacred values are fundamental to understanding why people are willing to martyr their lives for a cause. While these values are often rooted in religion, they can also be related to sustaining traditions and values such as justice and honour. As they speak to the core of one's sense of self and security in the world (identity), efforts to protect them can provide the impetus for instigating violence.

This leads to a further understanding of culture which Ross (2009: 3) defines as:

> [A] worldview containing specific scripts that shape why and how individuals and groups behave as they do, and includes both cognitive and affective beliefs about social reality as well as assumptions about when, where, and how people in one's culture and those in other cultures are likely to act in particular ways.

There are several observations to be made from this definition of culture. Firstly, it can be understood to be that which drives and informs behaviour (Geertz 1973; Berger and Luckmann 1966). This raises the issue of structure and agency. The cultural world in which we are brought up in has structure, as defined by a society's cultural expressions and social institutions, which is engrained in us. Although these structures are not fixed, they do have certain rigidity to them. For example, it has required decades of activism, campaigning and awareness-raising to shift the nature of racial, class and gendered roles in the society and for them to become more equal. However, within these cultural structures, every individual has, to a certain extent, the agency to choose how to live and engage with it.

Secondly, culture also informs what one might perceive as logical or common sense. Avruch and Black (1993: 132) link this to the development of negative stereotypes and group polarisation which they argue are rooted in cross-cultural encounters that either challenge or do not fit one's own sense of familiarity and logic. This was made evident in the research process underpinning this book in which several respondents made reference to the actions of others as illogical or confusing which, in turn, acted to entrench existing (and often racist) stereotypes of the 'other'.

Consequently, phrases and words such as 'confusing' and 'illogical' act as identifiers to interrogate the extent to which groups are interpreting the 'other' through their worldview and understanding of reality that may not necessarily be racist in itself, but in the context of South Africa is interpreted as such. For societies in transition the extent to which divided groups will be able to understand the logic of others is brought into question. As this book will show, a failure to understand the 'other' can be counterproductive to the goals of reconciliation and sustainable peace.

Pointing to a lack of conceptual clarity within the literature between culture and worldview, a third observation relates to how Ross likens culture to worldview. If culture is all encompassing of our social world, as suggested in this definition of culture, it can be rendered useless. By differentiating between worldview and culture, it allows one to look more deeply at how people within a particular group interpret the world around them. Thus, worldview can be understood to be embedded in culture and acts to inform the way a society is organised. Significantly, a society's cultural expressions including its institutes, rules, rituals, customs, symbols and language communicate a worldview held by an individual or group. Although deeply intertwined, this suggests that worldview has a deeper reach than culture. It is this deeper level of meaning-making and its impact on peace-building in multicultural and deeply divided societies that this book is addressing.

3.4 Worldview

Originating from the German word '*weltanschauung*' worldview refers to one's view of the world or universe that is 'used to describe one's total outlook on life, society and its institutions' (Wolman 1973: 406).[3]

[3]The concept of worldview has been used by a scholars across a range of academic disciplines including: philosophy (Pepper 1942; Nietzsche 1956; Dilthey 1970; Goodman 1978), psychology (Koltko-Rivera 2004; Kelly 1963; Clark 1989), sociology (Berger and Luckmann 1966; Goffman 1986; Bourdieu 1984), anthropology (Kearney 1984; Redfield 1953; Kluckhohn and Strodtbeck 1961; Hall 1959; Palmer 1996), theology (Naugle 2002; Balcomb 2014; Nürnberger 2007; Heslam 1998), and most recently within peace studies and conflict resolution (Nudler 1993; Docherty 2001; Krog 2008a, 2015).

The concept first emerged as a means of explaining the expansion of cultural, religious and philosophical diversity that was taking place within societies (Naugle 2002). It is a complex term to define and has been referred to in several different ways by scholars including among others: 'worlds' (Goodman 1978); 'world hypotheses' (Pepper 1942); 'habitus' (Bourdieu 1984); 'frames' (Goffman 1986); 'cosmologies' (Douglas 1996) and 'symbolic universes' (Berger and Luckmann 1966).

There are several features integral to understanding worldview. Firstly, worldview is a flexible and socially constructed entity that is nurtured through social processes and new experiences (Berger and Luckmann 1966; Bourdieu 1984; Navarro 2006). Drawing from Bourdieu's concept of habitus, it can be understood as 'a set of dispositions which generate practices and perceptions' (Jenkins 1992: 74). In other words, worldview is connected to one's social environment and rooted in the historical and collective memory of a social group that shapes how one engages with and interprets their social reality (Naugle 2002; Clark 1989). Consequently, there can be multiple interpretations of reality recognised across social groups; these have the capacity to develop in relation to the shifting nature of one's social environment and experiences.

Leading to the second feature, worldview is the ontology and epistemology that informs one 'truth' and what can be known about the social world (Naugle 2002; Pepper 1942; Clark 1989; Berger and Luckmann 1966). It houses the script or rules that give order to and justify one's actions, practices, social priorities and perceptions. These inform the way in which the behaviours of the 'other' are interpreted. Connecting worldview to identity and the need for a sense of security in the world, worldview is the 'set of assumptions' (Goffman 1986) or beliefs that provide meaning and coherence to the world without which reality cannot be understood and which determine what one can come to expect from their lived reality. Significantly, there is growing recognition of the way in which ontological and epistemological differences are contributing to the breakdown of transitional justice and peace-building processes in non-Western societies (Palmer et al. 2015; Merry 2006, Sriram 2007; Kelsall 2009; Krog 2008a, 2015).

Thirdly, worldview is a component of culture (Ross 2007, 2009). Underscoring how deeply intertwined and inseparable these two concepts are Redfield (1953: 103) argues that culture is the way in which an anthropologist (or researcher) perceives people; and worldview the way in which people perceive the world. They are maintained through a society's culture (i.e. its symbolic landscape, social institutions, rituals, beliefs and sacred values) and are deeply embedded within the psyche of an individual (Docherty 2001; Clark 1989). Worldview can also be related to power and serving the interests of those exercising it as evident in both the colonial enterprise and the way in which it supported the Apartheid machinery (see Chapter 2). Nonetheless, as a subconscious entity, worldview can only be studied indirectly through cultural practices, institutions and behaviours which act as signals or indicators of the worldview(s) held by the individual or group.

In addition to these core features, worldview comprises numerous attributes that can coalesce to form a complex system of meaning-making. To study worldviews, it is helpful to delineate these attributes so they can act as indicators for interpreting and understanding the relationship between the process of meaning-making and how peace is interpreted (see Chapters 5–6). While these attributes tend to be defined in binary terms, worldviews that are held by individuals are more complex and can sometimes appear contradictory. The attributes listed below do not form an exhaustive list but are some of the more dominant ones.

The first attribute of worldview relates to one's ontological and epistemological orientation (Koltko-Rivera 2004). This refers to the way in which the nature of reality is interpreted and how knowledge is attained and can be known (Guba and Lincoln 1998). This has led to the distinction between a material or scientific worldview and spiritual worldview. Materialism is closely associated with the Enlightenment, and more generally a scientific and a Western worldview. Spiritualism, in which the physical and spiritual realms are believed to be interconnected, is associated with a spiritual or interconnected worldview. For example, the belief in curses is closely related to an interconnected worldview. Significantly, these dimensions are where one places one's sense of security and well-being: i.e. in scientific knowledge or in the spiritual realm (Koltko-Rivera 2004). This attribute also relates to one's locus of control at the heart of which lies the question: Am I in control of my destiny or is my destiny in control of me (Blankenburgh 2013: 27)? People whose locus of control is internal will tend to rely on their own abilities and to look to themselves when making decisions. Those whose locus of control is external will usually look to the spiritual realm for support, guidance and general well-being in their life. Here, protection from curses and malevolent spirits takes on great significance. Chapter 4 will explore this dimension in more detail and examine the way it shaped the TRC and the criticisms it received.

A second attribute centres on the unit of survival and accountability and whether this is internal to the individual or within the collective group (Oyserman et al. 2002; Blankenburgh 2013; Somech 2000; Eaton and Louw 2000). Individualism emphasises the individual who is expected to look after him or herself and to pursue their own needs, goals and interest. The individualist will look to their awareness of self and independence for their sense of survival and prioritise personal achievements and personal responsibility. Conflict will be perceived on an interpersonal level (Oyserman 1993). Within collectivism the group and closely connected relationships are prioritised. Consequently, conflict is perceived at an intergroup level. The collectivist will also focus on maintaining social traditions inculcated in common beliefs, attitudes and practices. It emphasises values such as honour authority, respect, duty, loyalty, purity and sanctity (Shweder et al. 1997; Atran 2010).

A third attribute of worldview relates to how societies are organised; are relationships orientated hierarchically or more laterally (Kluckhohn and Strodtbeck 1961; Schwartz 1999; Koltko-Rivera 2004; Blankenburgh 2013). Within the hierarchical orientation, a stronger value is given to respecting and protecting the seniority of a person and those in authority. It also emphasises the use of formal titles when addressing individuals and places the needs of the leader first. In contrast, a lateral orientation, while still giving due respect to elders and those in authority, promotes a more informal context where those in authority can be addressed on a first name basis and a more informal dress code is socially appropriate. Its significance was highlighted in a conversation when I (the author) inadvertently addressed a more senior 'black' man by his first name causing him great offence. While in my culture calling a senior person by their first name is socially acceptable, in this instant I should have added the prefix 'Baba' to his name, the Zulu word for father, thus showing respect. Further to this, a hierarchical orientation will also tend to emphasise the importance of maintaining traditions and following protocols. Many collective societies follow this form of social organisation.

Temporal orientation is a fourth attribute of worldview (Kluckhohn and Strodtbeck 1961; Koltko-Rivera 2004; Blankenburgh 2013). This refers to whether one's outlook is orientated towards the past, present or future. Those who prioritise the past emphasise the importance of history and tradition and tend to be associated with collective societies. Reflecting individualism, those who prioritise the future tend to be more concerned with their achievements, personal growth and the setting of goals.

A fifth attribute of worldview refers to one's activity orientation and whether rules or relationships are prioritised (Hall 1959; Spencer-Oatey 2000; Hofstede 1980; Blankenburgh 2013). In societies that prioritise relationships, social rules are adhered to the extent they support the relationship. In contrast, in rule-based societies adherence to rules, codes of conduct and public policies is prioritised. Furthermore, relationally orientated communities will tend to prioritise relationships over time in the planning of their daily schedules while rule-based societies, who are more task-orientated, will emphasise the need to schedule events and starting and finishing a meeting on time. A relationship priority is generally associated with collectivism and hierarchically structured societies while a rule-based priority tends to be associated with individualist societies.

The last attribute of worldview to be considered are the value paradigms that shape how one interacts with one's social reality namely, the guilt-innocence paradigm, the shame-honour paradigm and the fear-power paradigm (Benedict 1946; Muller 2001; Blankenburgh 2013; James and McLeod 2014). Drawing from Blankenburgh's description of these paradigms, the guilt-innocence paradigm prioritises being right. This lends itself to the Western legal system which is built around proving the guilt of an individual or party, i.e. innocent until proven guilty.

Because being right or innocent is so strongly valued he explains that these societies will emphasise meticulous policies, laws, contracts and procedures to ensure innocence can be maintained. The guilt-innocence paradigm also lends itself to a rule-based orientation. For societies orientated towards a shame-honour paradigm, the rules of social engagement will be driven by maintaining honour above being right and will be built around the avoidance of shame. Within this paradigm, it is usually the honour of the society as whole and not just the individual that is at stake. This paradigm speaks to the correlation that Atran (2010) makes between suicide bombers and the need for a society to protect their sacred values, of which honour is one. The fear-power paradigm speaks to a spiritual epistemology and the need to find protection from spiritual insecurity. The statement made by former South African President Jacob Zuma as a means to gain political support highlights this paradigm: 'If you don't respect those in leadership, if you don't respect authority then you are bordering on a curse' (Pillay 2013).

These attributes can be used to study worldview through the cultural expressions of a society including the narratives, language, metaphors and stories that people tell as they illustrate what people use to construct and legitimise their realities (Docherty 2001, 2004a, b; Lakoff and Johnson 1980; Goldberg 2009). Such cultural expressions also communicate a worldview and provide insight into values that people hold. Furthermore, worldviews can be studied through the non-verbal language of a society (Hall 1959). For example, in traditional Zulu culture, to show respect to an elder or authority one's gaze needs to be directed downwards. In other cultures, respect is shown by looking directly at a person's face. Thus, the absence or presence of eye contact provides insight into whether a society is orientated towards a hierarchical or lateral form of social organisation respectively.

While worldview attributes are depicted in binary terms, it is important to note that most societies will evidence aspects of all these attributes. However, some will be more dominant and given greater priority than others. The binary within each attribute should be understood as the poles of a spectrum along which individuals can move. As an individual's context or experience changes, they may move towards either pole. This means worldviews can overlap with each other and that an individual can display a hybrid identity. For example, the former South African President Jacob Zuma, as the head of state, can be seen to function within a more Western interpretation of reality. However, he also functions within a non-Western worldview as suggested by his practice of the Zulu custom which supports polygamous marriage.

To understand the relationship between identity, culture and worldview, it is useful to conceptualise it diagrammatically using interlocking cogs (Fig. 3.1). These depict the way the concepts are interconnected, dynamic and embedded within a context which they can both influence and be influenced by. Identity is a system of beliefs for making sense of the world. It is also the unit of survival that speaks to one's sense of survival, safety and belonging in the world. Culture is defined as a shared system of beliefs for making sense of one's reality and is expressed in a society's social institutes, its social rules and values, as well as through its symbolic landscape. For the purpose of this research, culture refers to those expressions that are visible. Inseparably intertwined from culture, worldview contains the scripts and assumptions through which one's social reality is interpreted and which informs what can be known

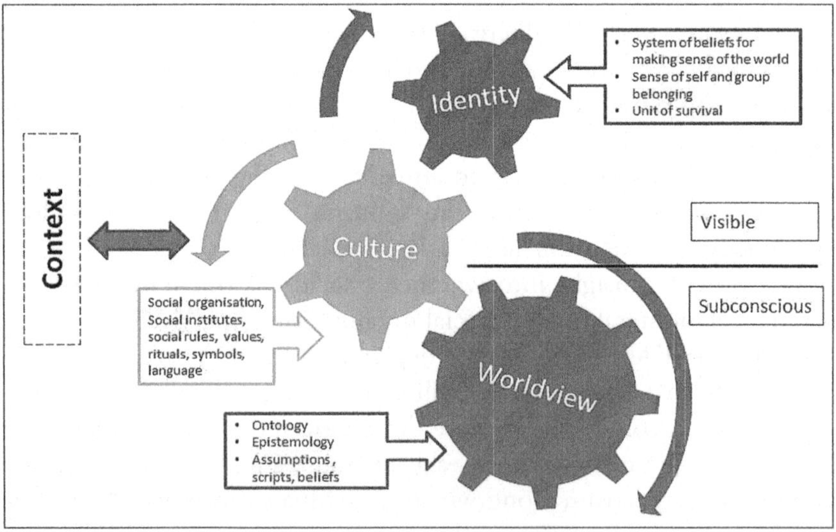

Fig. 3.1 The identity–culture–worldview nexus

about the world, i.e. it is the infrastructure for deeper meaning-making. It comprises a range of attributes which are manifested through culture and which act as the 'lens' that shapes how one engages with and interprets the world. For example, an interconnected ontology (worldview) might result in social rules, values and rituals that give primacy to one's ancestors (culture). These cultural expressions are forms of meaning-making that ensure the survival of the group and create a sense of well-being and safety in the world (identity). In this way, worldviews shape and support the social environment in which they are embedded, as was the case with the development of Apartheid (see Chapter 2). As they are flexible they can shift and develop through changes in environment and experience.

3.5 The Relationship Between Identity, Culture, Worldview and Intergroup Conflict

To build a positive peace, Johan Galtung (1969, 1990), the father of peace studies, argues that one needs to address each of the three interconnected vertices in his models of conflict and violence. Conflict, he argues, comprises three interconnected components namely: the contradiction, the attitude and behaviours that support the conflict.[4] His definition of violence comprises three categories namely: direct, structural and cultural. Direct violence is expressed in physical acts directed towards people (or property). Structural violence refers to institutional structures and policies which promote injustice in the political, social and economic realms thus denying people their inherent dignity and precluding them from being able to satisfy their basic needs, i.e. South Africa's policy of Apartheid. Cultural violence refers to those aspects of culture such as religion, ideology, language and narratives that seek to

[4]Contradiction, is defined as the 'incompatibility of goals' whether these are perceived or actual. Attitudes refer to the perceptions (or misperceptions) and stereotypes one has of the 'other'; these serve to legitimise the conflict and can include emotions of hatred, insecurity, fear, anger and the beliefs one holds towards a conflict. Behaviour is defined as the actions, such as violent attacks or threats, which serve to perpetuate a conflict.

justify violence which speaks to the influence of worldview in shaping attitudes and behaviours in group conflicts.

Further to this, in his theory of protracted social conflict (PSC), Edward Azar (1990: 12) argues that protracted conflicts occur 'when communities are deprived of satisfaction of their basic needs [including security, recognition and acceptance, fair access to political institutions and economic participation] on the basis of the communal identity [including racial, religious, ethnic, cultural among others]'. The legacy of colonialism and efforts at political domination by a single identity group over others can also act to exacerbate such conflicts. Given the dimension of identity in PSC, it follows that the influence of culture and worldview in shaping such conflicts needs to be understood.

The point is that understanding the causes of group conflict is crucial to their successful transformation and building a peace that can be sustained. Drawing on Galtung's definition of positive peace and Azar's theory of protracted social conflict, this book recognises the way in which structural violence, state actors, and histories of oppression and inequality contribute to exacerbating intergroup conflict. However, this book is concerned with exploring the role of worldview as an under-appreciated (and under theorised) cause of conflict which can act to reinforce other contributing factors.

The challenge with worldview as the cause of conflict is that it is not based on material evidence but rather on one's interpretation of reality and chosen truth (Nudler 1993). Thus, it is useful to refer to Gestalt ambiguous figures to conceptualise it. Depending on which elements are focused on, the figure can be viewed as two distinctly different images. Without evidence to support viewing the figure in only one way, the 'truth' of the image is derived by locating it within a world or social context. As these can differ across groups, it makes it possible that no agreement will be reached on what the figures represent. Indeed, as Nudler (1990) points out, in the real world the worldview of the 'other' may not be readily accepted as valid or even recognised as having the right to exist. Recognising that culture and shared systems of meaning-making determine what is seen as logical (or common sense) means that worldview conflicts are not easily resolved through perceived rational logic. Referring to such conflicts as 'radical disagreements',

Ramsbotham (2010) explains that they encompass deep value differences regarding beliefs about how one should live and prioritise one's decisions. This can extend to disputes surrounding the issue of abortion and homosexuality, as well as to everyday interactions with the 'other'.

To understand the relationship between worldview and conflict, one must bear in mind that worldview is inextricably linked to identity and one's sense of safety and security in the world. Drawing from Terror Management Theory (TMT), a branch of social psychology, encountering a different way of being in the world can solicit several (and sometimes violent) responses including denigrating and discrediting the 'other'; convincing the 'other' to assimilate one's own beliefs into their own, as is the approach of missionary religions; or asserting the superiority and 'truth' of one's own worldview and beliefs in an effort to eradicate the 'other' (Solomon et al. 2000).

These responses resonate with social identity theory which argues that one's sense of self is derived by comparing one's own group to the 'other' using discriminatory narratives and negative stereotypes that negate the credibility of the 'other' (Tajfel and Turner 1986). When encountering an understanding of reality that is different to one's own, the superiority of one's own reality over the 'other' will be defended (Berger and Luckmann 1966). Taking this a step further, TMT explains such an encounter can result in 'terror' and anxiety as it serves to destabilise one's sense of safety and security (Lieberman et al. 2001; Solomon et al. 2000; Hayes et al. 2008). For example, the theory argues that hate crimes aimed at those with a different belief system, such as religion or beliefs towards abortion, stem from a deep-rooted instinct for self-preservation (Lieberman et al. 2001). Consequently, this can contribute to a lack of awareness and distortion of the 'other', the perpetuation of group polarisation, and, potentially, to the eruption of intergroup violence (Northrup 1989; Ashmore et al. 2001). This is often supported by several beliefs which groups can use to interpret their shared experience and which act to justify the use of violence (physical or structural) against the 'other' namely: superiority, injustice, vulnerability, distrust and helplessness (Eidelson and Eidelson 2003; Rouhana and Bar-Tel 1998; Staub 1996). For example, superiority, which is defined by Eidelson and Eidelson (2003), as the conviction that one's group is morally superior, chosen, entitled and destined, was used by the Afrikaans to interpret their experience of British colonialism and to justify the adoption of the policy of Apartheid. While these beliefs serve to legitimise violence, they also act as the power base to racism, classism, sexism and other forms of structural violence.

To further illustrate the relationship between worldview and intergroup conflict, it is useful to apply the schematic depicting the nexus between identity, culture and worldview (Fig. 3.1) to South Africa and the development of Apartheid (see Fig. 3.2). As outlined in Chapter 2, this was shaped by the sociopolitical context and events taking place in nineteenth-century Europe and the impact this had on relations between the British and the Dutch in South Africa. Integral to the European colonial enterprise was a scientific worldview and values that promoted progress and improvement. While these are neutral values when coupled with beliefs in scientific racism, racial superiority, Social Darwinism, religious injunctions that supported racial purity, beliefs in one's divine chosen-ness, and the memory of being victims of

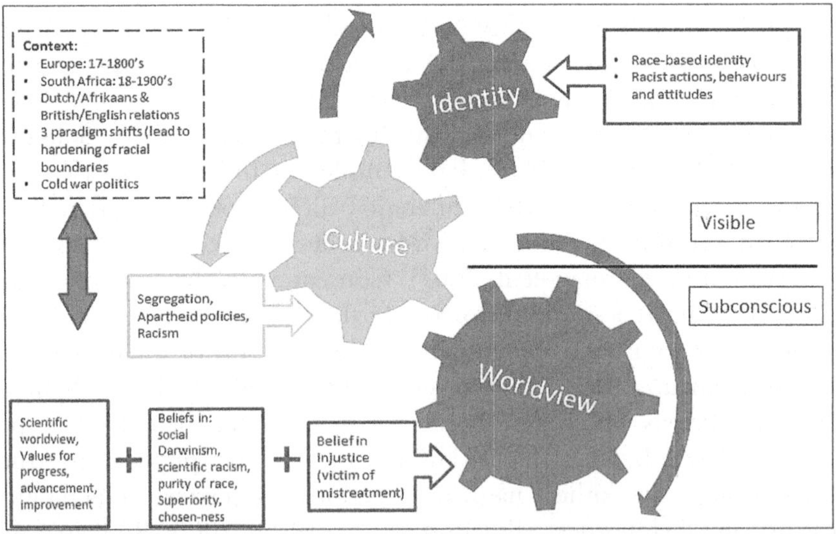

Fig. 3.2 Schematic diagram depicting the interplay between worldview and racism in South Africa

mistreatment, it leads to the structuring of an unequal society, the adoption of racist policies, and the implementation of racist and segregated social institutions (culture). Ultimately, this informed the construction of racist and race-based identities which continue to shape intergroup relations in the society.

To counter group polarisation, 'contact theory' is often used. It argues that direct contact and encounter with the 'other' will act to minimise the prejudices that groups hold of the 'other' and thereby reduce intergroup conflict (Hewstone 1996; Pettigrew 1998). Although the contact hypothesis is generally seen as an effective strategy for improving intergroup relations, several conditions are required to improve its chances of success. These include equal status of members across groups and the desire for a closer cooperation to achieve a common goal (Pettigrew and Tropp 2006). However, what contact theory fails to consider is the influence of worldview and deeper systems of meaning-making on intergroup relations. While it may be useful for improving tolerance, there is little evidence of contact being able to shift deeply held beliefs that might have divided groups in the first instance (Jackman and Crane 1986; Malešević 2011a, b). Indeed, research by Dixon et al. (2007) on intergroup contact and attitudes towards policies aimed at racial redress in South Africa shows that despite many 'whites' theoretically supporting the principle of equality encapsulated in these policies their implementation was still widely opposed to many 'whites' still holding onto an identity based on privilege and superiority. Moreover, contact theory fails to consider the potential implications contact between groups with different systems of meaning-making might have on interpreting the 'other' and promoting reconciliation.

Finally, given the focus of this discussion on worldview and intergroup conflict Samuel Huntington's theory developed in *The Clash of Civilizations* should be acknowledged (Huntington 1993, 1996). Recognising the significance of worldview in conflict, he argues that the 'dominating source of [global] conflict will be cultural' and future international conflict will mostly be between Western and non-Western countries, as non-Western countries seek to assert themselves against imposed Western values (Huntington 1993: 22). However, there are several cautionary points arising from criticisms of his theory (Sen 1999;

Fox 2005; Said 2001). The first relates to rendering non-Western societies as culturally homogenous; it is important to bear in mind that non-Western societies are as culturally diverse as are Western societies, perhaps more so. Failure to do so risks speaking about identity in binary terms when, in fact, it is much more complex and flexible that Huntington's theory suggests. Secondly, it gives primacy to culture to the exclusion of the argument that states act out of self-interest and in the interests of national security. Although one can argue that how national security is interpreted is rooted in worldview, the point is that even though worldview is an infrastructure for deeper meaning-making not everything can be attributed to it. Lastly, critics argue his theory does not account for other types of conflicts (such as conflicts over resources or territory) which may in fact be more prevalent. While not all conflicts are worldview conflicts, the attitudes and beliefs that justify one's behaviours are rooted in worldview. Furthermore, all parties to a conflict carry an identity which, by definition, is embedded in culture and worldview.

Notwithstanding these criticisms, this book argues that to promote positive intergroup relations and build a sustainable peace, different systems for interpreting reality need to be taken into account. Recognising that most societies are culturally diverse, with a variety of interpretations of reality, underscores the relevance of worldview in peace-building and transitional justice. The following chapter will review the significance of worldview in the context of South Africa's Truth and Reconciliation Commission.

References

Abrams, Dominic, and Michael A. Hogg. 1998. Comments on the motivational status of self-esteem in social identity and intergroup discrimination. *European Journal of Social Psychology* 18: 317–334.

Aiken, Nevin T. 2010. Learning to live together: Transitional justice and intergroup reconciliation in Northern Ireland. *International Journal of Transitional Justice* 4 (2): 166–188.

Aiken, Nevin T. 2013. *Identity, reconciliation and transitional justice: Overcoming intractability in divided societies*. London and New York: Routledge.

Arthur, Paige. 2011a. Introduction: Identities in transition. In *Identities in transition: Challenges for transitional justice in divided societies*, ed. Paige Arthur, 1–16. New York: Cambridge University Press.

Arthur, Paige. 2011b. *Identities in transition: Challenges for transitional justice in divided societies*. New York: Cambridge University Press.

Ashmore, Richard D., Lee Jussim, and David Wilder. 2001. *Social identity, intergroup conflict, and conflict reduction*. New York: Oxford University Press.

Atran, Scott. 2010. *Talking to the enemy: Violent extremism, sacred values, and what it means to be human*. Bristol and New York: Allen Lane and Harper Collins Publishers.

Auerbach, Yehudith. 2004. The role of forgiveness in reconciliation. In *From conflict resolution to reconciliation*, ed. Yaacov Bar-Siman-Tov, 149–175. Oxford and New York: Oxford University Press.

Avruch, Kevin, and Peter W. Black. 1993. Conflict resolution in intercultural settings: Problems and prospects. In *Conflict resolution theory and practice: Integration and application*, ed. Dennis J.D. Sandole and Hugo van der Merwe, 131–145. Manchester: Manchester University Press.

Avruch, Kevin. 1998. *Culture and conflict resolution*. Washington, DC: United States Institute of Peace Press.

Azar, Edward. 1990. *The management of protracted social conflict: Theory and cases*. Aldershot: Dartmouth.

Babo-Soares, Dionisio. 2004. *Nahe biti:* The philosophy and process of grassroots reconciliation (and justice) in East Timor. *Asia Pacific Journal of Anthropology* 5 (1): 15–33.

Balcomb, Anthony. 2014. *Journey into the African sun: Soundings in search of another way of being in the world*. Pretoria: University of South Africa.

Bar-Siman-Tov, Yaacov. 2004. *From conflict resolution to reconciliation*. Oxford and New York: Oxford University Press.

Bell, Christine. 2000. *Peace agreements and human rights*. Oxford: Oxford University Press.

Benedict, Ruth. 1946. *The chrysanthemum and the sword*. Boston: Tuttle Publishing.

Berger, Peter L., and Thomas Luckmann. 1966. *The social construction of reality: A treatise in the sociology of knowledge*. London: Allen Lane.

Bhabha, Homi K. 1994. *The location of culture*. London and New York: Routledge.

Blankenburgh, Marco. 2013. *Inter-cultural intelligence: From surviving to thriving in the global space*. Dubai: KnowledgeWorkx.

Bloomfield, David, Teresa Barnes, and Luc Huyse. 2003. *Reconciliation after violent conflict: A handbook*. Stockholm: International IDEA.

Borer, Tristan Anne. 2003. A taxonomy of victims and perpetrators: Human rights and reconciliation in South Africa. *Human Rights Quarterly* 25 (4): 1088–1116.

Bourdieu, Pierre. 1984. *Distinction: A social critique of the judgement of taste*, trans. Richard Nice. Cambridge, MA: Harvard University Press.

Brigg, Morgan. 2010. Culture: Challenges and possibilities. In *Palgrave advances in peace-building: Critical developments and approaches*, ed. Oliver Richmond, 329–346. Basingstoke: Palgrave Macmillan.

Brown, M. Anne. 2013. Anthropology and peacebuilding. In *Handbook of peacebuilding*, ed. Roger Mac Ginty, 132–146. London and New York: Routledge.

Bryan, Dominic. 2000. *Orange parades: The politics of ritual, tradition and control*. London: Pluto Press.

Bryan, Dominic, and Gillian McIntosh. 2005. Symbols: Sites of creation and contest in Northern Ireland. *SAIS Review* 25 (2): 127–138.

Bryden, Alan, and Heiner Hänggi. 2005. *Security governance in post-conflict peacebuilding*. Piscataway, NJ: Transaction Publishers.

Buchanan, Ruth Margaret, and Peer Zumbansen. 2014. *Law in transition: Human rights, development and transitional justice*. Oxford and Portland, OR: Hart Publishing.

Centre for Chinese Studies. 2008. *South Africa's recent court ruling on black economic empowerment*. Stellenbosch: *The China Monitor* 31.

Chapman, Audrey R., and Hugo van der Merwe. 2008. *Truth and reconciliation in South Africa: Did the TRC deliver?* Philadelphia: University of Pennsylvania Press.

Clark, Mary E. 1989. *Ariandne's thread: The search for new modes of thinking*. Hampshire and London: Macmillan.

Clark, Phil. 2007. Hybridity, holism, and traditional justice: The case of the *Gacaca* courts in postgenocide Rwanda. *George Washington International Law Review* 39 (4): 765–837.

Cohen, Raymond. 2004. Apology and reconciliation in international relations. In *From conflict resolution to reconciliation*, ed. Yaacov Bar-Siman-Tov, 177–195. Oxford and New York: Oxford University Press.

Cohen, Robin, and Paul Kennedy. 2000. *Global sociology*. London: Macmillan.

Curle, Adam. 1999. *To tame the hydra: Undermining the culture of violence*. Oxfordshire: Jon Carpenter Publishing.

Darby, John, and Roger Mac Ginty. 2003. *Contemporary peace making: Conflict, violence and peace processes*. Basingstoke and New York: Palgrave Macmillan.

David, Roman, and Susanne Y.P. Choi. 2006. Forgiveness and transitional justice in the Czech Republic. *Journal of Conflict Resolution* 50 (3): 339–367.

de Greiff, Pablo. 2006. *The handbook of reparations*. Oxford: Oxford University Press.

Dilthey, William. 1970. Culture and the production of worldviews. In *Man and culture: A philosophical anthology*, ed. Donald Phillip Verene, 103–132. New York: Laurel.

Dixon, John, Kevin Durrheim, and Colin Tredoux. 2007. Intergroup contact and attitudes toward the principle and practice of racial equality. *Psychological Science* 18 (10) (October 1): 867–872.

Docherty, Jayne Seminare. 2001. *Learning lessons from Waco: When the parties bring their gods to the negotiation table*. Syracuse: Syracuse University Press.

Docherty, Jayne Seminare. 2004a. Culture and negotiation: Symmetrical anthropology for negotiators. *Marquette Law Review* 87: 711–722.

Docherty, Jayne Seminare. 2004b. Narratives, metaphors, and negotiation. *Marquette Law Review* 87: 847–851.

Douglas, Mary. 1996. *Natural symbols: Explorations in cosmology*. New York: Routledge.

Drumbl, Mark A. 2007. *Atrocity, punishment, and international law*. New York: Cambridge University Press.

Easthope, Antony. 1998. Bhabha, hybridity and identity. *Textual Practice* 12 (2): 341–348.

Eaton, Liberty, and Johann Louw. 2000. Culture and self in South Africa: Individualism-collectivism predictions. *Journal of Social Psychology* 140: 210–217.

Eidelson, Roy J., and Judy Eidelson. 2003. Dangerous ideas: Five beliefs that propel groups toward conflict. *American Psychologist* 58 (3): 182–192.

Eriksen, Thomas Hylland. 2001. Ethnic identity, national identity, and intergroup conflict. In *Social identity, intergroup conflict, and conflict reduction*, ed. Richard D. Ashmore, Lee Jussim, and David Wilder, 42–70. New York: Oxford University Press.

Eriksen, Thomas Hylland. 2010. *Small places, large issues: An introduction to social and cultural anthropology*, 3rd ed. London and New York: Pluto Press.

Fletcher, Laurel, and Harvey Weinstein. 2002. Violence and social repair: Rethinking the contribution of justice to reconciliation. *Human Rights Quarterly* 24 (3): 573–639.

Fox, Jonathan. 2005. Paradigm lost: Huntington's unfulfilled clash of civilizations prediction into the 21st century. *International Politics* 42: 428–457.

Galtung, Johan. 1969. Violence, peace, and peace research. *Journal of Peace Research* 6: 167–191.

Galtung, Johan. 1990. Cultural violence. *Journal of Peace Research* 27 (3): 291–305.

Geertz, Clifford. 1973. *The interpretation of cultures: Selected essays*. New York: Fontana Press.

Gibson, James L. 2004. *Overcoming Apartheid: Can truth reconcile a divided nation?* New York: Russel Sage Foundation.

Goffman, Erving. 1986. *Frame analysis: An essay on the organization of experience*. Boston: North Eastern University Press.

Goldberg, Rachel M. 2009. How our worldviews shape our practice. *Conflict Resolution Quarterly* 26 (4): 405–431.

Goodman, Nelson. 1978. *Ways of worldmaking*. Hassocks: Harvester Press.

Gross, Oren, and Fionnuala Ní Aoláin. 2006. *Law in times of crisis: Emergency powers in theory and practice*. Cambridge: Cambridge University Press.

Guba, Egon G., and Yvonna S. Lincoln. 1998. Competing paradigms in qualitative research. In *The landscape of qualitative research: Theories and issues*, ed. Norman K. Denzin and Yvonna S. Lincoln, 195–220. Thousand Oaks, London, and New Delhi: Sage.

Guba, Egon G., and Yvonna S. Lincoln. 2008. Paradigmatic controversies, contradictions, and emerging confluences. In *The landscape of qualitative research*, ed. Norman K. Denzin and Yvonna S. Lincoln, 255–286. Thousand Oaks, CA: Sage.

Hall, Edward T. 1959. *The silent language*. New York: Anchor Books.

Hamber, Brandon. 2009. *Transforming societies after political violence: Truth, reconciliation, and mental health*. New York: Springer.

Hamber, Brandon. 2012. Transitional justice and intergroup conflict. In *Oxford handbook of intergroup conflict*, ed. Linda Tropp, 328–343. New York: Oxford University Press.

Hamber, Brandon, and Grainne Kelly. 2009. Beyond coexistence: Towards a working definition of reconciliation. In *Reconciliation(s): Transitional justice in postconflict societies*, ed. Quinn R. Joanna, 286–310. Montreal: McGill University Press.

Hayes, Joseph, Jeff Schimel, and Todd J. Williams. 2008. Fighting death with death: The buffering effects of learning that worldview violators have died. *Psychological Science* 19 (5): 501–507.

Hayner, Priscilla B. 2001. *Unspeakable truths: Confronting state terror and atrocity*. New York: Routledge.

Hazan, Pierre. 2006. Measuring the impact of punishment and forgiveness: A framework for evaluating transitional justice. *International Review of the Red Cross* 88 (861) (March): 19–47.

Hendry, Joy. 2008. *An introduction to social anthropology: Sharing our worlds*, 2nd ed. Basingstoke: Palgrave Macmillan.

Heslam, Peter S. 1998. *Creating a Christian worldview: Abraham Kuyper's lectures on Calvinism*. Grand Rapids: W. B. Eerdmans.

Hewstone, Miles. 1996. Contact and categorization: Social-psychological interventions to change intergroup relations. In *Foundations of stereotypes and stereotyping*, ed. C. Neil Macrae, Charles Stangor, and Miles Hewstone, 323–368. New York: Guilford.

Hicks, David, and Margaret A. Gwynne. 1996. *Cultural anthropology*, 2nd ed. New York: HarperCollins.

Hofstede, Geert. 1980. *Culture's consequences: International differences in work related values*. Beverly Hills, CA: Sage.

Huntington, Samuel P. 1993. The clash of civilizations. *Foreign Affairs* 72 (3): 22–49.

Huntington, Samuel P. 1996. *The clash of civilizations and the remaking of world order*. New York, London, Toronto, and Sydney: Simon & Schuster Paperbacks.

Huyse, Luc, and Mark Salter. 2008. *Traditional justice and reconciliation after violent conflict: Learning from African experiences*. Stockholm: International IDEA.

Jackman, Mary R., and Marie Crane. 1986. 'Some of my best friends are black': Interracial friendship and whites' racial attitudes. *Public Opinion Quarterly* 50: 459–486.

James, Aleya, and Candy McLeod. 2014. An analysis of the three colors worldview mapping tool: Contrasting Emirati and non-Emirati worldviews. *Intercultural Communication Studies* 23 (1): 165–186.

Jenkins, Richard. 1992. *Pierre Bourdieu*. New York: Routledge.

Jeong, Ho-Won. 2005. *Peacebuilding in postconflict societies: Strategy and process*. Boulder and London: Lynne Rienner Publishers.

Kearney, Michael. 1984. *Worldview*. Novato: Chandler and Sharp Publications.

Kelly, George A. 1963. *A theory of personality: The psychology of personal constructs*. New York: The Norton Library.

Kelsall, Tim. 2009. *Culture under cross-examination: International justice and the special court for Sierra Leone*. New York: Cambridge University Press.

Kent, Lia. 2011. Local memory practices in East Timor: Disrupting transitional justice narratives. *The International Journal of Transitional Justice* 5: 434–455.

Kirby, Paul. 2015. Paris attacks: France grapples with freedom of speech. *BBC News*, January 15. http://www.bbc.co.uk/news/blogs-eu-30829005. Accessed 27 August 2018.

Kluckhohn, Florence Rockwood, and Fred L. Strodtbeck. 1961. *Variations in value orientations*. Westport, CT: Greenwood Press.

Koltko-Rivera, Mark E. 2004. The psychology of worldviews. *Review of General Psychology* 8 (1): 3–58.

Kritz, Neil J. 1995. *Transitional justice: How emerging democracies reckon with former regimes*. Washington, DC: United States Institute of Peace.

Krog, Antjie. 2008a. '…if it means he gets his humanity back…': The worldview underpinning the South African Truth and Reconciliation Commission. *Journal of Multicultural Discourses* 3 (3): 204–220.

Krog, Antjie. 2008b. 'My heart is on my tongue': The untranslated self in a translated world. *Journal of Analytical Psychology* 53: 225–239.

Krog, Antjie. 2015. Research into reconciliation and forgiveness at the South African Truth and Reconciliation Commission and Homi Bhabha's architecture of the new. *Canadian Journal of Law and Society* 30 (2): 203–217.

Lakoff, George, and Mark Johnson. 1980. *Metaphors we live by*. Chicago and London: University of Chicago Press.

Lambourne, Wendy. 2009. Transitional justice and peacebuilding after mass violence. *The International Journal of Transitional Justice*, 3: 28–48.

Laplante, Lisa J. 2008. Transitional justice and peace building: Diagnosing and addressing the socioeconomic roots of violence through a human rights framework. *International Journal of Transitional Justice* 2 (3): 331–355.

Laplante, Lisa J. 2014. The plural justice aims of reparations. In *Transitional justice theories*, ed. Susanne Buckley-Zistel, Teresa Koloma Beck, Christian Braun, and Friederike Mieth, 66–84. London and New York: Routledge.

Lawler, Steph. 2008. *Identity: Sociological perspectives*. Cambridge: Polity.

Lederach, John Paul. 1997. *Building peace: Sustainable reconciliation in divided societies*. Washington, DC: United States Institute of Peace Press.

Lidén, Kristoffer, Roger Mac Ginty, and Oliver P. Richmond. 2009. Introduction: Beyond northern epistemologies of peace—Peacebuilding reconstructed? *International Peacekeeping* 16 (5): 587–598.

Lieberman, Joel D., Jamie Arndt, Jennifer Personius, and Alison Cook. 2001. Vicarious annihilation: The effect of mortality salience on perceptions of hate crimes. *Law and Human Behavior* 25 (6): 547–566.
Long, William J., and Peter Brecke. 2003. *War and reconciliation: Reason and emotion in conflict resolution*. Cambridge, MA and London: MIT Press.
Lundy, Patricia, and Mark Mcgovern. 2008. Whose justice? Rethinking transitional justice from the bottom up. *Journal of Law and Society* 35 (2): 265–292.
Mac Ginty, Roger. 2008. Indigenous peace-making versus liberal peace. *Cooperation and Conflict: Journal of the Nordic International Studies Association* 43 (2): 139–163.
Mac Ginty, Roger. 2010. Hybrid peace: The interaction between top-down and bottom-up peace. *Security Dialogue* 41 (4): 391–412.
Mac Ginty, Roger. 2011. *International peace-building and local resistance: Hybrid forms of peace*. Basingstoke: Palgrave Macmillan.
Mac Ginty, Roger. 2013. Introduction: The transcripts of peace—Public, hidden or non-obvious? *Journal of Intervention and Statebuilding* 7 (4): 423–430.
Malešević, Siniša. 2011a. Nationalism, war and social cohesion. *Ethnic and Racial Studies* 34 (1): 142–161.
Malešević, Siniša. 2011b. The chimera of national identity. *Nations and Nationalism* 17 (2): 272–290.
Mallinder, Louise. 2007. Can amnesties and international justice be reconciled? *International Journal of Transitional Justice* 1 (2): 208–230.
Mallinder, Louise. 2008. *Amnesty, human rights and political transitions: Bridging the peace and justice divide*. Oxford and Portland, OR: Hart Publishing.
Mallinder, Louise, and Kieran McEvoy. 2011. Rethinking amnesties: Atrocity, accountability, and impunity in post-conflict societies. *Contemporary Social Science* 6 (1): 107–128.
Mani, Rama. 2005. Rebuilding an inclusive political community after war. *Security Dialogue* 36 (4): 511–526.
Mani, Rama. 2008. Dilemmas of expanding transitional justice, or forging the nexus between transitional justice and development. *International Journal of Transitional Justice* 2 (3): 253–265.
Maslow, Abraham. 1954. *Motivation and personality*. New York: Harper Bros.
Mbeki, Thabo. 1998. Statement of Deputy President Thabo Mbeki at the opening of the debate in the National Assembly. *Reconciliation and Nation Building*, May 29. Department of International Relations and Cooperation.

McEvoy, Kieran, and Lorna McGregor. 2008. *Transitional justice from below: Grassroots activism and the struggle for change*. Portland, OR: Hart.

Merry, Sally Engle. 2006. *Human rights and gender violence: Translating international law into local justice*. Chicago and London: University of Chicago Press.

Miller, Zinaida. 2008. Effects of invisibility: In search of the 'economic' in transitional justice. *International Journal of Transitional Justice* 2 (3): 266–291.

Moon, Claire. 2004. Prelapsarian state: Forgiveness and reconciliation in transitional justice. *International Journal for the Semiotics of Law* 17: 185–197.

Muller, Roland. 2001. *Honor and shame: Unlocking the door*. Bloomington, IN: XLibris Corporation.

Muvingi, Ismael. 2009. Sitting on power kegs: Socioeconomic rights in transitional societies. *International Journal of Transitional Justice* 3: 163–182.

Naugle, David K. 2002. *Worldview: The history of a concept*. Grand Rapids and Cambridge: W. B. Eerdmans.

Navarro, Zander. 2006. In search of a cultural interpretation of power: The contribution of Pierre Bourdieu. *IDS Bulletin* 32 (6): 11–22.

Nietzsche, Friedrich. 1956. *The birth of tragedy and the genealogy of morals*. Garden City: Doubleday.

Northrup, Terrell A. 1989. The dynamic of identity in personal and social conflict. In *Intractable conflicts and their transformation*, ed. Louis Kriesberg, Terrell A. Northrup, and Stuart J. Thorson, 68–76. New York: Syracuse University Press.

Nudler, Oscar. 1990. On conflicts and metaphors: Toward an extended rationality. In *Conflict: Human Needs Theory*, ed. Burton John, 177–201. The Conflict Series. London: Palgrave Macmillan.

Nudler, Oscar. 1993. In search of a theory for conflict resolution: Taking a new look at world view analysis. *ICAR Newsletter* 5 (5): 1–5.

Nürnberger, Klaus. 2007. *The living dead and the living God: Christ and the ancestors in a changing Africa*. Pietermaritzburg: Cluster Publications.

Oberschall, Anthony. 2007. *Conflict and peace building in divided societies: Responses to ethnic violence*. London and New York: Routeledge.

Orentlicher, Diane. 2007. Settling accounts revisited: Reconciling global norms with local agency. *International Journal of Transitional Justice* 1 (1): 10–22.

Oyserman, Daphna. 1993. The lens of personhood: Viewing the self and others in a multicultural society. *Journal of Personality and Social Psychology* 65 (5): 993–1009.

Oyserman, Daphna, Heather M. Coon, and Markus Kemmelmeier. 2002. Rethinking individualism and collectivism: Evaluation of theoretical assumptions and meta-analysis. *Psychological Bulletin* 128: 3–72.

Palmer, Gary B. 1996. *Toward a theory of cultural linguistics*. Austin: The University of Texas Press.

Palmer, Nicola, Briony Jones, and Julia Viebach. 2015. Introduction: Ways of knowing atrocity—A methodological enquiry into the formulation, implementation, and assessment of transitional justice. *Canadian Journal of Law and Society* 30 (2): 173–182.

Parmentier, Stephan, Koen De Feyter, Paul Lemmens, and Marc Bossuyt. 2006. *Out of the ashes: Reparation for victims of gross and systematic human rights violations*. Antwerp: Intersentia.

Pepper, Stephen C. 1942. *World hypothesis: A study in evidence*. Berkeley, Los Angeles, and London: University of California Press.

Pettigrew, Thomas F. 1998. Intergroup contact theory. *Annual Review of Psychology* 49: 65–85.

Pettigrew, Thomas F., and Linda R. Tropp. 2006. A meta-analytic test of intergroup contact theory. *Journal of Personality and Social Psychology* 90: 751–783.

Pillay, Verashni. 2013. Cursed if we criticise Zuma? Think again. *Mail & Guardian Online*, October 8. http://mg.co.za/article/2013-10-08-cursed-if-we-criticise-zuma-think-again/. Accessed 28 August 2018.

Quinn, Joanna R. 2007. Social reconstruction in Uganda: The role of customary mechanisms in transitional justice. *Human Rights Review* 8 (4): 389–407.

Quinn, Joanna R. 2009. *Reconciliation(s): Transitional justice in postconflict societies*. Montreal and Kingston: McGill-Queen's University Press.

Ramsbotham, Oliver. 2010. *Transforming violent conflict: Radical disagreement, dialogue and survival*. London and New York.: Routledge.

Redfield, Robert. 1953. *The primitive world and its transformation*. Ithaca, NY: Cornell University Press.

Richmond, Oliver P. 2010. *Palgrave advances in peacebuilding: Critical developments and approaches*. Basingstoke: Palgrave Macmillan.

Richmond, Oliver P. 2011. *A post-liberal peace*. London and New York: Routledge.

Robinson, Darryl. 2003. Serving the interests of justice: Amnesties, truth commissions, and the International Criminal Court. *European Journal of International Law* 14 (3): 481–505.

Roht-Arriaza, Naomi, and Javier Mariezcurrena. 2006. *Transitional justice in the twenty-first century*. Cambridge: Cambridge University Press.

Ross, Marc Howard. 2007. *Cultural contestation in ethnic conflict*. Cambridge: Cambridge University Press.

Ross, Marc Howard. 2009. Cultural contestation and the symbolic landscape: Politics by other means? In *Culture and belonging in societies: Contestation and symbolic landscapes*, ed. Marc Howard Ross, 1–23. Philadelphia: University of Pennsylvania Press.

Rotberg, Robert I., and Dennis Thompson. 2000. *Truth v justice: The morality of truth commissions*. Princeton: Princeton University Press.

Rouhana, Nadim N., and Daniel Bar-Tel. 1998. Psychological dynamics of intractable ethnonational conflicts: The Israeli-Palestinian case. *American Psychologist* 53 (7): 761–770.

Said, Edward W. 2001. The clash of ignorance. *The Nation*, October 4. http://www.thenation.com/article/clash-ignorance/. Accessed 29 August 2018.

Sarkin, Jeremy. 1998. The development of a human rights culture in South Africa. *Human Rights Quarterly* 20 (3): 628–665.

Schabas, William A. 2011. *An introduction to the International Criminal Court*, 4th ed. Cambridge: Cambridge University Press.

Schabas, William A., and Shane Darcy. 2004. *Truth commissions and courts: The tension between criminal justice and the search for truth*. Dordrecht: Kluwer.

Schwartz, Shalom H. 1999. A theory of cultural values and some implications for work. *Applied Psychology* 48 (1): 23–47.

Schweder, Richard, and Robert A. Levine. 1984. *Culture theory: Essays on mind, self and emotion*. Cambridge: Cambridge University Press.

Sen, Amartya. 1999. Democracy as a universal value. *Journal of Democracy* 10 (3): 3–17.

Shriver, Donald W. 2001. Forgiveness: A bridge across abysses of revenge. In *Forgiveness and reconciliation: Religion, public policy, and conflict transformation*, ed. R.G. Helmick and R.L. Petersen, 151–167. Radnor, PA: Templeton Foundation Press.

Shweder, Richard, Nancy Much, Manamohan Mahapatra, and Lawrence Park. 1997. The big three of morality (autonomy, community, divinity) and the big three explanation of suffering. In *Morality and health: Interdisciplinary perspectives*, ed. Allan Brandt and Paul Rozin, 119–169. New York: Routledge.

Solomon, Sheldon, Jeff Greenberg, and Tom Pyszczynski. 2000. Pride and prejudice: Fear of death and social behavior. *Current Directions in Psychological Science* 9 (6): 200–204.

Somech, Anit. 2000. The independent and interdependent selves: Different meanings in different cultures. *International Journal of Intercultural Relations* 24: 161–172.

Spencer-Oatey, Helen. 2000. *Culturally speaking: Managing rapport through talk across cultures*. London: Continuum.

Sriram, Chandra Lekha. 2007. Justice as peace? Liberal peacebuilding and strategies of transitional justice. *Global Society* 21 (4): 579–591.

Staub, Ervin. 1996. Cultural-societal roots of violence: The examples of genocidal violence and of contemporary youth violence in the United States. *American Psychologist* 51 (2): 117–132.

Tajfel, Henri. 1981. *Social identity and intergroup relations*. London: Cambridge University Press.

Tajfel, Henri, and John C. Turner. 1986. The Social Identity Theory of intergroup behaviour. In *Psychology of intergroup relations*, ed. Stephen Worchel and William G. Austin, 33–48. Chicago: Nelson-Hall.

Teitel, Ruti G. 2000. *Transitional justice*. New York: Oxford University Press.

Thomas, Laurence. 2009. Forgiveness as righteousness. In *Reconciliation(s): Transitional justice in postconflict societies*, ed. Joanna R. Quinn, 17–25. Montreal and Kingston: McGill-Queen's University Press.

Torpey, John. 2003. *Politics of the past: On repairing historical injustices*. Lanham, MD: Rowman & Littlefield.

Tutu, Desmond M. 1999. *No future without forgiveness*. London: Rider.

Weedon, Chris. 2004. *Identity and culture*. Maidenhead: Open University Press.

Wilson, Richard A. 2001. *The politics of truth and reconciliation in South Africa: Legitimizing the post-Apartheid state*. Cambridge: Cambridge University Press.

Wolman, Benjamin B. 1973. *Dictionary of behavioural science*. New York: Van Nostrand Reinhold.

Yazdiha, Haj. 2010. Conceptualizing hybridity: Deconstructing boundaries through the hybrid. *Formations* 1 (1): 31–38.

4

Worldview Diversity Within South Africa's Truth and Reconciliation Commission

There is growing recognition within the peace-building and transitional justice discourse of the influence that ontological and epistemological differences have in shaping these processes (Palmer et al. 2015; Merry 2006; Sriram 2007, 2012; Kelsall 2009; Doe 2009). This is partly due to the criticism that Western liberal approaches to peace-building and transitional justice have been disconnected from the lived reality of individuals and communities affected by mass atrocities and their inappropriateness in non-Western contexts and to local culture (McEvoy 2007; Richmond 2011; McEvoy and McGregor 2008). In addition, there is also growing recognition that in divided societies these ontological differences contribute to peace (or conflict) at a local level in everyday intergroup interactions (Mac Ginty 2014; Richmond and Mitchell 2012). These differences were made apparent through South Africa's truth recovery process (Tutu 1999; Krog 2008, 2015; Shutte 2009a).

Recognising South Africa is an amalgam of diverse cultures, this chapter deconstructs the idealised forms of a Western liberal, nationalist and interconnected worldview (as exemplified within the African philosophy of *ubuntu*) that intertwine to shape South African society. Due to their European origins, it is likely that Western worldviews

C. Bollaert, *Reconciliation and Building a Sustainable Peace*,
Palgrave Studies in Compromise after Conflict,
https://doi.org/10.1007/978-3-030-03655-3_4

will be more dominant among 'white' South Africans while an interconnected worldview will be more reflective of an indigenous African way of being in the world. Understanding that worldviews are not as fixed as such a depiction might suggest, the aim is to develop a more nuanced understanding of these core strands of worldview and understand how they weave together, overlap and contradict each other simultaneously. The chapter applies this analysis to investigate the way in which they shaped the proceedings of the Truth and Reconciliation Commission (TRC) and to interpret some of the criticisms it received. It shows how key concepts such as reconciliation, accountability and nation-building can be interpreted differently highlighting the inherent assumptions worldview brings to how peace-building is approached.

4.1 Western Worldviews: Western Liberalism and Nationalism

Western liberalism and nationalism are two of the more dominant philosophies shaping Western societies. The Western liberal worldview is rooted in the Enlightenment, a period in European history (1600s–1700s) which challenged the authority of the Church, its perceived ignorance and superstitious beliefs. Interpreting reality and 'truth' from an objectivist ontological position, it served to separate the scientific world from the spiritual. In doing so, the Enlightenment promoted rationalism, secularism, truth that could be scientifically quantified, individualism and freedom (Tarnas 1991; Gay 1971; Nürnberger 2007). It also prioritised justice, equality and social order which provided the basis for what was referred to as the 'ideal society'; a vision for a secular society that followed the rule of law for political and legal purposes and not on the basis of religion or tribe (Gay 1971). Max Weber's notion of rational-legal authority in which claims to legitimacy or authority is rooted in rules that are legally or contractually determined can be traced back to this vision of society (Bendix 1977). Moreover, such a view of reality also had a significant influence on Western liberal approaches to peace-building which emphasises individual freedom and prioritises the rule of law, human rights, good governance, social and economic development, the building of state institutions and concern for social justice (Richmond 2011; Richmond and Mitchell 2012). Significantly, such an interpretation of the social world reflects the rule-based attribute of worldview which prioritises adherence to rules (over relationships), codes of conduct, contracts and policies and, more generally, the structural pillars of sustainable peace (see Chapter 3).

The Enlightenment also influenced the development of nationalism, as did Romanticism which challenged the Enlightenment in that it maintained a more spiritual view of the world. With the formation of the secular society, a new sense of community, which nationalism spoke to, was needed (Anderson 1983). It interpreted individualism and freedom within an autonomous but unified community and promoted a national identity and the right for every group to defend its language, religion and other aspects of its culture (Eriksen 1997; Gelvin 2005; Halliday 2006). Within this interpretation of the social world, national pride, loyalty to the state or collective, cultural and national unity, and attachment to one's ancestral history are prioritised (Smith 2001). Significantly, while civic nationalism emphasises the individual within a unified collective that is bound by common laws, ethnic nationalism emphasises the collective above the individual (Smith 2001: 39). In many respects, Western liberalism and nationalism espouse contradictory values in that one appears to promote the individual and the other, community. However, although a Western liberal worldview emphasises the individual, there is also a collective element in that it sees itself working for the security and well-being of the collective (Hernández-Truyol 2004; Dunne 2006).

4.2 Interconnected Worldviews: The *Ubuntu* Philosophy

Unlike Western worldviews, an interconnected worldview does not separate the spiritual world from the material or scientific world but rather sees the physical and spiritual world as unified (Turner 1977; Mbiti 1969; Bediako 2004; Krog 2008, 2015; Ashforth 2005; Nürnberger 2007). Within an interconnected worldview, there is a deep-rooted belief in a spiritual world which consists of benevolent and malevolent spiritual forces or beings greater and more powerful than oneself (Turner 1977). Benevolent forces include one's ancestors among other spirits and divinities while malevolent forces include evil spirits, demons and the occult power of witches and wizards. Malevolent forces are linked to witchcraft, which is widely understood as akin to jealousy, and can be used to deter those who are seen to be successful. Consequently, to maintain a sense of security in the world anything that may provoke jealousy should be avoided. This contrasts with individualism in which success and personal achievement are lauded. To maintain a sense of safety and security in such a world, a greater power outside oneself is needed. Thus, to protect one's self from malevolent spirits and misfortune, protocols, customs and rituals are closely observed. The contemporary relevance of this is illustrated in the incident surrounding a rescue mission of South African mineworkers trapped in a container (Saba 2016). Oversight in conducting a particular ritual, which is said to be carried out at all mines in the region, was interpreted by the families of those who were trapped as contributing to failed rescue attempts. Significantly, this speaks to the fear-power paradigm (see Chapter 3) and an identity rooted in 'spiritual insecurity'.

Furthermore, in an interconnected worldview the physical world is seen as a reflection of the spiritual world whereby the physical acts as a vehicle through which spiritual power can be accessed (Turner 1977). To strengthen an individual and society's resistance to potential malice, it is possible to share in the power of these forces both while alive and after death and form a relationship with the benevolent spirits to protect oneself against malevolent forces. Ancestors have an important role in maintaining their benevolent support of the community in which they formerly lived as they act as mediators between the spiritual world and family members who are still physically alive. While their physical bodies are dead, they are nonetheless perceived in some respects as being alive (i.e. the 'living-dead') (Nürnberger 2007). For example, among migrants to the city of Johannesburg a person's misfortune is interpreted either as a result of 'metaphysical disorder', which can include ancestors who are angry with the living for failing to observe necessary cultural rituals, or from exposure to malevolent spirits

(Zulu and Wilhelm-Solomon 2015). Thus, within this worldview security and well-being in the world are linked with submission to one's ancestors, elders and those in authority. It is also closely associated with a hierarchical structure of social organisation which is maintained by a strong connection and loyalty to the past.

Significantly, within this worldview ill health, poverty, suffering, early death and other personal difficulties are interpreted and resolved through the lens of motive (Ashforth 2005). This is illustrated in the examples of a migrant woman living in poverty who interpreted the miscarriage of her twins as the result of being bewitched or cursed by someone living in the same building as her and a labourer who attributed the swelling of his feet to someone who had bewitched him following the disappearance and then sudden reappearance of his work boots (Zulu and Wilhelm-Solomon 2015). When experiencing such difficulties, protection and resolution are usually sought through an *inyanga* or *sangoma* who use a medicine known as *muthi,* which can either be a herbal remedy or poison depending on the context in which it is administered.[1] Used in conjunction with occult powers, it can provide access to power and wealth (Ashforth 2005). In extreme cases, people can be killed for their body parts and the power they are perceived to contain (*Daily Sun* 2013a, b). The strength of these beliefs is well evidenced in the Marikana shootings where, following a consultation with a *sangoma,* some of the victims believed that *muthi* would give them protection by turning the bullets into water (Bond 2014; ENCA 2014; Maromo 2014).

Significantly, within an interconnected worldview the question of *who* (motive) is central to interpreting one's difficulties, misfortune and their solution. This is in contrast to an objectivist ontology which approaches social and personal problems with the question of *what,* i.e. *what* are the factors causing one's suffering as opposed to *who* is behind one's

[1]An *inyanga* is defined as 'a person who uses herbal and other medicinal preparations for treating disease' and a *sangoma* as someone who is 'trained to communicate with and utilise the powers of ancestors in diagnosing a disease or mishap' (Ashforth 2005: 53). An *inyanga* or *sangoma* can be used for either malevolent or benevolent purposes including gaining protection from one's enemy or for harming one's enemy.

suffering. These are two fundamentally different approaches to meaning-making. It raises important questions around how accountability, a key value within individualism and Western liberalism, is interpreted and around the extent to which peace-building interventions are asking the right questions to implement contextually relevant solutions.

The philosophy of *ubuntu* is an expression of an interconnected worldview that shaped the TRC (Munyaka and Motlhabi 2009; Krog 2008; Tutu 1999; Shutte 2009b).[2] Recognising that the well-being of one's society, community and spiritual worlds are inextricably intertwined, it encapsulates what it means to be human and speaks to an identity that only makes sense in relation to others; that is, one's sense of value, dignity and fulfilment in life is found in relationship with others (Munyaka and Motlhabi 2009; Shutte 2009a, b; Tutu 1999; Krog 2008; Metz 2011). Within this worldview, strong emphasis is given to placing communal interests above individual interests and on maintaining positive relationships. Respect and compassion for others are considered the most essential values from which other values such as loyalty, hospitality, tolerance, generosity and courtesy stem (Munyaka and Motlhabi 2009; Shutte 2009b; Metz 2011; Masina 2000). Thus, the notion of the collective from this perspective is organic and maintained by an interconnected understanding of relationships. This contrasts with the understanding of the collective in Western worldviews in which a society is comprised of individuals who are organised and controlled using mechanical forms of social structuring Shutte (2009b: 93).

This *ubuntu* worldview has received large amounts of criticism as a result of the crime and violence committed by individuals said to be functioning within this worldview (Shutte 2009a; Wilson 2001). Recognising this, Munyaka and Motlhabi (2009) explain that many of the values articulated within the *ubuntu* worldview have been degraded as a result of multiple factors including colonialism and the loss of land that accompanied it; the way in which Apartheid stripped 'black'

[2]Although the term *ubuntu* is an isiZulu term, the concept is expressed in a number of languages in South Africa and across Africa (Mbiti 1969; Munyaka and Motlhabi 2009; Kanwangamalu 1999).

South Africans of their dignity and delegitimised the African worldview; the influence of Western systems of meaning-making; and the way conflict acts to diminish the value of life. This, they argue, accounts for the extent of the violence witnessed in many South African communities laying claim to it and in which *ubuntu* was not operative. While this might suggest that an interconnected worldview may no longer be applicable or relevant in the contemporary world, a closer look at 'black' African engagement with ancestors and traditional healing, despite its hiddenness, points to a world that remains deeply interconnected shaping notions of social relationships.

Finally, although it was necessary to depict idealised versions of Western and interconnected worldviews to understand the South African social landscape, in reality the worldviews that are held within the society will (and do) shift, fuse and even contradict each other. For example, in post-Apartheid South Africa the merging of an interconnected worldview with capitalism and Western liberalism has led to a growth in occult economies in which supernatural techniques are used as a means of gaining access to wealth (Comaroff and Comaroff 1999; Ashforth 2005; Ralushai Commission 1996). Such practices can include ritual murders and the selling of body parts for use in *muthi* as a means of ensuring, for example fertility, romantic and business success.[3] However, it can also result in the use of lethal violence against those accused of using witchcraft to accumulate wealth. To illustrate this Comaroff and Comaroff (1999) cite, the example of an elderly lady living in a rural community who allowed a group of young men to watch her TV. The men then accused her of being a witch; this was their explanation as to how she came to be the owner of a TV and why they were unemployed and unable to find jobs. In this way, witchcraft becomes the *effect* of unemployment and a response to socio-economic difficulties and spiritual insecurity (Ashforth 2005; Comaroff and Comaroff 1999; Zulu and Wilhelm-Solomon 2015). Arguably, these practices are exacerbated by the way the Apartheid state controlled the

[3]*Muthi* related murders are regularly reported on in the news. For example, *Daily Sun* (2013c) and Vilakazi (2015).

political, material and even romantic life of 'black' South Africans; the promise of access to wealth the new democracy offered and the failure of these promises to materialise; and the sense of hopelessness that comes from persisting poverty (Comaroff and Comaroff 1999). So, unless the gravity of these beliefs is understood, Ashforth (2005: xiv) warns, 'the social and political dynamics of vast portions of humanity will remain incomprehensible'. Similarly, the way peace-building interventions are approached will lack contextual relevance and sustainability.

4.3 A Worldview Analysis of the Truth and Reconciliation Commission

The South African TRC, while heralded for its contribution to the society's peaceful transition, has received extensive criticism for the way it interpreted its mandate and approached, among others, the issue of reconciliation, accountability and nation-building. However, Krog (2008), one of the main journalists to cover the TRC proceedings asserts that to understand the working of the Commission it needs to be interpreted from the perspective of an interconnected worldview. With this in mind, it is useful to use the idealised depictions of Western and interconnected worldviews presented above as an analytical framework for interpreting the approach taken by the Commission and the criticisms it received. In doing so, it will show the way worldview shaped the proceedings underscoring its significance in peace-building and transitional justice mechanisms.

One of the challenges faced by the Commission relates to how the concept of reconciliation was interpreted (Wilson 2001; Hamber 2002; Chapman 2008a). Broadly speaking, there were two competing views, i.e. those who prioritised human rights and the rule of law and those prioritised the restoration of relationship. Reflecting the values within the Western liberal worldview, a human rights perspective saw reconciliation as possible only if social interactions were regulated through the rule of law. In contrast, for those coming from a relational perspective, reconciliation was only possibly on the basis of fostering positive interpersonal relationships and discovering the humanity in the 'other'. This speaks to an interconnected worldview in which the way to deal with the abuse of political power and prevent the reoccurrence of widespread human rights violations is to restore the humanity and relationship of the individuals involved (Shutte 2009a). Significantly, this debate reflects the structural and relational pillars of building a sustainable peace (see Chapter 3). Taking a relational approach, the Commission focused on the relationship between the victim and perpetrator and emphasised their interconnectedness and common humanity (Tutu 1999; Krog 2008). In doing so, it was criticised for creating a victim identity that failed to hold perpetrators and beneficiaries accountable for the wrongs of the past and for failing to deliver on victims' rights to justice (Valji 2004; Mamdani 2000; Chapman 2008a, b; Wilson 2001).

This debate also raises questions about how peace-building and transitional justice interprets the notion of nation-building. Within the human rights school of thought, a new national identity needed to be constructed on the basis of human rights and as embedded in the South African Constitution. In contrast, those emphasising relationships saw the nation as a body in need of healing and interpreted the construction of a national identity from a more interpersonal level (Wilson 2001). This was the approach taken by the TRC, as informed by *ubuntu*, for which it received several criticisms. Firstly, as *ubuntu* emphasises consensus building it was seen to refrain from addressing the hard choices a court of law is required to make (Cockrell 1996; Wilson 2001). Secondly, as nations are political constructs it was argued that applying the logic of interpersonal reconciliation to nations was flawed; only individuals, and not nations, can be reconciled (Cockrell 1996; Borer 2004). In turn, this raises the question of how peace-building and transitional justice interprets the notion of the community, i.e. a mechanical political construct as a means of organising a large number of individuals or an interconnected collective. Notwithstanding these criticisms, one can argue that both approaches were concerned with restoring peace and stability to the country. A human rights perspective emphasises the importance of applying the rule of law to individuals as a means of securing the future stability of the country, while *ubuntu* emphasises the restoration of relationships for achieving the same ends.

The difference lies in that the one focuses on the structural aspects of building a sustainable peace and the other on the relational aspects.

A second critique relates to the way the Commission individualised responsibility which raises the question of how accountability in transitional justice is interpreted. Indeed, the Western justice system is founded on a scientific and objectivist view of reality that is geared towards the individual (Hernández-Truyol 2004; Kelsall 2009; Kaschula and Ralarala 2004). However, accountability from an interconnected worldview is geared more towards the collective. Reflecting a more restorative approach to justice, it emphasises the relationship between the victim and perpetrator and seeks to maintain coherency of the collective by restoring the dignity and humanity of the individuals involved (Masina 2000; Murithi 2006; Tutu 1999; Munyaka and Motlhabi 2009). Arising from how justice was interpreted by the Commission is the way in which the concept of *ubuntu* became synonymous with 'justice proper' while retributive justice and punishment were interpreted as damaging to the well-being of the society (Wilson 2001: 10, 164). Challenging the way in which *ubuntu* has been romanticised, Wilson points out that despite its rejection of revenge, numerous acts of violence were carried out by people to whom this worldview was attributed. However, as previously noted, a person cannot be said to be acting with *ubuntu* when carrying out such acts but are rather the result of being dehumanised which, in its endeavour to promote a peaceful society, an *ubuntu* approach to justice seeks to rectify.

A third critique relates the issue of forgiveness and whether or not it was something that the Commission imposed on victims (Krog 2008; Chapman 2008a, b). Although there is very little empirical evidence for this, there was a strong perception that the Commission was about forgiveness (Chapman 2008b). This could be due, at least in part, to the emphasis placed by Commissioners on restoring relationships between victims and perpetrators and what was perceived as the TRC's Christian ethic. However, Krog (2008, 2015) argues that the misunderstandings surrounding the relationship between reconciliation and forgiveness were not a question of imposition but of ontological differences. While acknowledging the conflation between Christianity and *ubuntu*, she explains that the Commission's emphasis on forgiveness derives from the priority given to human interconnectedness as informed by the *ubuntu* worldview. This would account for why 'black' more so than 'white' South Africans saw forgiveness as a requisite for reconciliation (Chapman 2008b). Speaking to the significance of worldview in peace-building and transitional justice, Krog (2008, 2015) attributes these ontological divides to the breakdown in reconciliation during the Commissions proceedings as different interpretations and expectations were applied to the process.

The way in which an *ubuntu* approach was given primacy within the TRC also suggests an attempt at asserting an African identity and reclaiming an African way of being in the world that was overshadowed by Apartheid. Whether it is within peace-building processes or other systems, such as the legal system, taking different systems of meaning-making into account is particularly important to avoid reducing alternative forms of reason to 'cosmic error' (Comaroff and Comaroff 2004: 194). Consequently, integrating worldview into peace-building and transitional justice is also about recognising the equality of formerly oppressed groups and a means of restoring their dignity. Recognising the impact of the colonial presence on African identity, Balcomb (2014) argues that lying at the heart of African approaches to engaging with reality is the need to assert an African identity. Examples include the works of Frantz Fanon and his theories of decolonisation (Fanon 1990); Steve Biko and the Black Consciousness Movement which promoted psychological liberation from Apartheid and promoted the dignity of 'black' people (Biko and Stubbs 1987); and the rejection by the African Union of Western institutes such as the International Criminal Court (ICC). It is also seen in Thabo Mbeki's (former president of South Africa) attempt at resurrecting the discourse on the African Renaissance summarised in the slogan 'African solutions to African problems' and on the emphasis that the former president, Jacob Zuma, placed on African traditional customs such as polygamous marriage. Most recently, it has been demonstrated in student protests in South Africa surrounding the 'Rhodes Must Fall' campaign calling for the removal of statues symbolising South Africa's colonial past and the need for a higher education curriculum that reflects African values and way of being in the world (Boroughs 2015).

In conclusion, this section demonstrates how ontological disparities and different processes of meaning-making led to competing interpretations of South Africa's truth recovery process. Applying a worldview analysis to some of the criticisms directed to the TRC raises an important issue about how transitional justice deals with the past and interprets key concepts such as reconciliation, accountability and nation-building. It also suggests that a failure to understand different systems of meaning-making present within a peace-building process can contribute, alongside other complicating factors such as legacies of oppression, to the breakdown in reconciliation. Against this backdrop, the question of how the concept of peace might be interpreted within different systems of meaning-making; an important consideration in fostering reconciliation and promoting positive intergroup relations to which the following chapters will now turn.

References

Anderson, Benedict. 1983. *Imagined communities: Reflections on the origin and spread of nationalism*. London: Verso.

Ashforth, Adam. 2005. *Witchcraft, violence, and democracy in South Africa*. Chicago: The University of Chicago Press.

Balcomb, Anthony. 2014. *Journey into the African sun: Soundings in search of another way of being in the world*. Pretoria: University of South Africa.

Bediako, Kwame. 2004. *Jesus and the gospel in Africa: History and experience*. Maryknoll: Orbis Books.

Bendix, Reinhard. 1977. *Max Weber: An intellectual portrait*. Berkeley, Los Angeles, and London: University of California Press.

Biko, Steve, and Aelred Stubbs. 1987. *I write what I like: Selected writings*. London: Heinemann Educational.

Bond, Patrick. 2014. Marikana's meaning for crisis management: An instance of South Africa's resource curse. In *Global management, local resistances: Theoretical discussion and empirical case studies*, ed. Ulrike Schuerkens, 192–219. London: Routledge.

Borer, Tristan Anne. 2004. Reconciling South Africa or South Africans? Cautionary notes from the TRC. *African Studies Quarterly* 8 (1): 23–26.

Boroughs, Don. 2015. Why South African students say the statue of Rhodes must fall. *National Public Radio,* March 28. http://www.npr.org/sections/goatsandsoda/2015/03/28/395608605/why-south-african-students-say-the-statue-of-rhodes-must-fall. Accessed 30 August 2018.

Chapman, Audrey R. 2008a. The TRC's approach to promoting reconciliation in the human rights violations hearings. In *Truth and reconciliation in South Africa: Did the TRC deliver?*, ed. Audrey R. Chapman and Hugo van der Merwe, 43–65. Philadelphia: University of Pennsylvania Press.

Chapman, Audrey R. 2008b. Perspectives on the role of forgiveness in the human rights violations hearings. In *Truth and reconciliation in South Africa: Did the TRC deliver?*, ed. Audrey R. Chapman and Hugo van der Merwe, 66–89. Philadelphia: University of Pennsylvania Press.

Cockrell, Alfred. 1996. Rainbow jurisprudence. *South African Journal on Human Rights* 12 (1): 1–38.

Comaroff, Jean, and John Comaroff. 1999. Occult economies and the violence of abstraction: Notes from the South African postcolony. *American Ethnologist* 26 (2): 279–303.

Comaroff, Jean, and John Comaroff. 2004. Criminal justice, cultural justice: The limits of liberalism and the pragmatics of difference in the new South Africa. *American Ethnologist* 31 (2): 188–204.

Daily Sun. 2013a. Buried without his head! Tears for Madala after *muthi* murder. *Daily Sun,* May 6. http://www.politicsweb.co.za/politicsweb/view/politicsweb/en/page71627?oid=374646&sn=Detail&pid=71627. Accessed 30 August 2018.

Daily Sun. 2013b. Murder mayhem! *Muthi* killing sparks outrage—And more death! *Daily Sun,* August 27. http://politicsweb.co.za/opinion/murder-mayhem-muthi-killing-sparks-outrage--and-mo. Accessed 30 August 2018.

Daily Sun. 2013c. Bloody *muthi* madness! *Politics Web,* August 2. http://www.politicsweb.co.za/iservice/bloody-muthi-madness–daily-sun. Accessed 30 August 2018.

Doe, Samuel Gbaydee. 2009. Indigenizing post-conflict state reconstruction in Africa: A conceptual framework. *Africa Peace and Conflict Journal* 2 (1): 1–16.

Dunne, Tim. 2006. Liberalism. In *The globalization of world politics: An introduction to international relations,* ed. John Baylis and Steve Smith, 185–201. Oxford: Oxford University Press.

ENCA. 2014. Marikana commission: Cracks begin to show. *ENCA,* March. http://www.enca.com/south-africa/marikana-commission-cracks-begin-show. Accessed 30 August 2018.

Eriksen, Thomas Hylland. 1997. Multiculturalism, individualism and human rights: Romanticism, the Enlightenment and lessons from Mauritius. In *Human rights, culture and context: Anthropological perspectives*, ed. R. A. WILSON, 49–69. London & Sterling, Virginia: Pluto Press.

Fanon, Frantz. 1990. *The wretched of the earth*. London: Penguin.

Gay, Peter. 1971. *Great ages of man: Age of the enlightenment*. The Netherlands: Time-Life International.

Gelvin, James L. 2005. *The Israel-Palestine conflict: One hundred years of war*. New York: Cambridge University Press.

Halliday, Fred. 2006. Nationalism. In *The globalization of world politics: An introduction to international relations*, ed. John Baylis and Steve Smith, 521–538. Oxford: Oxford University Press.

Hamber, Brandon. 2002. 'Ere their story die': Truth, justice and reconciliation in South Africa. *Race & Class* 44 (1): 61–79.

Hernández-Truyol, Berta Esperanza. 2004. Panel V. Human rights commitments in the Americas: From the global to the local—The rule of law and human rights. *Florida Journal of International Law* 16: 167–194.

Kamwangamalu, Nkonko M. 1999. *Ubuntu* in South Africa: A sociolinguistic perspective to a pan-African concept. *Critical Arts: South-North Cultural and Media Studies* 13 (2): 24–41.

Kaschula, Russell H., and Monwabisi K. Ralarala. 2004. Language rights, intercultural communication and the law in South Africa. *South African Journal of African Languages* 24 (4): 252–261.

Kelsall, Tim. 2009. *Culture under cross-examination: International justice and the special court for Sierra Leone*. New York: Cambridge University Press.

Krog, Antjie. 2008. '…if it means he gets his humanity back…': The worldview underpinning the South African truth and reconciliation commission. *Journal of Multicultural Discourses* 3 (3): 204–220.

Krog, Antjie. 2015. Research into reconciliation and forgiveness at the South African Truth and Reconciliation Commission and Homi Bhabha's architecture of the new. *Canadian Journal of Law and Society* 30 (2): 203–217.

Mac Ginty, Roger. 2014. Everyday peace: Bottom-up and local agency in conflict-affected societies. *Security Dialogue* 45 (6): 548–564.

Mamdani, Mahmood. 2000. The truth according to the TRC. In *The politics of memory: Truth, healing and social justice,* ed. Ifi Amadiume and Abdullahi An-Na'im, 177–190. London and New York: Zed Books.

Maromo, Jonisayi. 2014. Marikana cops amateurs: Vermaak. *IOL News,* March 24. http://www.iol.co.za/news/special-features/marikana-cops-amateurs-vermaak-1.1665632#.VaPMnl9VhHw. Accessed 30 August 2018.

Masina, Nomonde. 2000. Xhosa practices of *ubuntu* for South Africa. In *Traditional cures for modern conflicts: African conflict 'medicine'*, ed. William I. Zartman, 169–181. London: Lynne Rienner Publishers Inc.

Mbiti, John. 1969. *African religions & philosophy*. London: Heinemann.

McEvoy, Kieran. 2007. Beyond legalism: Towards a thicker understanding of transitional justice. *Journal of Law and Society* 4 (4): 411–440.

McEvoy, Kieran, and Lorna McGregor. 2008. *Transitional justice from below: Grassroots activism and the struggle for change*. Portland, OR: Hart.

Merry, Sally Engle. 2006. *Human rights and gender violence: Translating international law into local justice*. Chicago and London: University of Chicago Press.

Metz, Thaddeus. 2011. *Ubuntu* as a moral theory and human rights in South Africa. *African Human Rights Law Journal* 11: 532–559.

Munyaka, Mluleki, and Mokgethi Motlhabi. 2009. *Ubuntu* and its socio-moral significance. In *African ethics: An anthology of comparative and applied ethics*, ed. Munyaradzi Felix Murove, 63–84. Scottsville: University of KwaZulu-Natal Press.

Murithi, Tim. 2006. Practical peacemaking wisdom from Africa: Reflections on *ubuntu*. *The Journal of Pan African Studies* 1 (4): 25–34.

Nürnberger, Klaus. 2007. *The living dead and the living God: Christ and the ancestors in a changing Africa*. Pietermaritzburg: Cluster Publications.

Palmer, Nicola, Briony Jones, and Julia Viebach. 2015. Introduction: Ways of knowing atrocity: A methodological enquiry into the formulation, implementation, and assessment of transitional justice. *Canadian Journal of Law and Society* 30 (2): 173–182.

Ralushai, Commission. 1996. *Report of the commission of inquiry into witchcraft violence and ritual murders in the Northern Province of the Republic of South Africa*. South Africa: Ministry of Safety and Security.

Richmond, Oliver P. 2011. *A post-liberal peace*. London and New York: Routledge.

Richmond, Oliver P., and Audra Mitchell. 2012. *Hybrid forms of peace: From everyday agency to post-liberalism*. Basingstoke: Palgrave Macmillan.

Saba, Athandiwe. 2016. Desperate Lily Mine families seek supernatural help. *Mail & Guardian Online*, February 17. http://mg.co.za/article/2016-02-17-desperate-lily-mine-families-seek-supernatural-help. Accessed 30 August 2018.

Shutte, Augustine. 2009a. Politics and the ethic of *ubuntu*. In *African ethics: An anthology of comparative and applied ethics*, ed. Munyaradzi Felix Murove, 375–390. Scottsville: University of KwaZulu-Natal Press.

Shutte, Augustine. 2009b. *Ubuntu* as the African ethical vision. In *African ethics: An anthology of comparative and applied ethics*, ed. Munyaradzi Felix Murove, 85–99. Scottsville: University of KwaZulu-Natal Press.
Smith, Anthony D. 2001. *Nationalism: Theory, ideology, history*. Cambridge: Polity Press.
Sriram, Chandra Lekha. 2007. Justice as peace? Liberal peacebuilding and strategies of transitional justice. *Global Society* 21 (4): 579–591.
Sriram, Chandra Lekha. 2012. Post-conflict justice and hybridity in peacebuilding: Resistance or cooptation? In *Hybrid forms of peace: From everyday agency to post-liberalism*, ed. Oliver P. Richmond and Audra Mitchell, 58–72. Basingstoke: Palgrave Macmillan.
Tarnas, Richard. 1991. *The passion of the Western mind: Understanding the ideas that have shaped our worldview*. New York: Harmony Books.
Turner, Harold W. 1977. The primal religions of the world and their study. In *Australian essays in world religions*, ed. Victor C. Hayes, 27–37. Bedford Park: The Australian Association for the Study of Religions.
Tutu, Desmond M. 1999. *No future without forgiveness*. London: Rider.
Valji, Nahla. 2004. *Race and reconciliation in a post-TRC South Africa*. Paper presented at a conference entitled Ten Years of Democracy in Southern Africa, organized by the Southern African Research Centre, Queens University, Canada, May, 2004.
Vilakazi, Zimbili. 2015. She was killed for *muthi*! *Daily Sun*, November 12. http://www.dailysun.co.za/News/National/she-was-killed-for-muthi-20151112. Accessed 30 August 2018.
Wilson, Richard A. 2001. *The politics of truth and reconciliation in South Africa: Legitimizing the post-apartheid state*. Cambridge: Cambridge University Press.
Zulu, Melekias, and Matthew Wilhelm-Solomon. 2015. Tormented by *umnyama*: An urban cosmology of migration and misfortune in inner-city Johannesburg. In *Healing and change in the city of gold: Case studies of coping and support in Johannesburg*, ed. Nicola Palmer, Brandon Hamber, and Lorena Núñez, 135–148. Cham, Heildelberg, New York, Dordrecht, and London: Springer.

5

Exploring the Diversity of Worldviews in South Africa

In the same way a forest is comprised of an entangled mass of different trees and undergrowth culturally diverse societies are comprised of different systems of meaning-making (worldview). When viewed from a distance the forest may appear to look uniform. However, when one begins to cut away the overgrowth the forest is clearly comprised of multiple layers and types of vegetation, all interacting to form a complex environment. The same is true with worldview. Unlike the metaphor of a forest, the difficulty with disentangling worldviews is that historically, culture was tied to biology and (ab)used to support colonialism and justify the subjugation of Africans and other forms of racism. Consequently, talking about cultural differences can sometimes be seen as politically incorrect, possibly even racist. In moving away from theories that reinforce racial difference, the language of universalism, as expressed in 'universal values' and 'universal rights' which emphasise similarity, is increasingly being used. While this is important for protecting human dignity, implicit in such language is the assumption that all societies share similar systems of (often Western) meaning-making. By failing to uncover and understand the worldviews within which other

C. Bollaert, *Reconciliation and Building a Sustainable Peace*,
Palgrave Studies in Compromise after Conflict,
https://doi.org/10.1007/978-3-030-03655-3_5

societies live finding contextually relevant solutions to peace-building is impeded. It also undermines a person's sense of identity and dignity; particularly those from previously oppressed groups. This raises the question of how to engage with sensitive issues in deeply divided societies in a way that is politically correct but does not compromise the rigour of the research or prevent research on crucial issues, such as those affecting intergroup conflict.

Against this backdrop, the chapter seeks to untangle the various strands of worldview held by the respondents in the study by drawing on the worldview attributes described in Chapters 3 and 4, namely: one's ontological orientation, unit of survival and accountability, form of social organisation, and activity and temporal orientation. It explores how worldviews can be similar yet quite different at the same time; both fixed and flexible and able to change. It raises questions about how peace-building interventions are contextualised and the impact that different social values might have on the goal of reconciliation. Recognising that identities shift over time, the worldviews represented by the respondents are a window into the diversity of South African identities at a given point in time.

5.1 Ontological Orientation: Scientific or Interconnected?

The ontological orientation refers to the nature of reality and what can be known about it, i.e. is it objective and scientific or spiritual and interconnected, and to what extent is it a combination of both ontological assumptions? In South Africa, an interconnected worldview is one of the more dominant worldviews shaping the society (see Chapter 4). In the research informing the study, this was largely evidenced in the role that ancestors were seen to play in shaping one's interpretation of reality. Indeed, there was unanimous agreement, particularly among 'black' respondents, that the world of the 'living dead' (ancestors) was real and a normative part of the everyday. Elucidating on this the following respondent explains:

> You must remember that black people believe that their ancestors have a hand in the way. So, the way in which most black people are brought up is that you need to respect your elders and your forefathers. And you need to praise your forefathers; you need to praise your current leaders and so forth, while they're still alive… If the ancestors are unhappy about your behaviour then they can curse you in trying to make sure that you understand that what you are doing is wrong, because if they don't teach you how to do things then you will not understand. And obviously we're talking about dead people now. So the only way in which I can make sense of that is they're not here but bad things can happen to you. But if you go back to your ancestors and seek help then they will show you what is happening to you and they will show you how to get out of the curse. You've got to always make sure that whatever you're doing is the right thing and that if they were here that they would approve of what you are doing. (Respondent 56, Xhosa)

Within this system of meaning-making one's social conduct, such as showing respect to elders, becomes more than a simple case of exercising 'good manners' but is intricately linked with one's sense of safety and well-being in the world and an identity rooted in spiritual insecurity. From this perspective, it forms an integral part of building a sustainable peace (see Chapter 6).

Related to an interconnected worldview and one's interaction with ancestors is the belief in (and fear of) curses and the need for protection from malevolent spirits. While this is usually sought through traditional healers, it is also found through the Christian faith which is seen as a greater power (Bediako 2004). Sometimes both a Christian pastor and a *sangoma* can be consulted. Nonetheless, the prevalence of these beliefs is suggested in the growing number of advertisements for 'doctors' and traditional/spiritual healers offering spiritual protection and help for a range of problems relating to finances, health, success, love and even sex (see Fig. 5.1). Speaking to the prevalence of such beliefs Rev Moss Ntlha (General Secretary of the Evangelical Alliance) exclaims 'you can always find a *sangoma* who can offer to "solve" your problem, whether it is to get rid of a rival (be it in politics, romance, sports, or at work). Does it work? You bet it does!' (Personal correspondence, 2013).

Fig. 5.1 Flyer advertising spiritual power and protection

While the belief in ancestors applies more to 'black' indigenous populations, the reality of curses also extends to other race groups sharing an interconnected worldview. In this research, 'Indians' more so than 'coloured' or 'white' South Africans expressed such beliefs. Significantly, it is also not limited to people with little or no formal education. For example, in seeking to find a comprehensible reason for how someone like Jacob Zuma (former president of South Africa) could come to power a Zulu business woman educated within a Western schooling system turns to the spiritual world for an explanation:

> I believe that Zuma must have his own *Nyanga* [traditional doctor/herbalist] and probably just a whole lot more to give him power and strength. For the life of me I just can't believe why someone who is not educated from Nkandla, not to say anything disrespectful towards him, but someone who all of a sudden they become president of this country. For them to just be able to be a president of the country and stand and say you know, I'm the South African president and, I just feel that to get to that point you must have really acquired some strength somewhere. (Respondent 18, Zulu)

While education can certainly influence and shape one's worldview, it does not necessary follow that it will cause one to depart from an interconnected worldview. Dispelling the colonial myth that beliefs in curses belong to the 'uncivilised' world the following respondent remarks:

> It depends, of course, on the way that you were brought up. I've seen people who were at a very high level of education but they still believe they can be bewitched or that people are bewitching them. (Respondent 17, Zulu)

Notwithstanding the extent to which one interacts with ancestors and believes in curses, there is a general acceptance in South Africa that these different ontologies coexist and sometimes fuse and overlap. This has implications on the everyday. For example, within the business sector, a 'white' business owner explains how it can result in extended periods of staff absence as spiritual healers (traditional and Christian) are consulted (above medical doctors) for health-related problems.

It also has implications for peace-building and transitional justice, beyond those discussed in Chapter 4. For many people, Apartheid was interpreted as an evil that needed to be exorcised from the land (Tutu 2008). From the perspective of an interconnected worldview, Ashforth (2005) argues that part of the Commission's role should have been to expose the source of evil, which required confession and full disclosure. By failing to persuade, the leadership of the National Party to confess to their full activities, he further argues the source of evil that is seen to account for the poverty and oppression 'black' South Africans continue to experience remains hidden and alive. Given the failure of the post-Apartheid government to significantly reduce levels of poverty and inequality, individuals may experience a greater sense of insecurity in the world. The result is that more time and money will be spent on consulting traditional healers which, as Chapter 6 shows, is seen to contribute to the cycle of poverty. It also risks an increase in witchcraft-related violence. For example, there is speculation that the recent incident in which three men attempted to cut off the legs of the South African triathlete Mhlengi Gwala (with a chainsaw), is related to jealousy and beliefs in witchcraft (Singh 2018). The challenge for peace-building is to build a society that recognises the legitimacy of such belief systems and at the same can protect its citizens from the threat of witchcraft-related violence (Comaroff and Comaroff 2003, 2004, 2005; Ashforth 2005).

5.2 Unit of Survival and Accountability: The Individual or the Collective?

Individualism and collectivism refer to where a person's sense of survival and well-being is placed, whether this is within the individual or within the collective group. The analysis underpinning this research suggests that English-speaking 'whites' most strongly expressed an individual identity as did the Afrikaans group, albeit to a lesser extent. Significantly, given the history of Afrikaans nationalism, one would have expected the Afrikaans respondents to show a stronger value for collectivism. That they did not could be indicative of how worldviews can shift over time. However, it could also be reflective of the mechanically constructed nature of the nationalist community which, although it emphasises the group, also places a strong value on the individual. The 'black', 'coloured', 'Indian' and migrant groups all presented an identity that was more strongly located within the collective. Statements that demonstrated valuing the group (referred to as a 'group priority') were interpreted as indicating a collective worldview. The following interview extract explaining how *ubuntu* is expressed within a community exemplifies this:

> When there's a bereavement in the family, the family won't be the one who's providing food. When black people come together they eat. So the neighbours would cook from their own homes. When they come, it's them [the neighbours] who will be providing [food]. It goes to an issue of raising a child. As Africans a child is not raised by a parent but it's raised by the entire community, by the entire society. (Respondent 17, Zulu)

This narrative shows how the wider community, and not just the immediate family, is accountable for the well-being of the society. Indeed, obeying and respecting one's elders in the same way as one's parents was commonly expressed by those who appeared to have a more collective worldview. In addition, a collective worldview was evidenced by a sense of interconnectedness as exemplified in the relationship that was drawn between poverty and the one's sense of well-being in the society:

> My freedom in a sense is dependent on the freedom of others so I cannot be comfortable when the levels [of poverty] are so great. I cannot be comfortable because I might be living a middle class existence. But someone who doesn't have will come and break in where I stay. I cannot live a comfortable life because if I go out here now I will be met with three homeless guys. I've got to; we've got to do things together. (Respondent 36, Coloured)

Prioritising slightly different values, individualism was evidenced within those narratives that emphasised the self and one's own well-being. For example, the following statement illustrates an individualistic outlook on life:

> The lady next door she wears that ninja outfit [*niqab*] which I don't understand because that's very suppressive… I mean, it's their problem. They have to deal with it. I hope she's happy with it. For me, it's important to be happy. So, if you're not happy with it then run away or something. (Respondent 26, Afrikaans)

Based on her negative (and perhaps even racist) response to the *niqab*, this quotation suggests the respondent is interpreting her neighbour's culture from the perspective of individualism and how individual freedom is interpreted. Furthermore, an individual worldview was indicated within narratives that prioritised personal responsibility:

> Rather educate yourself and lead a productive life. Don't go and sit somewhere on the top of the mountain and don't have water, don't have food and basically expect the government or somebody else to feel sorry for you and look after you. (Respondent 33, Afrikaans)

> So there's this 'I'll take what I can get and I'll help myself that way. I won't help myself through hard work or diligence'. Or it's about what I can get. And maybe that comes from a place of 'I'm so desperate'. Maybe, it comes from laziness. Maybe it's just cultural. I don't know. (Respondent 51, English-speaking white)

Significantly, as well as underscoring the respondents value for personal responsibility, these statements also point to a growing prejudice among 'whites' about a 'black' sense of self-entitlement and dependency on the government. This raises the question as the to the extent that a 'white' identity rooted in privilege persists. However, interpreting these statements through the lens of worldview suggests that if one is functioning within an individualist worldview then responsibility for getting out of poverty will largely be placed on the individual. While it may not be possible to disentangle racism from individualism in the above examples (both work to reinforce the other), a failure to understand difference will almost certainly act to reinforce racist attitudes within society.

Within South African society, the terms 'individualist' and 'collectivist' are generally not used in everyday conversations. However, these different ways of being in the world were readily recognised by the participants in their everyday lives. For example, the following extracts illustrate the distinction between individualist and collectivist rules for social engagement:

> You know, white culture is different to black culture. I will know everyone; I would know all the 202 houses, the 201 neighbours if I was staying in the black township. But because I'm in a white area I don't know my neighbours we just don't even greet each other. They don't even know

> who I am. I don't know them either. I wrote letters to greet them, they never replied. (Respondent 22, Zulu)

> In my neighbourhood, in a Zulu culture, my neighbour, I have to greet my neighbour. Mina [me] I have 'white' neighbours in Yellowwood Park, we never talk. And I had a 'white-black' next to me. You know I tried, because I'm very outspoken you know I'll speak to them. You could see that I'm really important. And I began to learn, no, let me not impose. Let me, even though she's standing outside, I'll just go into my house. (Respondent 17, Zulu)

This was a common narrative expressed by 'black' people who had moved into previously all 'white' suburbs. The implications that a collective worldview had on a Western structured business was also recognised:

> I've needed to very carefully balance HR and western contractual procedures which apply completely to them ['blacks'] but try and mesh that together in a way where you communicate it differently. So I'm saying you are working for me but we have to make this business succeed together because if you do something wrong it affects us all – which is the truth. But it resonates with them a lot more because of the understanding of community and the understanding of group think and the understanding of tribe...They want to be part of something and if they don't feel they are part of something then they will find something to be a part of as a group and as a body...You'll have faithful people for the rest of your life if you can treat them well. But if you don't, you can have an entire work force against you as an enemy and not just one. (Respondent 53, English-speaking white)

As well as the implications coexisting worldviews have on business and contract law (as expressed above) it also has important implications for democratic processes:

> Black people need to realise one thing about white people; most decisions are made from an individual perspective...So that's what we miss that white people are more individualistic when they come to decision making. And the reason we miss that is our approach is always the

> community. And then that's what the white people miss about us…Our thinking is always plural, not singular. So those two things always make problems when we try to form peace…when you guys want to talk to us you always want to attend to individuals and that's not the case with us, it's always the general community. (Respondent 24, Xhosa)

As the respondent explains, in 'black' communities an individual is speaking on behalf of the collective and is therefore the individual is representing more than one person. In a democratic process which looks at individual representation, the presence of one 'black' person could work against the community. This has implications for how decisions are reached within conflict transformation processes.

Returning to the broader themes of the book, this attribute of worldview underscores the reality of different systems for making sense of the world and determining the rules that guide social engagements. It also reflects the values represented within the Western liberal worldview and the interconnected worldview. Unfortunately, these differences are usually not well understood and the result is that the boundaries between the self and the other become entrenched and hardened (see Chapter 6).

5.3 Social Organisation: Hierarchical or Lateral?

The worldview indicator, social organisation, speaks to the extent a community structures itself hierarchically or laterally. A hierarchical form of social organisational was more evident among 'black' respondents while a lateral form of social organisation was more evident among the 'white' groups (particularly, English-speaking 'whites'). One way of identifying a hierarchical worldview was to apply Lakoff and Johnson's (1980) metaphorical analysis of worldviews to the narratives. This is well-exemplified within the following interview extract in which the individual consistently uses the preposition 'under' to locate themselves within their community:

> I like being a citizen in my rural area *under* tradition, following my culture. *Under* the chief, I am also living *under* the chief... because most of our country or these rural places are now *under* councillors who are now *under* political parties. (Respondent 19, Zulu, emphasis mine)

Linking it to an interconnected ontology, a culture associated with a hierarchical worldview was also evidenced in relation to protocols surrounding respect. As the following extract explains, a person's age is fundamental to how one engages with the 'other' and what can or cannot be said:

> Being an elder in my culture as a Xhosa, being an elder you can speak publically whichever way you like because with age comes wisdom, so as an elder you're respected, so your views are respected. So as an elder you can stand on any platform and speak your mind. It would be a problem if as a young person I would have done what Tutu did, then that's a problem, its disrespect. (Respondent 24, Xhosa)

Furthermore, suggested within the above statement is that in hierarchically structured societies, one's status or authority is something that is arrived at through age. This differs in lateral forms of social organisation in which authority is usually signified through a person's office or level of qualification, irrespective of age. The implications of this aspect of worldview had a strong influence in parliamentary proceedings in South Africa. Referring to Lindiwe Mazibuko, the DA parliamentary leader from 2009 to 2014, who in parliamentary terms was very young (aged 29 when she began her term), the following respondent explains:

> She's absolutely not accepted because she's black on the outside and white on the inside. She's got all these beliefs and things that white people do because that's the way she went to school. That's the way she was educated. And she's left her black culture completely behind her. And then across the spectrum you've got Jacob sitting directly opposite her in parliament. And he's like 'You are child, you're a woman, you can't do what I'm telling you to do: you've got no respect'...and if you look at it they're both Zulu's...Then you have the minister and speakers [who say] 'Oh, you're a child, you mustn't speak like that'. (Respondent 39, Coloured)

This interview excerpt raises several important points. Firstly, it suggests that the ANC, as represented by the reference to Jacob Zuma, is functioning within a hierarchical worldview. This is in contrast to the DA, as represented by Mazibuko, which holds a more individualist and linear view of society. Complicating the matter further is that Mazibuko is functioning within an assigned status and authority meaning that it's her office that carries authority, and not her being. The result is that Mazibuko's authority is not readily received and her actions as a leader in the formal opposition in parliament appear to be discredited and interpreted as disrespectful.

This aspect of social organisation raises important questions for peace-building and transitional justice. What is the age profile of the actors involved? To what extent does it impact the effectiveness peace-building mechanisms? Moreover, it has implications on inter-group relations. What may be appropriate forms of showing respect for a person from a lateral social orientation may not be so for someone from a hierarchical social orientation as it can quickly lead to feelings of disrespect together with the breakdown in communication. This is an especially important consideration for transitional justice and peace-building given that respect is fundamental to a person's sense of dignity and building positive relations. It takes on even greater significance in post-conflict societies where oppressive regimes associated with the gross violations of human rights served to undermine and erode one's sense of dignity, as was the case in South Africa.

Further to this, the above extract is points to how identities are socially constructed and strongly influenced by one's context and experience. Mazibuko, who could be assumed to be functioning from a collectivist and hierarchical worldview by virtue of her Zulu ethnicity, is seen here to be functioning within an individualist and lateral worldview. Further evidencing how identities can shift, an Afrikaans respondent notes how historically within the Afrikaner community a greater emphasis was placed on hierarchy and on showing respect to elders:

> Most of the older people can't say my name; they can't call me by my name. I'm *Dominee* [Afrikaans for ordained minister of religion]. For

> them it's a big status thing that I've got the name *Dominee*. For the younger people I'm Penny.[1] (Respondent 31, Afrikaans)

Similar shifts were seen to be happening within the 'Indian' community. This raises a number of important points. While the literature often treats 'black' and 'white' groups as mutually exclusive, this interview points to a common understanding of how societies are organised. Moreover, it gives further evidence of how, over time, worldviews can shift underscoring the need for peace-building and transitional justice processes to remain dynamic.

5.4 Activity Orientation: Relationship or Rule Priority?

The activity orientation relates to the way in which rules and relationships are prioritised in determining how one's activities are ordered. Closely associated with individualism, a rule priority can be seen in those persons who show a value for 'sticking to the rules' and the way 'things should be done' above serving the interests of the relationship. This does not suggest that for those with a rule priority relationships do not matter, they do, but not as the primary framework through which decisions are filtered. Nonetheless, it was more apparent among 'white' groups and was evidenced through a number of statements such as:

> Respecting values and rules as well, not that I'm a goody two shoes, but you know there are rules that have been put into place for certain reasons. (Respondent 26, Afrikaans)

> Rules are there for a reason because you get hurt if you don't follow them. (Respondent 31, Afrikaans)

> Working in a government sector for many years as a doctor: that was very hard. That was very frustrating because of the lack of efficiency and just basic management skills and doing the things the correct way. Sometimes,

[1] Not her real name.

> all of us were so frustrated because of the lack of equipment, the lack of just doing things the right way. (Respondent 48, Afrikaans)

Bearing in mind that nationalism has a strong communal focus, and given their history, one would have expected a stronger emphasis on relationship from Afrikaner respondents. While this could be indicative of a worldview shift taking place within the Afrikaner community, it could also be the result of a mechanically engineered understanding of community which requires adherence to rules to enable it to function.

A relationship priority, on the other hand, can be identified by the way preference is given to personal interaction, the respect shown to elders (as per an interconnected and hierarchical worldview), loyalty to the group, and the priority that is given to putting relationships before personal goals. A relationship priority is also associated with a collective worldview and understood as a means of protecting the unity and survival of the group. It was more apparent among the 'black', 'Indian' and migrant groups. Among the 'coloured' group a more mixed approach was evidenced which could be due to this group historically having a more culturally varied background. Nonetheless, a relationship priority was seen in the way interaction with one's neighbours was valued (as per a collective worldview described above). It was also seen in the way the group (rather than the individual) was given priority as the following interview extract indicates:

> Most of our leadership is now is black people. And you find that when, like for example, a meeting is called or a gathering is called some of our white brothers they don't even pitch up…I think maybe there is still within some of them to say I cannot be told by a black person, or be led by a black person. I think that's the thing. You find that you've sent an invitation in a good time, you know. And they don't pitch; with no apology… We're trying because when they called us into their events we do attend. You know we do attend. It's like they don't care. (Respondent 2, Zulu)

The emphasis placed on attendance at a social gathering suggests the respondent is prioritising relationships. However, it also demonstrates how a failure to understand different worldviews can contribute to the hardening of intergroup relations. If relationship is not prioritised by an individual then not attending a social function might be perceived as acceptable to them. Due to the racist narrative in South Africa, such a misunderstanding can quickly be interpreted within a racist framework. Thus, it begs the question as to extent the non-attendance of the 'white brothers' comes from a racist position or from functioning within a different paradigm?

This hardening of boundaries as a potential result of different activity orientations at play is further expressed in an interview with an English-speaking 'white' businessman:

> So we would say to the landlord, 'Barry,[2] we want to set up x, y and z'. 'No, you can't because that's earmarked for black business.' 'Ok, but we're saying why? Where's the black business offering you these ideas and business opportunities? Nowhere. So are you really just going to say no to us?' 'Yes, we're going to say no to you.'... So I think it's a number of combinations of things that have maybe resulted in our business from advancing and being stopped. So, therefore, from that point of view if we are not winning there then we've got to look elsewhere and see if there are other opportunities in different directions where people do want to see advancement...It's totally counterproductive because we're taking something they don't have to do anything for, we will take all the risks, we will take the land, we will develop it, and we will take the risk and they get paid for it. They get paid for doing nothing, just saying yes, that's what they get paid for. We're not taking anything from them. We're not wanting to be their enemies, we're just wanting to advance business. (Respondent 53, English-speaking white)

In this extract, the business owner appears to be interpreting the business transaction on the basis of a rule priority and a value for advancement (individualism). Thus, the rejection he receives from the landlord to extend his business is interpreted as illogical. This social transaction is further complicated by the history of inequality, land ownership in South Africa and Black Economic Empowerment (BEE) policies, which 'white' South Africans generally interpret negatively. Although the respondent may be seen to be denigrating BEE policies and using this experience to legitimise their failures, his perception nonetheless stems

[2]Not his real name.

from his system of meaning-making and works to reinforce intergroup boundaries. While this book is focused on the influence of competing worldviews on peace-building, the above extract also shows that it is not one factor alone, such as past injustices or worldview differences, which contribute to intergroup conflict. Recognising they work together and are deeply intertwined emphasis is being given to the influence of worldview as an under researched area in peace-building.

Opposed modes of operating can be difficult to reconcile. Aware of the struggle between rules and relationship the following respondent keenly observes:

> [I'm] aware of cultural differences and the way that you deal with things. It's very western to say it like it is, to put it out there, to name and shame. That's not African at all. You don't name and shame. And that's hard because you've got a country of white people who are wanting people to be named and shamed and African culture deals with it differently…in my experience of white people is if you, if somebody messes up you say it. You put it out there and they have to take responsibility, deal with it. But not so, you don't shame your leaders in African culture. And that's hard. So how do you, how do you address leadership that's not fulfilling what it should be doing in a country that just deals with leaders so differently? I don't know. (Respondent 5, English-speaking white)

These differences in activity orientation are relevant in the context of transitional justice and have contributed to the credibility of the International Criminal Court (ICC) being undermined and seen by African states as a neo-colonial institution (Escritt 2015; IOL News 2015). It was also made evident in the criticisms arising from South Africa's failure to arrest al-Bashir, the president of Sudan on his visit to the country. He was attending the African Union summit meetings and was wanted by the ICC for crimes against humanity (Reuters 2015). Despite South Africa being signatories to the Rome Statute, he was not arrested. The reason for this, as the South African Justice Minister explains, was that 'we had obligations in relation to customary law insulting heads of state (from arrest)' (Escritt 2015). Here, South Africa is seen to be operating from a relationship priority while the ICC is operating from a rule priority. This raises important questions about how transitional justice approaches and interprets the concept of accountability in societies that do not operate strictly within a Western liberal worldview. The failure of peace-building and transitional justice to engage with worldview differences could significantly diminish the ICC's relevance and ability to prevent gross violations of human rights.

5.5 Temporal Orientation: Past or Future?

Temporal orientation refers to whether a person more orientated towards the future or towards the past? A past orientation is linked with an identity that is strongly located in one's history and traditions and tends to be associated with collectivism and loyalty to the group. For example, pointing to a past orientation, the following respondent went into elaborate detail to set himself within his historical context:

> Yes, I see myself as Xhosa…I'm a Xhosa; I belong under the Bhele's in Xhosa. Because basically because one of the reasons is as a Xhosa again, I'm identified as, you see as black people, as Xhosa's we also part of Xhosa people I'm also identified as Mfengu. So that is why I don't put the Xhosa thing there because as a Xhosa I'm also in a way being taken out as an Mfengu, as a different part of a Xhosa, not a fully Xhosa. My mother is a fully Xhosa…but because as Xhosa's or as blacks we tend to take the father's side when we identify yourself, you identify yourself more as from your father's perspective. As for my father's side, I'm seen as not as fully or as 100% Xhosa. I'm Mfengu which is not being 100% Xhosa. Basically I should be saying what I mean as Mfengu is that as Xhosa's my grandfather told me that there were Xhosa's who broke away and then chose education over their culture. So that's where I come from, that why part of the Xhosa are those who chose education over their culture, that's how I'm identified. (Respondent 24, Xhosa)

By contrast, a future orientated worldview is linked to an identity rooted in a sense of individual achievement, success and advancement. Like a rule priority, it emphasises the need for personal responsibility and is closely associated with individualism. The following interview extracts, in which the future and advancement are seen to be prioritised, illustrate how such a worldview might be indicated:

> So, therefore, from that point of view if we are not winning there then we've got to look elsewhere and see if there are other opportunities in different directions where people do want to see *advancement*. (Respondent 53, English-speaking white, emphasis mine)

> It does strike home to you, well certainly for me the fact that you are part of something. We are really *shaping the future* of not just the city but of South Africa and that *your decisions do impact on people's lives* and I mean Durban is a huge area. (Respondent 27, English-speaking white, emphasis mine)

In addition, a future orientation can be displayed by an antipathy to community history and an absence of any attachment to the group or its traditions:

> I encourage people going out there and seeing the world and earning passports because it's not about loyalty it's about the way we, the direction we going. (Respondent 45, Indian)

> I believe that there was absolutely nothing wrong with the old street names ... Sylvester Nthuli [new street name], who is he? He's nobody that I know; Sandile Thusi, whose he or she? (Respondent 39, Coloured)

> I think I should feel more but I don't. I think it's just a road name and people need to get over it...I mean in my head I know that a lot of people would feel like their history is being erased and replaced by somebody else's history or version of history. But it's just a road name. (Respondent 5, English-speaking white)

An analysis of the interviews underpinning this research suggests Afrikaans, but particularly English-speaking 'whites', had a strong future temporal orientation; almost none of the 'black' participants prioritised values in accordance with a future temporal orientation. Similarly, almost none of the 'white' participants identified with a past orientation, as defined in this inquiry. Interestingly, while holding strong communal and collective values, 'Indian' and migrant respondents expressed a future orientated priority. Among the 'coloured' respondents, there was a more varied expression of the temporal worldview attribute. This shows how worldviews across groups can be different but can also overlap and be shared.

Due to their strong collective and spiritual identity one would have expected migrants to express more of a past orientation. However, there were multiple instances among respondents from this group when their identity was articulated more in terms of their achievements and personal responsibility than in terms of their relationship to the collective. In addition, they often articulated their identity against their perception of 'black' South Africans who were perceived to be 'lazy'. Given the extent to which this group has been the target of xenophobic attitudes and violence, this might be expected. However, what is more significant is that like each of the groups expressing a future orientated worldview, the migrant population living in South Africa have also uprooted themselves from their land of origin. This raises the question as to whether their former contexts (many coming from conflict societies) forced a shift in worldview or whether it might also be that those who are future orientated are more likely to migrate. While further research would be needed to investigate this, it further points to how worldview is shaped by context and experience.

It is also surprising that some of the Afrikaner participants did not indicate a past orientation as historically they would have placed more emphasis on the past and tradition. This could be because the Apartheid past has been discredited and people feel they cannot talk publically about it which raises the question as to how much the lack of attachment to the past among 'whites' is just 'white talk' rather than an indicator of future orientation. In other words, the Apartheid past becomes the problem rather than the past being of less import. However, bearing in mind that worldview is about the process of deeper meaning-making, emphasising the future to avoid the past still indicates a move towards a future orientation. Moreover, given the sample group were not from the former Apartheid generation, this could be an indication of how a change in context and experience can result in worldviews shifting and changing over time. So, while worldview might not be a cause of conflict, when coupled with historical injustices it can become a contributing factor.

Combined with South Africa's legacy of Apartheid, one's temporal orientation has implications for how a peaceful future might be interpreted. For example, in the following interview extract the future is emphasised:

> Years ago when it was all Apartheid, they still ride that little boat, that Apartheid and they suffered and whatever. Get over it then. Go forward you know. Move on. (Respondent 26, Afrikaans)

Compared to this extract which suggests a past orientation and stronger emphasis on the history:

> I just feel that there was a need for a people to understand the situation where we come from and the situation where we are today. (Respondent 19, Zulu)

This attribute of worldview is particularly relevant in the context of transitional justice which straddles the temporal orientation in that it seeks to address the past while forging a new future. From a race-based perspective one might argue that one's emphasis on the past or future is determined by one's experience of conflict, i.e. those who were formerly oppressed or sympathised with the oppressed will emphasise the past. However, from a worldview perspective, the primacy given to history, traditions and rituals among those with a past orientation will be an important aspect of how a country's symbolic landscape is recreated and a new future is built. Similarly, understanding that values such as achievement and advancement are prioritised among those with a future orientation is important for understanding why, at least in part, the past is easily ignored or even devalued. This raises questions as to whether or not mechanisms such as truth commissions may be more acceptable or appropriate among cultural groups with an orientation towards the past. This would partly account for Tutu's (1999) assertion that restorative justice in the form of truth commissions speak to an African worldview.

5.6 Worldview Diversity in South Africa

To further explore, the relationship between group identity and systems of meaning-making worldview attributes can be amalgamated, as depicted in Fig. 5.2. Being reminded that this uses an interpretative

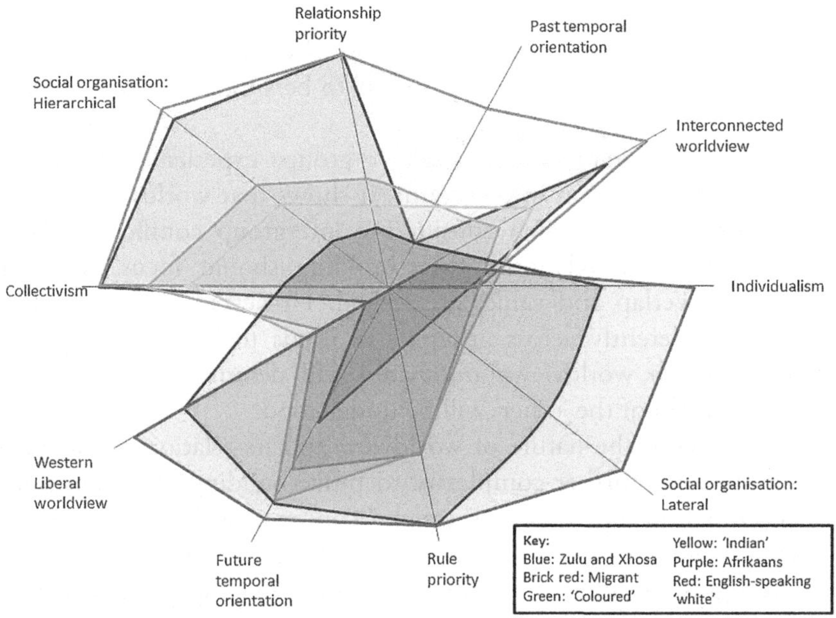

Fig. 5.2 The relationship between worldview and group identities

methodology (and not an exact science), the diagram should be seen as a broad conceptualisation of the relationship between worldview and identity groups. Using a series of intersecting lines that represent the different worldview attributes, it conceptualises the dominant worldviews around which each group gravitates. As illustrated throughout the chapter these worldviews are not fixed but are able to shift and change. However, this diagram is limited in its ability to show their flexibility.

While each group has a unique combination of dominant worldview attributes, it also depicts how worldviews across groups can overlap showing that groups can have certain worldview attributes and values in common, and how they can simultaneously differ. For example, both the 'white' groups shared numerous worldview attributes; as did the migrant and 'black' groups and the 'Indian' and 'coloured' groups. However, although the Afrikaans group shared some worldview attributes with the 'black' group, the 'white' and 'black' groups tended to gravitate around a distinctly different combination of worldviews while the 'Indian' and 'coloured' groups tended to overlap with all the groups. This contributes to understanding why interpretations of reality in culturally diverse societies may appear to be similar and yet different simultaneously.

While this diagram does not take a groups experience of conflict, injustice and oppression into account, it shows that worldview is a real and important factor when considering intergroup conflict. To build positive intergroup relations, peace-building should focus on where worldviews overlap and values are shared. However, where values are prioritised differently across groups also needs to be considered. The extent to which worldviews are shared will determine the extent to which the world of the 'other' will be understood.

In conclusion, the nature of worldview and its relationship to identity groups adds further complexity to peace-building and transitional justice, and how interventions can be contextualised. In as much as a human rights approach to justice seeks to give dignity back to victims, recognising different systems of meaning-making (in that they are deeply intertwined with identity) will further support this endeavour. To support this, practitioners need to learn how to identify worldview indicators through the process of everyday conversation. As the next chapter will show, different interpretations of peace can act to harden intergroup boundaries.

References

Ashforth, Adam. 2005. *Witchcraft, violence, and democracy in South Africa.* Chicago: The University of Chicago Press.

Bediako, Kwame. 2004. *Jesus and the gospel in Africa: History and experience.* Maryknoll: Orbis Books.

Comaroff, Jean, and John Comaroff. 2003. Reflections on liberalism, policulturalism, and ID-ology: Citizenship and difference in South Africa. *Social Identities* 9 (4): 445–473.

Comaroff, Jean, and John Comaroff. 2004. Criminal justice, cultural justice: The limits of liberalism and the pragmatics of difference in the new South Africa. *American Ethnologist* 31 (2): 188–204.

Comaroff, Jean, and John Comaroff. 2005. The struggle between the constitution and 'things African'. *Interventions: International Journal of Postcolonial Studies* 7 (3): 299–303.

Escritt, Thomas. 2015. International court urged to reform or risk losing Africa. *Reuters Africa*, November 20. http://af.reuters.com/article/topNews/idAFKCN0T90JQ20151120. Accessed 31 August 2018.

IOL News. 2015. ICC is dangerous: Mantashe. *IOL News*, June 22. https://www.iol.co.za/news/politics/icc-is-dangerous-mantashe-1874842. Accessed 31 August 2018.

Lakoff, George, and Mark Johnson. 1980. *Metaphors we live by*. Chicago and London: The University of Chicago Press.

Reuters. 2015. ICC asks South Africa to explain failure to arrest Bashir. *Reuters*, September 9. https://www.reuters.com/article/us-safrica-icc-bashir/icc-asks-south-africa-to-explain-failure-to-arrest-bashir-idUSKCN0R71A120150907. Accessed 31 August 2018.

Singh, Kaveel. 2018. Chainsaw attack—'They couldn't get through his bone'—Training partner, friend of SA Triathlete. *News24*, March 7. https://www.news24.com/SouthAfrica/News/chainsaw-attack-they-couldnt-get-through-his-bone-training-partner-friend-of-sa-triathlete-20180307. Accessed 31 August 2018.

Tutu, Desmond. 1999. *No future without forgiveness*. London: Rider.

Tutu, Desmond. 2008. Interview. In *Truth, justice, memory: South Africa's truth and reconciliation process*. Cape Town: Institute of Justice and Reconciliation.

6

Through the Eyes of the 'Other': Interpreting Peace and What Is Required for Building a Sustainable Peace

Recognising the diversity of worldview's in South African society raises the question of how different identity groups understand what is required for building a peace that can be sustained. For some, such an investigation may seem obvious and redundant given the pervasiveness of issues such as poverty, crime, unemployment and corruption. However, as articulated in the debates raised by the discourses on sustainable peace (Chapter 3) and those surrounding Western and non-Western approaches to peace-building (Chapter 4), a shared interpretation of peace cannot be assumed. Indeed, by definition, one's system of meaning-making influences how one interprets the world around them, in this case, one's view of intergroup conflict and, therefore, the strategy through which it should be addressed.

Using the worldview framework developed in Chapters 3–5, this chapter provides an in-depth analysis on the nexus between worldview and what this means for peace-building in multicultural societies. The research uncovered six themes associated with the relational pillars of sustainable peace and five themes relating to the structural pillars of sustainable peace (see Table 6.1). The relational pillars comprised the need for understanding, respect, encounter and engagement, peace

C. Bollaert, *Reconciliation and Building a Sustainable Peace*,
Palgrave Studies in Compromise after Conflict,
https://doi.org/10.1007/978-3-030-03655-3_6

Table 6.1 Comparing pillars for building a sustainable peace with group identity

	Xhosa	Zulu	Afrikaans	English-speaking white	Coloured	Indian	Migrant
Relational pillars							
1. Understanding the 'other'	Strongly emphasised	Strongly emphasised	Strongly emphasised	Moderately emphasised	Strongly emphasised	Moderately emphasised	Strongly emphasised
2. Respect	Strongly emphasised	Strongly emphasised	Not mentioned	Not mentioned	Not mentioned	Not mentioned	Moderately emphasised
3. Engagement and encounter	Strongly emphasised	Strongly emphasised	Moderately emphasised	Acknowledged	Strongly emphasised	Strongly emphasised	Strongly emphasised
4. Peace education	Strongly emphasised	Strongly emphasised	Acknowledged	Acknowledged	Acknowledged	Strongly emphasised	Strongly emphasised
5. Cultural equality	Strongly emphasised	Strongly emphasised	Not mentioned	Not mentioned	Moderately emphasised	Moderately emphasised	Acknowledged
6. Healing from the past	Strongly emphasised	Strongly emphasised	Acknowledged	Not mentioned	Moderately emphasised	Moderately emphasised	Moderately emphasised
Structural pillars							
7. Good governance and accountability	Acknowledged	Acknowledged	Strongly emphasised	Strongly emphasised	Moderately emphasised	Strongly emphasised	Moderately emphasised
8. Civic responsibility	Acknowledged	Moderately emphasised	Strongly emphasised	Strongly emphasised	Moderately emphasised	Not mentioned	Not mentioned
9. National unity	Moderately emphasised	Moderately emphasised	Strongly emphasised	Strongly emphasised	Moderately emphasised	Moderately emphasised	Acknowledged
10. Past redress	Strongly emphasised	Strongly emphasised	Acknowledged	Acknowledged	Moderately emphasised	Acknowledged	Moderately emphasised
11. Socio-economic development	Strongly emphasised	Strongly emphasised	Strongly emphasised	Strongly emphasised	Strongly emphasised	Strongly emphasised	Strongly emphasised

Key:

Strongly emphasised — Acknowledged

Moderately emphasised — Not mentioned

education, cultural equality and healing from the past. The structural pillars included good governance and accountability, civic responsibility, national unity, past redress and socio-economic development. The chapter shows that when a person's own interpretation of peace was not readily demonstrated in the actions and behaviour of the 'other' or when a person's actions did not seem to make sense, it reinforced existing stereotypes of the 'other' and hardened intergroup boundaries. Significantly, the chapter also shows how the various pillars resonated with different worldview attributes. This was useful for shifting the discourse surrounding conflict analysis and reconciliation in South Africa from one which essentialises and reinforces race-based identities to one that has a deeper reach than race and is more complex, dynamic and contextually relevant.

Table 6.1 broadly reflects the pillars each identity group emphasised with the colours representing the varying levels of support. One should be mindful that the difficulty with a tabulated form of analysis is it can suggest the idea of fixed identities and interpretations of peace, which is not the case. Consequently, this table is useful to the extent it visualises which aspects of peace were prioritised across the groups. For example, it reflects how, across all the groups, an understanding of the 'other' and the need for socio-economic development was emphasised. It also indicates that 'white' groups tended to prioritise the structural pillars of sustainable peace while the 'black' and migrant groups mostly prioritised the relational pillars (see also Adams et al. 2012). The remainder of the chapter will speak to each of these pillars, paying particular attention to its relationship to worldview.

6.1 Relational Pillars of Sustainable Peace

The relational pillars of sustainable peace emphasise the interpersonal aspects of building a lasting peace. Within the body of literature, this includes among others: social rehabilitation, the need for truth, acknowledgement, apology and forgiveness, rebuilding positive relationships and creating a culture of trust, and developing a shared vision of the future. These pillars are reflected in the priorities for peace that were uncovered in the research including the themes relating to understanding the 'other', encounter and engagement, and healing from the past. Less readily reflected in literature were those themes relating to respect, cultural equality and peace education. Bearing this in mind, each of the themes uncovered in the research is explored below:

Understanding the 'Other'

Given South Africa's history of Apartheid, it is not surprising that one of the strongest themes to emerge from the interviews was a need for an understanding of the 'other'. While 'black' South Africans would have had greater exposure to the 'white' way of life, albeit within the confines of authoritarian power relationships, the Apartheid architecture meant that most 'whites' lived in a segregated bubble with limited awareness of the 'black' reality. Recognising that democracy forces 'one' to encounter the 'other' meant that for many people South Africa's transition would require meeting the 'other' as an equal citizen for the first time. A 'white' respondent captures the impact of this very well in what she refers to as her 'awakening' which took place a number of years after she left high school:

> My awakening has been recognising that even within South Africa culturally we're different…The time I was in the North West [province], I mean I might as well have been in another country. It was a complete culture shock; I could have been in Japan it was that foreign…So, that for me was a time of recognising that there is another world, leaving my bubble I guess. (Respondent 5, English-speaking white)

Indeed, there was a strong awareness among the majority of participants interviewed for this research of how the culturally diverse South African society is. The focus on difference and the challenges surrounding understanding the 'other' was seen as one of the primary causes of intergroup conflict which was reiterated across all the groups represented in the study. Significantly, even after 20 years of democracy the need for understanding the 'other' was still seen as something crucial to peace-building in South Africa.

In explaining the importance for cultural understanding in the everyday participants drew on their personal experiences:

> For example, for a black person you can just pop into their office and say 'Oh, can I talk to you about this'. Even if the person was doing something he will stop and listen. But for white people you must make an

> appointment. You cannot just pop into their office. They will tell you 'did you make an appointment?' So, the culture and understanding each other, you know, to say we're created differently and we need to understand each other. (Respondent 2, Zulu)

> When we [a coloured business owner] employed that white guy, Sheldon,[1] into our stores, there was no peace here. The black guys in the stores didn't get on with him: two different cultures. And I can't say it's because you're black and because you're white, they just think differently, they do things differently. They're more ambitious than black people are, although the black people are more loyal than the white people are. It's different; they just don't get on…It's just the cultural thing. (Respondent 34, Coloured)

While these two interview excerpts underscore the familiarity of South Africans with the challenges of living in a multicultural society, they also point to the challenge of culture in the everyday interpersonal relationships that contribute to the nature of peace in any given community. It is also notable that racial differences are interpreted within cultural terms which previous studies have also shown (Durrheim and Dixon 2005; Seekings 2008; Bhana and Pattman 2010). While this may indicate a movement away from racism, it could also be a means of couching racial prejudices in the language of non-racialism and more socially accepted terms of discourse (Steyn and Foster 2008; Durrheim and Dixon 2005). It also shows how deeply entrenched racial categories are in the society. This raises the question as to the extent the language of culture continues to reinforce a social understanding that group identities are fixed (as per the primordial school of thought) further entrenching racially defined intergroup boundaries.

Moreover, the strong emphasis that is given to this theme 'the need for understanding' suggests that different systems of meaning-making, with their accompanying social rules, are at play. This is well illustrated in the following narrative which reflects a Zulu respondent grappling with the nature of intergroup relations in South Africa:

[1]Not his real name.

> There are some occasions… [for example] Freedom Day on 27th April where you only see black people there filling the stadium. Then you try to understand really what is wrong with this thing of trying to make 'unity in diversity'[2] …it brings about some negative attitude. Sometimes it tells us that after this hard won freedom there are some people, especially some whites, that were not or are not happy at all with what happened or who are still trying to perpetuate their own agenda, who are not trying to help or support this freedom to grow. So those feelings come when you get into the gatherings and you feel that only blacks come into those gatherings, why? To see that unity in diversity we need to be mixed… When you go around you find them [whites] the beach doing their own thing, others sitting, others braaing [BBQing]. So there is still that thing that worries, it really worries. And it really tells and makes someone ask herself or himself where are we going as South Africa or as a country if we say we are free and we want a unity in diversity but we don't see people at the gatherings that are very important to uplift our country or to develop or to show the world that really this is South Africa, a new South Africa… Maybe, it's how they understand, or how they grew up, or what deep-seated views they have about the blacks. There's still that understanding that blacks are dangerous people or are people you cannot come close to… But there is that element that others do not like to come closer to understand a black person better in this post-Apartheid era. (Respondent 19, Zulu)

A closer review of this narrative shows, in the first instance, the respondent grappling with why 'whites' are not turning up to what he sees as significant events central to the well-being and future of the country. Furthermore, the respondent expresses the desire to believe that 'whites' want to participate and contribute to building the country. In failing to find evidence for this, he is reluctantly forced to find meaning within a racial framework, the normative interpretation of intergroup relations in South Africa. This reinforces his perception of 'white' superiority against his perceived inferiority and further serves to consolidate intergroup boundaries along racial lines.

---

[2]'Unity in Diversity' is the motto inscribed in the South African coat of arms (South African History Online 2011).

While a racial interpretation may well be a plausible and influencing factor within the South African context, a worldview interpretation can help to open the discourse to move beyond race. Firstly, the emphasis the respondent gives to the group indicates he is interpreting his reality through a collectivist worldview in which the group is the location of one's sense of self and survival. Consequently, participation in mass events, such as the Freedom Day celebrations, would be critical to the survival of the group and evidence of trying to build peace. The failure of 'whites' coming to these events can then take on a negative interpretation. Given that worldviews do not function in isolation of other factors, this response to mass rallies could also be compounded by 'white' beliefs of superiority and persisting racism. However, for 'whites', who are largely individualists, supporting the collective in this way carries little meaning and indeed they would fail to realise, unless it was pointed out, how this would signify their commitment to South Africa. Furthermore, in any given election campaign political rallies are held by parties typically supported by 'black' South Africans. Consequently, 'white' South Africans do not have a history of attending such events. While the situation that is narrated by the respondent may well include elements of political and racial bias, this underscores the influence and significance of competing worldviews for societies in transition and building sustainable peace. Without an alternative framework for understanding, one is 'forced' to interpret the 'other' through the lens of race which can act to exacerbate historical lines of division.

Encounter and Engagement

The need for engagement and encounter with the 'other' was recognised by participants in the study as an important means to building a lasting peace (see also Lederach 1997). This was accompanied with an underlying sense of anger associated with the role the Apartheid structures had on keeping people separated. Although this is closely related to the first theme 'understanding the "other"', engagement and encounter connotes a deeper and more personal relationship with the 'other'. Interestingly, numerous respondents, and in particular 'black' respondents, pointed to their experience in racially mixed schools as the space in which they learned to accept and interact with 'whites'. Whether or not this suggests the sample was skewed towards more liberal thinking individuals is difficult to evaluate. However, as the participants were part of South Africa's transitional generation, it could also be an indication of a shift in attitudes across the generations. Nonetheless, supporting contact theory, this theme emerged largely due to the formative impact that people's personal experiences of encounter with the 'other' had on challenging their view of the world and shaping the nature of their relationships with the 'other' (Dixon et al. 2005, 2007).

Significantly, within this theme, emphasis was placed on the need for dialogue and cultural or worldview translation. For example, the following respondent explains how what his group had interpreted as showing a lack of respect leading to a hostile situation between 'black' and 'white' students had been transformed through dialogue and engagement with the 'other':

> When I started studying black students had just started coming into Potchefstroom University; there were some tensions between white students and black students in my faculty. And then we realised its real plain and simple cultural things: for example, there were a lot of Venda students studying and in Venda culture you give a very soft hand when you greet because it's seen as being aggressive if you take a firm hand. While in Afrikaans culture its very disrespectful not to have a firm hand in greeting. So, needless to say that the Venda students immediately experienced Afrikaans students as being aggressive and the Afrikaans immediately experienced the Venda's as being disrespectful, purely because of a misunderstanding. (Respondent 47, Afrikaans)

Recognising the implications of cultural misunderstandings for the society and the country's democracy, one respondent brought a particularly interesting perspective to the discussion arguing for need of a 'multicultural committee' to assist with understanding how policy developments impact on the different social groups:

> In a multi-party democracy, like they claim that we have, there should be a multi-party cultural committee who actually sits down to revise policy that has been made by government in order that everybody is appeased. A multi-party cultural or appeasement committee or something like that where there's lots of policy that we have that is actually offensive to some societies…We are twenty years into democracy; we cannot still have offensive legislation in place, absolutely not. (Respondent 39, Coloured)

In an endeavour to make sense of their new post-Apartheid reality, both these respondents recognise the need for intercultural interpretation. This suggests that while sustained contact with the 'other' may be instrumental in promoting positive intergroup attitudes, it needs to be accompanied with efforts at translating cultural values and social rules for engagement. The failure to do so can risk reinforcing negative perceptions of the 'other' which further hardens intergroup boundaries, the antithesis of what encounter as requisite for reconciliation seeks to achieve.

Despite the priority that many participants gave to this theme, there was also a sense of fatigue and frustration among some participants (mostly English-speaking 'whites') about having to continually learn about the 'other'. Comparing this response to how different groups responded to intercultural reconciliation workshops I (the author) previously facilitated in South Africa, it was not out of the ordinary; 'white' individuals regularly showed little interest in engaging with the process. On the contrary, despite being cautioned by colleagues that my 'white' identity would hinder 'black' South Africans from engaging, they always showed an eagerness to participate. From a worldview perspective, this could indicate that an emphasis on encounter and engagement for building a sustainable peace appeals more to those who function within a relationship priority. The reticence of 'whites' could speak to an individualist sense of identity in conjunction with sustained beliefs in superiority. For societies in transition, this underscores the need for formal institutions, such as schools and universities to include intercultural education into their teaching curriculum. It also suggests that peace-building and transitional justice needs to consider how cultural and worldview translation can be included into its practices.

Peace Education

Following on from the previous theme, the need for peace education was seen as an important requisite for building a sustainable peace. It was primarily emphasised by the 'black', 'Indian' and migrant groups. Given the heinous acts of xenophobic violence migrant groups have had to face, it is easy to understand why this group might prioritise this theme. While this suggests that one's experiences contribute to how one might interpret what is required for building peace, this theme also supports the suggestion that processes focused on engaging the 'other' lend themselves to a relationship priority and collective worldview. As suggested in the following interview extract, this requires thinking about *who* should be involved in leading peace-building processes as it can act to either legitimise or undermine the strength of the process:

> If in the church they can have those sessions of peace it will help... Collaborate with pastors because people listen more to pastors. Because of our background when you see a pastor you think that he is God himself, he presents God. When the pastor says something people listen more... Because in the church you will have all the ages and then the message is going to be spread among all the ages. I think that is the way to do it because trying to do the workshops in the community, not everybody available. (Respondent 25, Migrant)

The recognition afforded to the pastor indicates a hierarchical form of social organisation and interconnected worldview. Within such a worldview, the role of the pastor is significantly powerful; not only must he be respected as an elder, but he has a responsibility to impart spiritual security and a sense of well-being in the world (see also Núñez 2015). This points to the church as an influential support mechanism (more so than secular community organisations). This should caution liberal peace-building approaches which tend to be secular in nature to not dismiss the role of spiritual leaders and seek to function separately from religious institutions.

Peace education also requires thinking about *what* needs to be taught. Among other aspects of peace-building, this needs to centre on how different concepts, such as reconciliation, accountability and nation-building, are interpreted across groups (see Chapter 4). Through the research process, the importance of understanding how democracy is interpreted in Africa was also underscored. This raises an important question around the extent to which African democratic states interpret the concept in the same way as Western and European states. Indeed, the current conditions in South Africa bring into question the ability of democracy as a political system to deliver on its values of equality and freedom. While the scope of this book does not permit further investigation into this, it points to the need for international politics, peace-keeping and peace-building interventions that are built around democratic rules of engagement to consider how interpretations of democracy impact the goal of building a peace that can be sustained.

Respect

The issue of respect was a dominant theme that emerged particularly among 'black' respondents. The importance of this theme is evidenced in the media through calls by the deputy president to respect Zuma (Makinana 2014) and from the current Minister of Education and Training, Blade Nzimande, to outlaw insults against the president (News24 2012). More recently, the African National Congress Women's League (ANCWL) organised a public protest in defence of Zuma's dignity (ENCA 2015; The Citizen 2015). Their support for the president was particularly fascinating (from a research perspective) bearing in mind previous rape allegations made against Zuma (although he was cleared of them) (BBC News 2006) and the criticisms levelled at him for his sexist views of women (Sapa 2015). Rather, one might have been expected that the ANCWL would be marching against the president and in support of gender equality. Although this criticism likely expresses a Western liberal interpretation of reality, it underscores the strength and importance of respect within this interpretation of reality.

The issue of respect became even more intriguing following a telephone conversation with a senior 'white' English-speaking politician. When explaining my research interest, she quickly and dismissively replied saying, 'They will tell you we just need to respect more'. Judging by the tone of her voice, she was clearly frustrated with what she considered would be the stock response from the 'black' community and dismissed it as superficial and effectively meaningless. Suggesting there are deeper issues at stake, these sentiments are also insinuated in a newspaper article written by a 'white' commentator and entitled: 'All that Emperor Zuma wants is respect, mon. Respect!' (Saunderson-Meyer 2014).

For a group to keep reiterating the need for respect suggests its members are not feeling respected and that it is a strong corporate value. Indeed, Dlamini (1998) explains that the practice of respect was integral to Zulu identity and contributed to former divisions between rival political parties, the Inkatha Freedom Party (IFP) and the United Democratic Front (UDF). In Zulu culture, children are taught to respect and be non-confrontational towards anyone older than them, even if only by one year. Thus, when the UDF began recruiting young people, many of whom were Zulu, it was seen as a threat to Zulu culture and identity. The reason for this, as Dlamini goes on to explain, was that many of the political activities undertaken by the UDF, such as workers' strikes which prevented people from going to work, would have been organised by Zulu youth and involved them requiring the compliance of Zulu adults, thereby showing them grave disrespect. Consequently, this led to the UDF and those living in urban areas being associated with disrespectful practices which were an affront to Zulu culture. Although the UDF no longer exists, these divisions continue to polarise many of the communities today (Jarstad 2010).

Understanding that identity is about one's sense of self and survival can facilitate a better appreciation of why this issue of respect is so important. Given South Africa's Apartheid history in which 'blacks' were stripped of their dignity, it might be a reasonable expectation that the notion of respect was seen as a key aspect in building a sustainable peace. Significantly, none of the research participants referenced the Apartheid past in relation to the need for respect. This includes respondents from an Afrikaans background, despite the Apartheid state prosecuting people for disrespecting it. While undoubtedly exacerbated by the Apartheid past, the research findings indicate that the issue of respect extends beyond this. In the months running up to the 2014 national elections, Zuma made several statements which appealed to an interconnected worldview and a belief in malevolent spirits. Speaking to a group of 'black' church leaders, he stated: 'If you don't respect those in leadership, if you don't respect authority then you are bordering on a curse' (Pillay 2013). In his statement, Zuma is correlating respect with one's sense of survival and well-being in the world. Recognising that Zuma may be exploiting these beliefs for political gain, he nonetheless understands the worldview of his electorate and is appealing to a deep-rooted fear of being cursed. In the light of this statement and contributing to a deeper understanding of why showing respect is so imperative, the following respondent explains:

> God curses people that don't respect adults. Respect your father and your mother so that your days in the world can be increased, that's the Bible. So, if you don't do that, you don't respect your elders what then happens. Your days won't increase; then you'll die prematurely. Then if you die prematurely, then what does that mean, you were cursed…If you are challenging elders then indirectly you are challenging God… But I understood the President very well and he was right. In fact, its Biblical principles, it's Christian. (Respondent 15, Xhosa)

That this respondent recognises the possibility of being cursed suggests he is functioning within an interconnected worldview and, as he says, is able to understand Zuma. It further suggests that in an interconnected worldview showing respect goes beyond simply treating someone with dignity but is connected with one's sense of well-being and longevity. Furthermore, this explanation speaks to a hierarchical form of social organisation, as respect is largely vertical, i.e. you respect the leader and those who are older, but not necessarily those who are lower in the hierarchy and younger in age.

Comparing the interpretation given to respect within an interconnected and hierarchical worldview with the response of the 'white' English-speaking politician suggests there are distinctly different interpretations of the notions of respect at play. This is well illustrated in the following excerpt from a conversation with an Afrikaans business woman:

> Basic ethics is for me very important. Like being on time for appointments, treating somebody else with respect…Some people don't even pitch for the appointment. They don't let you know. For me, in my business that's a big issue because time is money for me. If I book you for an appointment and you don't even let me know or don't pitch I lose money. And people don't seem to understand that, and unfortunately, yes, the black community don't. I think they grew up differently, they just rock up whenever. (Respondent 26, Afrikaans)

From this extract, it is significant to note the way in which the respondent relates respect to honouring appointments and being on time. Indeed, for an individualist functioning within a rule priority, timeliness is an important means of showing respect; failure to arrive on time would be interpreted as a form of disrespect. For someone with a relationship priority, being on time does not carry the same weight in terms of how respect is given and received. From this, broadly two different interpretations of respect are seen to emerge, i.e. one that comes from an individualistic worldview and the other from an interconnected and collective worldview. Again, as suggested by the tone of the interview extract, for a society in which racism is deeply rooted differences tend to get interpreted through the lens of race which can act to reproduce racist thinking and intergroup conflict.

Common sense dictates that if a person feels respected, the possibility of future positive communication, collaboration and success on any named project, including peace-building processes, is more likely. A difference in how respect is interpreted can have far-reaching implications on intergroup relations as illustrated, for example, in the furore that the painting of Zuma with his genitals exposed caused (Burbidge 2012; May et al. 2012). Coupled with other factors, such as historical forms of structural inequalities and oppression, differences in how respect is interpreted can also contribute to lethal violence. This exemplified in the violence that ensued following the drawing of the Prophet Mohamed by Danish and French magazines (Ross 2009; Kirby 2015). Consequently, this requires an investigation into how different groups experience respect. Interestingly, in its Programme for Government, the Northern Ireland Executive is developing a respect index as a means of measuring how far the society has come in reaching its outcome for building a society that respects diversity (Northern Ireland Executive 2016). However, for this to be effective, it would need to engage with how different groups experience respect.

Competing interpretations of respect can also pose serious challenges for Western liberal values that promote gender equality and freedom of speech. Underscoring the significance of this was the way in which South African newspapers were being threatened with punishment if they published anything that could be regarded as insulting to the president (Mataboge and Letsoalo 2014). In South Africa, this presents a challenge of how to negotiate the balance between promoting Western liberal values, such as equality and freedom of speech, as written into South Africa's constitution, and values that support an interconnected and collective worldview which doesn't permit the same liberties regarding political commentary. Competing interpretations of respect have also challenged the work of the International Criminal Court (ICC). At the risk of promoting a culture of impunity, African nations have agreed that 'sitting heads of state should not be put on trial by the International Criminal Court' (Reuters 2013; Al Jazeera 2014). It also relates to South Africa's decision not to arrest the Sudanese President Omar al-Bashir during his visit to South Africa, despite being signatories to the Rome Statute (Maru 2015). Defending South Africa's decision, the Secretary General of the African National Congress (ANC), Gwede Mantashe, argued that the ICC was 'a dangerous tool in the hands of the powerful to destroy the weak' and seen to be a neo-colonial construct (Reuters 2015a). Complicated by histories of colonialism and Western hegemony, the decision was also based on customary law which prohibits heads of state from being insulted, in this case through his arrest (Reuters 2015b). This raises serious concerns for the protection of human rights in Africa and brings into question how accountability in non-Western contexts is interpreted.

Cultural Equality

A strong theme emerging particularly from 'black' respondents relates to the need for cultural equality. It is widely recognised that with South Africa's transition to democracy political equality and transformation was reached. The lack of economic transformation has more recently been identified as one of the failures of the new South Africa despite policies aimed at economic redress (Durrheim et al. 2011). However, the research process uncovered the need for a cultural transformation in the context of continued unresolved issues of racism, its associated power relations and persisting attitudes of superiority. The importance of cultural equality and the need for cultural transformation is well expressed in the following interview extract:

> Back in those days their focus was more on political equality and they didn't focus on the economic equality, and that's where they lost it...Cultural equality is also very important. My belief is that the western culture is as important as the African culture, for example. None is more superior to the other. You see, it's like in the world of business we adopt a western culture to a large degree. It's primarily a western culture. Even in the work that we do it's primarily western, even in the pieces of legislation that we have, they favour primarily western culture. For instance, in the profession that I'm in, the planning profession, most of our approaches to planning are western ideas. The problem is we are in Africa. We are unique. We have African issues. And our approach to addressing our issues should also be an African approach. (Respondent 46, Xhosa)

This theme raises important considerations for transitional justice and Western liberal approaches to peace-building which tend to focus more on the structural aspects of sustainable peace-building such as political and institutional reform. While economic transformation is addressed through policies aimed at past redress, peace-building and transitional justice fails to engage with the issue of cultural reform. Given that Apartheid sought to strip 'black' Africans of their identity and dignity, recognising different ways of being in the world not only contributes to restoring the dignity of formerly oppressed groups, but also contributes to strengthening local agency and promoting equality at an even deeper level. As noted by the Comaroffs (2004), this helps to ensure that African culture is not further denigrated or criminalised.

Healing from the Past

Underscoring the impact that South Africa's Apartheid past has on shaping the future, numerous 'black' respondents spoke of the continued need to acknowledge the pain caused by Apartheid. This included acknowledging the intergenerational consequences that Apartheid had on 'black' people, and the need for cultural equality, forgiveness and psychological liberation from the past. Significantly, failing to acknowledge the need for healing from the past was seen to contribute to the growing sense of anger in South Africa's current sociopolitical climate. This has led to it becoming a controversial topic particularly among many 'white' South Africans who are reticent about, and some completely opposed to, acknowledging the way in which they benefited from the past (Matthews 2010). Those who contested the need for healing argued the past was being exploited for political gain and that the country needed to move on from it (Mathambo 2015).

These competing claims about the past require further investigation. To what extent do they point to the failure of the TRC to implicate beneficiaries of the Apartheid and, in doing so, exempt 'whites' from their responsibility to contribute to reparations (Mamdani 2000)? How much of this assertion to move on is also a response to 'white' feelings of guilt associated with the Apartheid past? This debate raises the question of whether or not there are also competing worldviews at play here. While the failure to understand and acknowledge the consequences of the past points to persisting attitudes of racism and beliefs in superiority, it also questions the extent to which the call to move on is informed by a future temporal orientation? As depicted in Chapter 5, 'whites', 'coloureds' and 'Indians' all emphasised values which prioritised the future. This brings into question whether their calls to move on from the past and look to the future are rooted in racism or a future-orientated worldview, which, in itself, is not racist. However, when coupled with South Africa's oppressive history, an emphasis given to the past or future could be perceived negatively by one group or another. Given that transitional justice is concerned with both the past (in relation to human rights abuses) and building a more peaceful future, further consideration should be given to how worldview impacts on these goals. Is it sufficient to assume that formerly oppressed groups will want to focus on the past while beneficiaries and perpetrator groups will prioritise the future? While not accepting racist behaviour, failing to engage with worldview could risk entrenching racist stereotypes of the 'other'.

6.2 Structural Pillars

The structural pillars of building a sustainable peace refer to the institutional and policy aspects of peace-building such as institutional reform, the rule of law, socio-economic transformation and past redress. These pillars are reflected in themes relating to good governance, past redress and socio-economic development that emerged from the research. In addition, the need for national unity and civic responsibility were also seen by the respondents as important components of sustainable peace. Significantly, these are the pillars that tend to be emphasised in Western liberal approaches to peace-building (Richmond 2011).

Good Governance and Accountability

The need for good governance and accountability was the first theme relating to the structural pillars of sustainable peace that emerged from the research. Addressing corruption was seen to be integral to this. Significantly, it was most emphasised by the 'Indian', 'coloured' and 'white' research participants. This is not to suggest that 'black' groups did not recognise corruption and the lack of accountability as a problem, they did. However, it was not given the same priority as by these other groups. Examples of responses speaking to governance and accountability include the following interview extracts:

> Get rid of Zuma and the ANC. Yes, get rid of the corruption and that entitlement and being above the law. (Respondent 26, Afrikaans)

> I wish it could be a more proactive, more efficient country. I think that will be great…Corruption and a more efficient government. (Respondent 48, Afrikaans)

From a worldview perspective, these responses are particularly interesting. At first glance, they could be interpreted as a form of 'white talk' and a reaction to the loss of exclusive power (Steyn and Foster 2008; Verwey and Quayle 2012). Indeed, the language that is used could be seen as a form of racism which tries to show that 'black' South Africans are not capable of leading, which points to a worldview that continues to be supported by attitudes of superiority. The problem with this interpretation is that while it may hold true it can serve to reinforce racial lines of division and it dismisses the fact that there may well be corruption. However, a worldview analysis uncovers some deeper insights. The emphasis given to accountability, efficiency and being proactive suggests the respondents are functioning within an individualised sense of identity, a future temporal outlook and a rule-based priority. For those functioning within this worldview, these are the rules that must be followed if the society is to function; any breach of them could readily be interpreted as the person seeing themselves as entitled and above the law. The significance of worldview (and indeed competing worldviews) on intergroup relations is further illustrated by the following respondent who has a strong rule priority and is relating an incident in which a relationship priority and hierarchical interpretation of social reality are being lived out:

> Respondent: We, as white people, probably resent the government intensely for their abuse of power. I think for me peace will come when that abuse of power stops. So, just a simple example: when we see the blue light brigade driving up, flashing their blue lights on the freeway, we get angry, and we don't move over. And we become obstinate because in Apartheid days they didn't feel as important as that to have to drive with the blue light. And I don't believe that they have to drive with blue lights because they're threatened. I think that's an abuse of power. Because it's about 'look at me I'm important now whereas before I wasn't important'. It's that, arrogance is the word I'll use, and the abuse of power. When that is addressed and the money starts flowing in the right direction then we will, the whites will start feeling better about the government. Then you'll stop having this 'us and them' kind of situation. Then maybe we can call ourselves South Africans.
>
> Interviewer: What do you mean by the blue light brigade?

> Respondent: It's all these black cars ferrying a person of varying degrees of importance around and depending on how important it is, is whether he'll be in one car or whether it will be a motorcade of ten cars. And each of them will have their blue lights on and they'll be going 200 km's an hour because they're above the law.[3] And they'll come up behind you and if you don't pull over they have the right to make you pull over by law. They have hurt a couple of people, they've caused accidents and I think they did cause someone's death once. So there have been a few law suits around it. But back in Apartheid days that never happened…So they, to me, are the symbol of what's wrong with this country. (Respondent 51, English-speaking white)

Similar incidences pertaining to the 'blue-light brigade' are widely reported in the media (Keepile 2010; Da Costa 2011). For example, in 2010 a roadside jogger was arrested for disrespecting the president when he gave the middle finger to a presidential motorcade (Underhill 2010). In response to the allegations of bullying and disregard for road traffic regulations by government dignitaries, the ANC argue the Road Traffic Act gives provision for them to act accordingly during *any* official business (not only in the case of emergency) (Keepile 2010). This is being contested by the DA.

Together, these incidences point to clashes between a rule priority and a relationship priority, and a hierarchical and lateral form of social organisation. In a rule-based paradigm, there are road-safety rules and codes of conduct that need to be adhered to, unless in the case of an emergency. However, if interpreting this scenario from a relationship priority, and a hierarchical form of social organisation, the situation the respondent perceives as wrong is not in breach of the associated worldview rules. Within this worldview, it is not only important but it is necessary that appropriate power is exercised and that respect is shown to dignitaries. As worldview conflict theory supports, an affront to one's rules for being in the world impacts on one's sense of self and survival (Solomon et al. 2000; Lieberman et al. 2001; Ramsbotham 2010). When coupled with beliefs in superiority, this can elicit a violent response (Eidelson and Eidelson 2003).

[3] The speed limit on South African motorways is usually 120 km per hour.

For 'white' South Africans, this response to the so-called blue light brigade might be further compounded by the impact the loss of exclusive power had on their identity. Similarly, for 'black' South Africans in leadership this sense of entitlement could also be compounded by the way they were historically excluded and marginalised. Recent changes to the national budget which saw VIP protection services being allocated three times more money than the Department of Higher Education and Training (Flanagan 2015) are further evidence of this. Given that education has been identified as a priority by the ANC, such a budget allocation is alarming and contradictory. However, it underscores the potential of worldview in shaping society and contributing to group polarisation.

Civic Responsibility

Civic responsibility was another theme to emerge from the research process which speaks to the structural pillars of sustainable peace. It was mostly emphasised by 'white' and 'Indian' participants and to certain degree 'coloured' and migrant participants and raised in the context of what was perceived as 'black' people not paying taxes and not taking responsibility for keeping the government accountable. In this way, the 'black others' were viewed as irresponsible citizens. Emphasis on paying taxes and obeying the 'laws of the land' also suggests these respondents are functioning within a rule priority. This raises the question as to whether or not civic responsibility is interpreted differently across groups. In relation to this, a local politician makes a significant observation:

> I think there is a misunderstanding of what civil responsibility means. Many people think if I show up every four years, five years and cross the box I've done my responsibility, my duty, as a citizen. I do think that people need to understand that actually your, well our black population, is active all the time and involved and all of that. I mean it's interesting that Morningside [historically a white suburb] is a DA stronghold; I get a very high percentage of votes but I have one of the smallest branches in the city. I struggle to get my residents involved in politics while in a place like Mlazi [a nearby black township], where we don't get a lot of votes, but our branches there are very active; they come to meetings every week and

> they want to be involved. So, I also think it's that sort of cultural type of thing, almost like 'No, I don't want to get involved. I voted, what more do you want of me'...Even in my Morningside branch I've got more black members that white members. (Respondent 47, Afrikaans)

From a worldview perspective, this is a fascinating comparison of how civic responsibility is interpreted differently across groups. From a rule-based perspective, civic responsibility and being a good citizen is about paying taxes and keeping the government accountable. Such an understanding of civic responsibility is located more with the individual, and less with the collective. Moreover, those who do not hold to this point of view are seen to be neglecting their duty and contributing to the failure of the country. On the other hand, for those coming from a collective perspective and relationship priority civic responsibility is interpreted as needing to be actively engaged in politics and participating in the group. This interpretation was also evidenced in a previous example (see the theme 'understanding the "other"') in which a Zulu respondent spoke to the importance of attending mass meetings, a form of civic responsibility, in which he challenged the motives of 'whites' for their lack of participation and failure to be what he perceived as good citizenship. Notwithstanding this interpretation, it should also be recognised that the way a person participates in the sociopolitical life of the country may also be influenced by one's sense of agency and the consequence of living in an oppressive and racist state.

This theme raises important considerations for peace-building and transitional justice as it touches on the notion of national pride and identity and what it means to participate in building the nation. Again, a failure to understand how the 'other' expresses their responsibility to the society can act to harden intergroup boundaries and exacerbate racism.

National Unity

There is a continuing discourse in South Africa around the issue of national unity which emerged as a further requisite, particularly among 'white' South Africans, for building a sustainable peace. The notion of national unity is captured by the metaphor of the Rainbow Nation which was intended to facilitate the creation of a collective identity (see Chapter 2). However, the research underpinning this book suggests national unity was interpreted differently across groups and the notion of being separate but one (as depicted by the rainbow) appealed more to individualism, as suggested in the following interview extract:

> Government must say, 'Hey guys, you know what, whites you carry on doing what you doing, Indians you carrying on doing, coloureds you carry on doing what you doing. But you know what we are actually in charge here and we are going to do our thing – not despite you or ignoring you'. (Respondent 53, English-speaking white)

There were numerous responses similar to this one in which the respondents seemed to be comfortable and at ease with the notion of functioning individually and as separate entities within the broader collective. In contrast, those functioning within an interconnected worldview interpreted the creation of a new national identity from a more interpersonal perspective as suggested in the following narrative from a 'black' politician.

> Look, South Africa is a very complex country and one that is having a deep scarred inter-personal relationship which really one wants to believe was unfortunate. [Some] things you don't choose, you are given. It's nice when you go to China because in China they are Chinese. When you go to Japan, in Japan they are Japanese. And when you are saying Japanese they are Japanese, even the way you see, they are Japanese. But in South Africa it's very difficult to say that these are South Africans because you have to, before you call yourself a South African, definitely there are things that you need to mould so that you can get the identity that will reflect you as a South African. Even our code says 'Unity in Diversity', so we are forging the contradictions. So, it's a contradictory world, one that is inherited, but one needs to forge a new identity out of it. We don't have it, we don't have an identity. But if you are saying you going to identify with language, you are going to identify with our culture, we are going to identify with Chinese, everything its one. But with us, now we must start understanding your culture: Why you don't eat this? Why you eat this? Why? Why? Why? Why you don't talk Zulu? Why am I talking English?

> Even right now I'm supposed to be speaking Zulu for that matter but I'm talking to you in English. So, it's a problem. It's a serious contradiction of contradictions. And we are trying then to forge, and I want to believe we are forging. When we are saying forge it's something that has not been there…Therefore, we are a culture in diversity. So, can we have a culture in diversity? Then it's up to you how you want to interpret that. So that's where it becomes very difficult. You see before you try to identify who you are, you need to try and understand who you are with. But if you're Japanese you're Japanese. I think I'm trying to simplify what I'm trying to say. If I'm Japanese, from Japan and our culture is Sudoku, or whatever, I mean it just relates one culture… We have inherited the Hottentots that were in the Eastern Cape. After that there was Jan van Riebeeck. And after van Riebeeck, the Trek and all these things. So all that is an inheritance we got from history. It's not us. Where we are finding ourselves now is a mixture of everything that we got…To a point we have eleven official languages, that is a contradiction. You can't say a country is having eleven official languages…So in South Africa it's very difficult. You can't say in South Africa there is Shaka then others say they have Moshoeshoe, and have this all happening within one country. It's very difficult and all them they want to claim one identity. All of them, everyone here wants to claim South African identity. (Respondent 15, Xhosa)

Approaching this excerpt from a worldview perspective provides some useful insights for understanding the challenges associated with the struggle for national unity in culturally diverse societies. In his reflection, the respondent is grappling with the concept of a national identity which requires answering the question of how to forge one identity out of many identities and one collective out of many collectives. As he points out, in a collective there is a common language, a common king and a common culture. However, in South Africa there are multiple collectives each with their own language and king, i.e. Shaka and Moshoeshoe who, it is important to understand, represent different tribes, the Zulu and Basotho, respectively. This means that for the Zulu tribe King Shaka is one of their ancestors, whereas King Moshoeshoe is not. For those functioning within an interconnected worldview, maintaining a positive relationship with one's ancestors is central to one's sense of survival and well-being in the world (see Chapter 4). Furthermore, in collectivism, the unit of survival is the group. Therefore, if language, history and ancestors are integral to defining the collective, it follows that creating a new national identity for those with an interconnected and collective worldview is fraught with difficulties, if not impossible. This raises the question as to whether or not it is possible for a society shaped by an interconnected worldview (which has a more organic sense of social organisation compared to a mechanical form of social organisation within nationalism) to shift its sense of the collective to be more encompassing of diversity.

Overall, these interviews prompt discussion on the extent to which national unity and creating a new supra identity lends itself more to individualism. While this may be the case when forging a civic identity, it may not follow if trying to forge a shared narrative which would lend itself more to collectivism. Given that nationalism originated in Europe, it follows that the need for national unity speaks to the individualised worldview and a politically constructed notion of the collective. As noted in Chapter 4, it also raises the question of how transitional justice interprets the concept of nation-building.

Past Redress

Deeply intertwined with the need for healing from the memory of the past (see Sect. 6.1.6) is the need to redress the legacy of inequalities from the past. While these two categories are difficult to separate, the need for healing speaks to the relational pillars of sustainable peace with past redress speaking to the structural pillars. Tied to transitional policies, such as Black Economic Empowerment (BEE) and land reform (see Chapter 2), this theme is one of the most contested themes within the public sphere (Atuahene 2011; Vollgraaff 2015; Donnelly 2015). Indeed, there is a growing perception that these policies are the cause of instability and violence across the society (Du Toit 2000; Boraine 2014; Mashele and Qobo 2014). Significantly, it was mostly 'black' respondents who emphasised the need for past redress, as did 'coloured' and migrant participants—although to a lesser extent. Given their experience of oppression and injustice, such a response might be expected. However, while most of the participants in the sample group acknowledged the importance for redress, the way in which it was being pursued was strongly debated by 'white' and 'Indian' respondents in particular.

The need to redress injustices is not new to the transitional justice discourse. However, applying a worldview lens to this theme provides some useful insights. While most of the respondents agreed with the need for redress, the issue lies with where the emphasis was placed. Those who argued that redress is still needed for sustaining peace did so on the basis of the past injustices and as a means of righting wrongs and promoting equality and wealth distribution across the racial groups. A survey carried out by James Gibson shows that 66% of 'black' Africans agreed that 'land must be returned to blacks in South Africa, no matter what the consequences are for the owners and for political stability in the country' (Gibson 2009: 32). In contrast, those respondents who spoke about the failure of the policies aimed at redress emphasised future-orientated values such as achievement and development and did not readily admit the importance of these policies as a means of acknowledging the past.

Opposition to the transitional policies could indicate a subtle form of racism in that they challenge the normative racial hierarchies and pose a threat to identity (Bornman 2011; Durrheim et al. 2011; Verwey and Quayle 2012). However, the survey carried out by Gibson (2009) found that historical factors were an important consideration for 'black' South Africans in relation to land redress whereas for 'whites' property rights and contractual issues were of more concern. While this could be understood in the light of South Africa's Apartheid past, a more nuanced analysis suggests that worldview may also contribute to how these policies are interpreted. Collectivism and a past temporal orientation lend themselves to prioritising the need for past redress based on historical injustices while individualism lends itself to focusing on the future and on legal contracts (as per a rule-based priority). This further underscores how one's experience is deeply intertwined with worldview and how, due to South Africa's history of Apartheid, the social and political context tends to be interpreted through the lens of race.

This discussion also raises the question of the relationship between worldview and land. As noted in Chapter 2, land ownership was integral to shaping the Afrikaans collective identity and was supported by religious narratives and symbols. Although Afrikaners and English-speaking 'whites' shared a common understanding relating to land ownership, for Afrikaners, land was seen as sacred and deeply intertwined with Afrikaner ethno-nationalism (Akenson 1992). For English-speaking 'whites', land ownership was associated more with the colonial conquest and the capitalist agenda (Lambert 2009). This reflects a future-orientated worldview driven by economic interests. Significantly, both these interpretations differ from the way the ANC interpreted land under its policy of non-racialism which embraced a more shared understanding of property ownership. Such an interpretation is partly due to the way in which land is also deeply connected with ancestors; among those functioning within an interconnected worldview, the 'living-dead' are a vital force giving security to one's sense of survival and well-being in the world (see Chapter 4).

Significantly, in 1996 under the GEAR strategy (a macroeconomic policy framework called the Growth, Employment and Redistribution strategy), the ANC began to adopt more privatised notions about land and property ownership. This has been strongly criticised by some groups, such as National Union of Metalworkers of South Africa (NUMSA) and the Economic Freedom Front (EFF), for disenfranchising the working class who are mostly 'black' (The Mercury 2014a). Arguing in favour of the nationalisation of land and against 'white' majority ownership, Julius Malema, leader of the EFF, asserts, 'This monopoly of white imperialism has also created greedy Africans, something that goes against the meaning of the word 'African'. To be an African means to love to share' (The Mercury 2014b). Interestingly, by appealing to an African identity, Malema is also underscoring different ways of being in the world.

Consequently, land as a symbol of 'black' and Afrikaner identity involves a complex set of dynamics encompassing worldview, politics and political ideologies, sacred narratives and a history of inequality and racism. Being reminded of the relationship between identity, worldview and conflict (Chapter 3), this would account for land redistribution being such a contentious and increasingly volatile issue—perhaps more so than any other (Harding 2018).

Socio-Economic Development

Given the persisting high levels of poverty in South Africa, it is to be expected that the need for socio-economic development would emerge as a key theme in relation to what is required for building a sustainable peace. Indeed, it was one of the few themes upon which there was consensus across the groups. However, from a worldview perspective, it is significant to note the different causal factors attributed to poverty as this will shape the way it is addressed.

The first group of causal factors included the long-term consequences of Apartheid government policies and the current government policies which were perceived to be contributing to a dependency mentality, sense of self-entitlement, lack of personal responsibility and a poor work ethic particularly among 'black' South Africans. Limited access to quality education, as well as greed and government corruption, were also seen as contributing factors. Although these factors were, to a certain extent, reflected across all groups, they were most strongly emphasised by the 'white', 'coloured', 'Indian' and migrant groups. From a worldview perspective, such interpretations are insightful in that they reflect values relating to individualism, a future temporal orientation and a rule-based priority. Moreover, it suggests that these aspects of worldview resonate with the structural pillars of building a sustainable peace. However, reflecting the intertwined nature of worldview, context and experience, it is important to recognise that these interpretations may also be influenced by the current political situation and by persisting racist attitudes and beliefs in superiority.

In contrast to the more structural causal factors attributed to poverty, the second group of causal factors related to witchcraft, jealously, the fear of curses and beliefs in the malevolent spirit world (see also Nürnberger 2007; Ashforth 2005; Comaroff and Comaroff 1999). This interpretation of poverty was expressed by most 'black' South Africans, 'Indian' and migrants. It reflects an interconnected worldview which is well illustrated in the following interview extract:

> When people do witchcraft to someone, she or he wants to see that person not developing at all. She wants to see her going down, not becoming

> successful in any whatever way…I do understand it and I know it well. It does make people go down, really. This thing of witchcraft and jealousy it really has a very big impact on how we develop ourselves. Even me, I'm talking from experience, since now I'm a teacher [meaning that he is earning an income] it's very hard for me…And they understand that if you can get this boy or get this man down then that house or that home can perish, through jealousy. (Respondent 19, Zulu)

There were several reasons attributed to why such beliefs were seen to perpetuate poverty. Firstly, they are understood to remove a person's sense of agency and personal autonomy and thus prevent people from developing and progressing in life. Secondly, the time and financial costs associated with accessing the necessary spiritual protection or for carrying out acts of witchcraft were seen as a major contributing factor. This relationship between poverty and beliefs in witchcraft is well illustrated in an incident (that was personally recounted to me) which ultimately led to the death of young boy who was extremely malnourished. The grandfather, who was his primary carer, had been receiving government grants to help support the family. Although social workers and hospital staff had advised that the child needed good nutrition, instead of spending the money on food the grandfather sought help from traditional healers. From the grandfather's perspective, he was doing what he thought was best to help the child. However, it resulted in further impoverishment and the death of a child that might otherwise have been prevented.

Access to education, and, in particular, to quality education, is a common response in relation to South Africa's socio-economic development problems. Often, it is seen as a solution to the problem of witchcraft. While the benefit of education cannot be disputed, the danger is to limit beliefs in witchcraft to uneducated people living in rural areas. As a number of respondents pointed out, such beliefs also exist in middle-class areas and among well-educated people. Significantly, this demonstrates how worldviews can overlap. On the one hand, a person might be a well-educated lawyer, pointing to a Western way of being in the world, while on the other hand, the same person might also exercise practices that speak to beliefs in witchcraft and a malevolent spiritual world. In other words, an interconnected worldview is relevant to educated professionals living in urban environment and is not limited to rural parts of South Africa or Africa more generally. This is an important consideration for approaches to peace-building and reconciliation in multicultural societies, such as the UK and Europe more widely, that outwardly may reflect Western liberal values.

This theme also raises the question of how persons who believe in witchcraft (who are mostly 'black') relate to those who don't (who are mostly 'white') and whether those who are on the outside can be affected by witchcraft. Firstly, 'whites' tend not to be regarded by those who hold beliefs in witchcraft and curses (who are mostly 'black') with the same suspicion as someone from within an interconnected community who does. In this way, 'whites' may be perceived to be less of threat. However, it can also result in the scenario in which 'whites' are seen not to fully understand the complexities of life. If this is the case, it limits the ability of peace-building practitioners who do not carry an interconnected worldview, or at least have a good understanding of it, to develop processes that can lead to a lasting peace. This is important because with poverty and inequality persisting at a macro-level one can expect an increase in witchcraft-related violence and the cycle of poverty to be further entrenched. Structural solutions to peace-building addressing the 'what' question as opposed to the 'who' question relating to the cause of poverty and socio-economic problems become insufficient. For these approaches to become more sustainable in culturally diverse societies, strategies that restore the spiritual balance of a society and address the motivational issues behind poverty need to be incorporated.

6.3 Interpreting Peace Through the Lens of Worldview

This chapter has uncovered different interpretations of peace which reflect the relational and structural pillars of sustainable peace delineated in Chapter 3. These findings can be analysed in several ways. Due to South Africa's history of racism, a normative race-based lens is typically used to interpret the conflict (and its solution) (see Table 6.1). Through such a lens, one might expect certain themes (such as the need for healing and past redress) to be prioritised by those who experienced the discrimination and oppression of Apartheid (i.e. 'black' South Africans). For similar reasons, one might expect 'white' South Africans to want to forget the past and focus on the future. Recognising that such histories and experiences will certainly influence one's interpretation of peace, a race-based interpretation raises several challenges: it will produce race-based solutions to the conflict which will reinforce race-based and racist interpretations of the 'other'. As this chapter has shown, this acts to harden intergroup boundaries and reinforce racial identities and race-based lines of division. Although race has become a normative interpretation, the difficulty with it is that it draws on a primordial understanding of identity which fails to recognise the flexibility and ability of identities to shift and change (see Chapter 3). Indeed, such a fixed notion of identity is associated with racism, xenophobia, sectarianism and other forms of exclusion.

To move beyond racially based interpretations of identity in South Africa, this chapter applied the worldview framework (developed in Chapters 3–5) to interpret why certain aspects of peace were prioritised over others. Bearing in mind that, by definition, worldview informs how one interprets one's reality and interacts with the world; a 'worldview lens' effectively allows one to 'look through the eyes of the "other"'. The analysis shows how various worldview attributes support certain aspects of sustainable peace over others as outline in Table 6.2. This provides a more contextual analysis of the conflict which has the scope for more sustainable solutions to peace as it engages with the deeper systems of meaning-making that speak to ones' sense of security and well-being in the world.

Table 6.2 is based on an interpretative analysis and so is primarily illustrative. It shows certain themes resonate more closely with particular attributes of worldview. Broadly speaking, individualism, a rule priority, a future temporal orientation and a Western liberal worldview support structural approaches to peace-building. Collectivism, a relationship priority and an interconnected worldview support the relational pillars of peace-building. Given the historical Western roots of 'white' South Africans, it stands to reason that these groups would prioritise the structural pillars of sustainable peace and, similarly, that 'black' South Africans might prioritise the relational pillars given their experience of an interconnected worldview. However, the way in which peace was interpreted was also influenced by how respondents experienced Apartheid. This is suggested by the way healing from the past and the need for past redress were mostly prioritised by 'black' South Africans. Indeed, such an interpretation is consistent with a constructivist's understanding of worldview; in as much as worldviews can shape the social environment, the social environment can shape worldviews (see Fig. 3.1).

The table also reflects how worldviews can overlap, as was the case with the theme 'socio-economic development' which was supported by both collectivism and individualism. However, a closer review of the interviews shows that within this theme different causes were attributed to the issue of poverty and lack of development within the wider society. These included structural causes (generally supported by an individualist outlook) and spiritual causes associated with an interconnected worldview and beliefs in witchcraft. Nonetheless, as formerly divided groups encounter each other different aspects of the 'other's' worldview may be assimilated causing identity constructions to shift between generations. This will influence how social institutions and the future of the country are shaped. Therefore, as society changes it will have to find ways of accommodating different beliefs or alternatively belief systems will need to emerge to assimilate the new order.

Significantly, the analysis shows these different systems of meaning-making contributed to the hardening of group boundaries. When a respondent's own interpretation of peace was not seen to be lived out through the actions and behaviour of the 'other', or if their actions were not understood or did not make sense, it served to reinforce existing stereotypes of the 'other' as, for example, being racist, superior or lazy. Consequently, without an alternative framework through which to understand the 'other' a normative racial lens was applied. Understandably, this resulted in the negative reinforcement of intergroup boundaries. This is further complicated by South Africa's history of Apartheid and persisting beliefs in superiority and vulnerability. Consequently, when thinking about transitions, how key concepts relating to sustainable peace are interpreted across groups needs to be

Table 6.2 Comparing pillars for building a sustainable peace with worldview

	Unit of survival		Social organisation		Activity orientation		Temporal orientation		Ontology	
	Individualism	Collectivism	Lateral	Hierarchical	Rule-based	Relationship-based	Future	Past	Western liberal	Interconnected
Relational pillars										
1. Understanding the 'other'	X	X	X	X	X	X	X	X	X	X
2. Respect		X		X		X				X
3. Engagement and encounter		X				X				X
Peace education		X				X				
5. Cultural equality										X
6. Healing from the past		X				X	X	X		
Structural pillars										
7. Good governance and accountability	X				X		X			
8. Civic responsibility	X				X				X	
9. National unity	X	X								
10. Past redress		X			X	X	X	X		X
11. Socio-economic development	X	X			X	X	X	X	X	X

understood (Kelsall 2009; Merry 2006; Krog 2008, 2015; Sriram 2007; Palmer et al. 2015).

Looking through the eyes of the 'other' to understand how peace is interpreted across diverse groups in South Africa underscores the need to accommodate ontological difference and systems of meaning-making in peace-building and transitional justice. Historically, these disciplines (which are underpinned by a Western liberal worldview) have given primacy to the structural pillars of sustainable peace. While these are important for addressing the structural aspects of racism, inequality and oppression in South Africa, alone, they are insufficient in that they fail to take into account different ways of being in the world which is essential to one's sense of well-being and security. Therefore, building a sustainable peace requires going beyond strategies aimed at reforming the political and economic institutions to include strategies that also promote the relational pillars, such as the need for respect and cultural transformation. The last-minute inclusion of 'the Ethnic Chapter' into Colombia's 2016 Peace Agreement is reflective of this understanding in that it recognises for the peace process to succeed different ethnic perspectives and systems of meaning-making need to be acknowledged (The Institute on Race, Equality and Human Rights 2016; Sanchez-Garzoli 2017). Moreover, the inclusion of worldview into peace-building is integral to restoring the dignity of those who were historically oppressed. In conclusion, when thinking about transitions, consideration needs to be given to how the pillars of sustainable peace relate to the core identity of a society. Chapter 7 will now explore the nexus between identity and the policies that were implemented to facilitate South Africa's transition.

References

Adams, Byron G., Fons J. R. Van de Vijver, and Gideon P. de Bruin. 2012. Identity in South Africa: Examining self-descriptions across ethnic groups. *International Journal of Intercultural Relations* 38: 377–388.

Akenson, Donald Harman. 1992. *God's peoples: Covenant and land in South Africa, Israel and Ulster*. New York: Cornell University Press.

Al Jazeera. 2014. African Union urges united stand against ICC. *Al Jazeera*, February 1. http://www.aljazeera.com/news/africa/2014/02/african-union-urges-united-stand-against-icc-20142111727645567.html. Accessed 31 August 2018.

Ashforth, Adam. 2005. *Witchcraft, violence, and democracy in South Africa*. Chicago: The University of Chicago Press.

Atuahene, Bernadette. 2011. South Africa's land reform crisis: Eliminating the legacy of Apartheid. *Foreign Affairs* 90 (4): 121–129.

BBC News. 2006. S Africa's Zuma cleared of rape. *BBC*, May 8. http://news.bbc.co.uk/1/hi/4750731.stm. Accessed 31 August 2018.

Bhana, Deevia, and Rob Pattman. 2010. White South African school girls and their accounts of black girls at school and cross-racial heterosexual relations outside school. *Ethnicities* 10 (3): 371–386.

Boraine, Alex. 2014. *What's gone wrong? On the brink of a failed state*. Johannesburg and Cape Town: Jonathan Ball Publishers.

Bornman, Elirea. 2011. Patterns of intergroup attitudes in South Africa after 1994. *International Journal of Intercultural Relations* 35: 729–748.

Burbidge, Matthew. 2012. Gallery refuses to remove 'spear of the nation' artwork. *Mail & Guardian Online*, May 17. http://mg.co.za/article/2012-05-17-anc-irate-over-spear-of-the-nation-artwork. Accessed 23 August 2018.

Comaroff, Jean, and John Comaroff. 1999. Occult economies and the violence of abstraction: Notes from the South African postcolony. *American Ethnologist* 26 (2): 279–303.

Comaroff, Jean, and John Comaroff. 2004. Criminal justice, cultural justice: The limits of liberalism and the pragmatics of difference in the new South Africa. *American Ethnologist* 31 (2): 188–204.

Da Costa, Wendy Jasson. 2011. Blue light cops 'cause crash'. *IOL News*, October 24. http://www.iol.co.za/news/south-africa/kwazulu-natal/blue-light-cops-cause-crash-1.1163201#.VmhJgtLhDcs. Accessed 3 September 2018.

Dixon, John, Kevin Durrheim, and Colin Tredoux. 2005. Beyond the optimal contact strategy: A reality check for the contact hypothesis. *American Psychologist* 60: 697–711.

Dixon, John, Kevin Durrheim, and Colin Tredoux. 2007. Intergroup contact and attitudes toward the principle and practice of racial equality. *Psychological Science* 18 (10): 867–872.

Dlamini, Sibusisiwe Nombuso. 1998. The construction, meaning and negotiation of ethnic identities in KwaZulu Natal. *Social Identities* 4 (3): 473–497.

Donnelly, Lynley. 2015. Bitter fight looms over land. *Mail & Guardian Online*, May 15. http://mg.co.za/article/2015-05-14-bitter-fight-looms-over-land. Accessed 3 September 2018.

Durrheim, Kevin, and John Dixon. 2005. *Racial encounter: The social psychology of contact and desegregation*. London: Routledge.

Durrheim, Kevin, John Dixon, Colin Tredoux, Liberty Eaton, Michael Quayle, and Beverley Clack. 2011. Predicting support for racial transformation policies: Intergroup threat, racial prejudice, sense of group entitlement and strength of identification. *European Journal of Social Psychology* 41 (12–8): 23–41.

Du Toit, Pierre. 2000. In search of post-settlement peace. In *The management of peace processes*, ed. John Darby and Roger Mac Ginty, 16–60. Basingstoke, London, and New York: Macmillan Press.

Eidelson, Roy J., and Judy Eidelson. 2003. Dangerous ideas: Five beliefs that propel groups toward conflict. *American Psychologist* 58 (3): 182–192.

ENCA. 2015. ANCWL to march for Zuma. *ENCA*, October 30. http://www.enca.com/south-africa/ancwl-march-zuma. Accessed 31 August 2018.

Flanagan, Louise. 2015. VIP scores more money than varsity. *IOL News*, October 23. http://beta.iol.co.za/business/2.1742/vip-scores-more-money-than-varsity-1934487. Accessed 3 September 2018.

Gibson, James. 2009. *Overcoming historical injustices: Land reconciliation in South Africa*. Cambridge: Cambridge University Press.

Harding, Andrew. 2018. South Africans' anger over land set to explode. *BBC News*, May 30. https://www.bbc.co.uk/news/world-africa-44278164. Accessed 3 September 2018.

Jarstad, Anna K. 2010. Local peace agreements: The road to peace and democracy in KwaZulu Natal. *Statsvetenskaplig Tidskrift* 11 (1): 60–68.

Keepile, Karabo. 2010. Blue-light blunders. *Mail & Guardian Online*, May 4. http://mg.co.za/article/2010-05-04-bluelight-blunders. Accessed 3 September 2018.

Kelsall, Tim. 2009. *Culture under cross-examination: International justice and the special court for Sierra Leone*. New York: Cambridge University Press.

Kirby, Paul. 2015. Paris attacks: France grapples with freedom of speech. *BBC News*, January 15. http://www.bbc.co.uk/news/blogs-eu-30829005. Accessed 27 August 2018.

Krog, Antjie. 2008. '...if it means he gets his humanity back...': The worldview underpinning the South African Truth and Reconciliation Commission. *Journal of Multicultural Discourses* 3 (3): 204–220.

Krog, Antjie. 2015. Research into reconciliation and forgiveness at the South African Truth and Reconciliation Commission and Homi Bhabha's architecture of the new. *Canadian Journal of Law and Society* 30 (2): 203–217.

Lambert, John. 2009. 'An unknown people': Reconstructing British South African identity. *The Journal of Imperial and Commonwealth History* 37 (4): 599–617.

Lederach, John Paul. 1997. *Building peace: Sustainable reconciliation in divided societies*. Washington, DC: United States Institute of Peace Press.

Lieberman, Joel D., Jamie Arndt, Jennifer Personius, and Alison Cook. 2001. Vicarious annihilation: The effect of mortality salience on perceptions of hate crimes. *Law and Human Behavior* 25 (6): 547–566.

Makinana, Andisiwe. 2014. Ramaphosa: MPs must respect Zuma and his office. *Mail & Guardian Online*, November 5. http://mg.co.za/article/2014-11-05-ramaphosa-mps-must-respect-zuma-and-his-office. Accessed 31 August 2018.

Mamdani, Mahmood. 2000. The truth according to the TRC. In *The politics of memory: Truth, healing and social justice*, ed. Ifi Amadiume and Abdullahi An-Na'im, 177–190. London and New York: Zed Books.

Maru, Mehari Taddele. 2015. Why South Africa let Bashir get away. *Al Jazeera*, June 15. http://www.aljazeera.com/indepth/opinion/2015/06/south-africa-bashir-150615102211840.html. Accessed 3 September 2018.

Mashele, Prince, and Mzukisi Qobo. 2014. *The fall of the ANC: What next?* Johannesburg: Picador Africa.

Mataboge, Mmanaledi, and Matuma Letsoalo. 2014. State poised to wield advertising axe. *Mail & Guardian Online*, December 12. http://mg.co.za/article/2014-12-11-state-poised-to-wield-advertising-axe/. Accessed 31 August 2018.

Mathambo, Khanya. 2015. Why I can't 'get over' Apartheid. *Mail & Guardian Online*, July 15. http://thoughtleader.co.za/readerblog/2015/07/15/why-i-cant-get-over-apartheid/comment-page-2/. Accessed 3 September 2018.

Matthews, Sally. 2010. Differing interpretations of reconciliation in South Africa: A discussion of the home for all campaign. *Transformation* 74: 1–22.

May, Jackie, and Andrea Nagel. 2012. Ban the spear, stone its maker. *Times Live*, May 22. http://www.timeslive.co.za/politics/2012/05/22/ban-the-spear-stone-its-maker. Accessed 23 August 2018.

Merry, Sally Engle. 2006. *Human rights and gender violence: Translating international law into local justice*. Chicago and London: University of Chicago Press.

News24. 2012. Nzimande wants to outlaw Zuma insults. *News24*, November 15. http://www.news24.com/SouthAfrica/News/Nzimande-wants-to-outlaw-Zuma-insults-20121115. Accessed 31 August 2018.

Northern Ireland Executive. 2016. Draft Programme for Government: 2016–2021. https://www.northernireland.gov.uk/sites/default/files/consultations/newnigov/draft-pfg-framework-2016-21.pdf. Accessed 20 June 2018.

Núñez, Lorena. 2015. Faith healing, migration, and gendered conversions in Pentecostal churches in Johannesburg. In *Healing and change in the city of gold: Case studies of coping and support in Johannesburg*, ed. Nicola Palmer, Brandon Hamber, and Lorena Núñez, 149–168. Cham, Heildelberg, New York, Dordrecht, and London: Springer.

Nürnberger, Klaus. 2007. *The living dead and the living god: Christ and the ancestors in a changing Africa*. Pietermaritzburg: Cluster Publications.

Palmer, Nicola, Briony Jones, and Julia Viebach. 2015. Introduction: Ways of knowing atrocity: A methodological enquiry into the formulation, implementation, and assessment of transitional justice. *Canadian Journal of Law and Society* 30 (2): 173–182.

Pillay, Verashni. 2013. Cursed if we criticise Zuma? Think again. *Mail & Guardian Online*, October 8. http://mg.co.za/article/2013-10-08-cursed-if-we-criticise-zuma-think-again/. Accessed 28 August 2018.

Ramsbotham, Oliver. 2010. *Transforming violent conflict: Radical disagreement, dialogue and survival*. London and New York: Routledge.

Reuters. 2013. Africans tell ICC: Heads of state should not be tried. *Mail & Guardian Online*, October 12. http://mg.co.za/article/2013-10-12-africans-tell-icc-heads-of-state-should-not-be-tried/. Accessed 31 August 2018.

Reuters. 2015a. ICC is dangerous: Mantashe. *IOL News*, June 22. http://www.iol.co.za/news/politics/icc-is-dangerous-mantashe-1.1874842#.VZZxqBtVhHw. Accessed 3 September 2018.

Reuters. 2015b. ICC asks South Africa to explain failure to arrest Bashir. *Reuters*, September 7. https://www.reuters.com/article/us-safrica-icc-bashir/icc-asks-south-africa-to-explain-failure-to-arrest-bashir-idUSKCN0R71A120150907. Accessed 3 September 2018.

Richmond, Oliver P. 2011. *A post-liberal peace*. London and New York: Routledge.

Ross, Marc Howard. 2009. *Culture and belonging in societies: Contestation and symbolic landscapes*. Philadelphia: University of Pennsylvania Press.

Sanchez-Garzoli, Gimena. 2017. Colombia's peace implementation will only succeed with an ethnic perspective. *WOLA*, August 18. https://www.wola.org/analysis/colombias-peace-implementation-will-succeed-ethnic-perspective/. Accessed 3 September 2018.

Sapa. 2015. Zuma reprimanded for comments about women. *Mail & Guardian Online*, January 17. http://mg.co.za/article/2015-01-17-zuma-reprimanded-for-comments-about-women. Accessed 31 August 2018.

Saunderson-Meyer, William. 2014. All that emperor Zuma wants is respect, mon. respect! *Mail & Guardian Online*, November 8. http://thoughtleader.co.za/williamsaundersonmeyer/2014/11/08/all-that-emperor-zuma-wants-is-respect-mon-respect/. Accessed 31 August 2018.

Seekings, Jeremy. 2008. The continuing saliency of race: Discrimination and diversity in South Africa. *Journal of Contemporary African Studies* 26 (1): 1–25.

Solomon, Sheldon, Jeff Greenberg, and Tom Pyszczynski. 2000. Pride and prejudice: Fear of death and social behavior. *Current Directions in Psychological Science* 9 (6): 200–204.

South African History Online. 2011. The national coat of arms. *South African History Online*, March 22. http://www.sahistory.org.za/article/national-coat-arms. Accessed 31 August 2018.

Sriram, Chandra Lekha. 2007. Justice as peace? Liberal peacebuilding and strategies of transitional justice. *Global Society* 21 (4): 579–591.

Steyn, Melissa, and Don Foster. 2008. Repertoires for talking white: Resistant whiteness in post-Apartheid South Africa. *Ethnic and Racial Studies* 31 (1): 25–51.

The Citizen. 2015. ANCWL members march to protect Zuma's dignity. *The Citizen*, October 30. https://citizen.co.za/news/south-africa/843945/live-ancwl-march-for-zumas-dignity/. Accessed 31 August 2018.

The Institute on Race, Equality and Human Rights. 2016. Final peace accords in Colombia include ethnic chapter. http://raceandequality.org/en/english/final-peace-accords-in-colombia-include-ethnic-chapter/. Accessed 3 September 2018.

The Mercury. 2014a. Numsa moves to contest elections. *The Mercury*, May 16.

The Mercury. 2014b. Malema lashes out at 'land thieves'. *The Mercury*, April 17.

Underhill, Glynnis. 2010. No middle finger to prez. *Mail & Guardian Online*, February 19. http://mg.co.za/article/2010-02-19-no-middle-finger-to-prez. Accessed 3 September 2018.

Verwey, Cornel, and Michael Quayle. 2012. Whiteness, racism, and Afrikaner identity in post-Apartheid South Africa. *African Affairs* 111 (445): 551–575.

Vollgraaff, Rene. 2015. Lack of land reform fuels inequality in SA. *Fin24*, October 1. http://www.fin24.com/Economy/Lack-of-land-reform-fuels-inequality-in-SA-Piketty-20151001. Accessed 3 September 2018.

7

Transitional Policies, Group Identity and Intergroup Relations

The previous chapters provide evidence to suggest that one's interpretation of peace is informed by the structures of deeper meaning-making (worldview). While this includes one's experience of South Africa's Apartheid past, one's interpretation of the conflict and its solution are not as tied to race as normative race-based interpretations, which are based on fixed notions of identity, might suggest. Moreover, there was evidence to suggest that such interpretations contributed to hardening intergroup boundaries. Building on this, this chapter engages with how the policies that were implemented to redress the Apartheid past and promote equality across race, class and gender are shaping identity and intergroup relations. These policies (referred to as transitional policies) include: the Truth and Reconciliation Commission (TRC), affirmative action policies, Black Economic Empowerment (BEE), land reform, government grants, and the renaming of towns, stadiums and street names (see Chapter 2 for further detail).

The interview process asked participants for their views about the transitional policies. This proved to be very provocative and elicited some emotional responses which reflects how these policies are affecting the lives of every person in the country, both citizen and migrant

C. Bollaert, *Reconciliation and Building a Sustainable Peace*,
Palgrave Studies in Compromise after Conflict,
https://doi.org/10.1007/978-3-030-03655-3_7

(Southall 2007; Jeffery 2014). Nonetheless, there was a range of perceptions on how respondents interpreted these policies. At one end of the spectrum were those who saw the current transitional policies as beneficial and having a positive impact on society. This was the dominant perception held by 'black' respondents. Moving along the spectrum were those who argued the principles underpinning the policies were good but poorly implemented. This was a widely held view across all the represented identity groups. Further along the spectrum was another commonly held view that the policies were only benefitting 'black' South Africans and, moreover, only a minority of 'black' South Africans. This latter perspective was the view most widely expressed by all the respondents irrespective of group identity. Moving towards the opposite end of the spectrum were those who expressed a dilemma, wanting to support the policies but unable to do so because of the negative implications they perceived surrounding them. Finally, on the extreme end of the spectrum were those who interpreted the policies as unbeneficial, failed and promoting racism and xenophobia. This view was mostly among 'white', 'Indian', 'coloured' and migrant groups who attributed to them the growing sense of anger and hopelessness in the country:

> The way I defined it once is 'Why is it so frustrating to live in South Africa?' It's frustrating to live in South Africa, not because of crime and those things are obviously bad, but the worst thing for me entirely is shattered hope every single day. Hopeful for a moment, it gets shattered. Hopeful for another moment, it gets shattered. Wake up in the morning hopeful, you think your shower is going to work, there's no water. Hopeful that the electricity is all going to be fine, the power goes off. Going with a new business venture or business idea and you think it's going to work out, the guy tells you 'No, we're giving business to black businesses, not white. Sorry.'. Hope shattered. So that for me is probably is the hardest, hardest thing. Your hope gets shattered on every level. (Respondent 53, English-speaking white)

> Sometimes we feel like this guy in Greek mythology who was punished by the gods and had to roll this huge boulder up the hill. He had to pull this huge boulder up the hill and everyday just before sunset he would always get to the top of the hill but then he would be so tired and it

> would roll down. I think sometimes many of us feel like that. So you've got to find ways to stay energised. (Respondent 36, Coloured)

> When people don't have proper houses, they don't have access to water, they don't have a good education; they are not in peace. They are still living in a future that doesn't have a hope and that might break into violence any time….It makes you down, but you have nothing to do, you have to carry on with life. (Respondent 11, Migrant)

One might argue that having lost exclusive power and privilege this response from 'white' South Africans is to be expected. However, given this view was expressed by respondents across all of the groups it is not possible to argue that only 'disgruntled whites' held these views. Rather, it speaks more deeply to the sense of identity, survival and belonging that, across the groups, continues to be threatened for a variety of reasons, including the lack of socio-economic transformation, persisting inequality and poverty and the sense of victimisation and re-victimisation. This illustrates the beliefs that Eidelson and Eidelson (2003) argue propel groups to conflict including superiority, victimhood and sense of injustice, absence of trust and helplessness. Indeed, there is growing recognition that South Africa is an angry nation that is sitting on a ticking time bomb (The South African Depression and Anxiety Group, n.d.; IOL News 2014; Colpo 2013).

Using a worldview lens, the chapter is organised around the way worldview has shaped identities by promoting equality while introducing new class divisions, entrenching fixed notions of identity based on race and gender, and hardening intergroup boundaries. Despite transitional policies being aimed at promoting equality, which is seen as fundamental to reconciliation and sustainable peace, there have been some unintended consequences in that they have also introduced new forms of inequality and insecurity into the society. With South Africa continuing to be a landscape in a struggle over identity and belonging, the chapter also engages with what the impact of transitional policies on identity means for peace-building and how we think about reconciliation.

7.1 Shifting Identities: The Beginnings of Classism and the Division of 'Black' Identity

One of the most apparent themes to emerge from the research relates to the impact the transitional policies are having on 'black' South Africans. Firstly, reflecting one of the few positive outcomes of these policies, numerous Zulu and Xhosa respondents acknowledged being beneficiaries of BEE policies. For these respondents, this meant that previously unattainable business and employment opportunities had now become accessible. Consequently, these policies were seen as responsible for contributing to the spread of wealth and the growth the 'black' middle class (Glaser 2010; Seekings 2008; Seekings and Nattrass 2005; Vahed and Desai 2010). Although there is no statistical consensus on the extent of this growth (Business Tech 2015) one report indicates that in 2012 51% of adults classified as middle class were 'black' while only 34% were 'white' (Dürr 2013: 26). This is a rapid shift from 2004, which according to the same report, 'black' and 'white' South Africans constituted 32% and 52% respectively. Another study undertaken by the University of Stellenbosch shows that from 1993 until 2012 the 'black' middle class grew from about 350,000 individuals to almost 3 million, which is almost a nine-fold increase over a period of ten years (Business Tech 2015).

Secondly, in contributing to the upward mobility of some 'black' South Africans these policies are also dividing 'black' identity along class lines. They are seen to have facilitated both the development of former 'black' rural areas as well as the movement by 'black' South Africans into previously 'white' suburbs. This partly accounts for why class, and not race, is increasingly used to interpret current social divisions (Glaser 2010; Seekings 2008; Seekings and Nattrass 2005; Mpama 2007; Vahed and Desai 2010). Consequently, there is the perception that the policies are also contributing to the persisting levels of poverty in the country. The extent to which this is true is unclear. However, it is widely agreed the policies account for the persisting levels of inequality in the country (Ramsamy 2007; Seekings and Nattrass 2005; Seekings 2008; Davies 2009).

This leads to a third impact surrounding transitional policies in which they can be seen to be dividing previously disadvantaged groups (i.e. 'black', 'Indian' and 'coloured' groups) who were united under a broad 'black' identity in the struggle against Apartheid. This impact is mostly attributed to BEE policies which draw on the former Apartheid classification system in which South Africans were classified according to their perceived race, i.e. 'black', 'coloured', 'Indian' and 'white' (see Chapter 2). Using this classification system BEE provides graded incentives for trade i.e. employing a 'black' person carries greater benefit than employing a 'white' person, which carries the least incentive. Among 'coloured' participants there was a particularly strong perception that BEE policies were exclusionary and, as a group, they were being re-victimised. Under Apartheid there was a perception that 'coloureds' were seen as not 'white' enough to benefit and now, under BEE, they are not 'black' enough (Erasmus 2001; Hammett 2010; Adhikari 2005). Further to this, they were also seen to reinforce race-based identities (Sect. 7.3 will explore this further).

Finally, supporting the constructivist school of thought, this section points to how identities can shift as the context changes. With the growth of the 'black' middle class, new hybrid identities are emerging as aspects of other cultures are assimilated into their own (see Chapter 2) (Mckinney 2007; Rudwick 2008; Bangeni and Kapp 2007). Speaking to the deeper structures of meaning-making this is evidenced in the way some 'black' South Africans are seeking to encompass both Western and African worldviews as part of their identity. Mmusi Maimane, in his campaign for the DA (Democratic Alliance) leadership, captured this tension well in his speech on what it meant to be an African:

> I am proud to say that I am an individual. I am also proud to say that I am an African. Being an African is part of who I am; it is part of who I choose to be. You can believe in individualism and still have respect for culture and tradition, as long as culture and tradition are never abused to take away the individual rights of others. (Maimane 2014)

A shift in identity among 'black' South Africans was also evidenced in an African National Congress (ANC) election poster outside the University of KZN, Durban campus, which highlights the move towards individualism. The poster depicts a young, trendy woman behind the slogan 'step up for your individuality'. Although during the data collection period campaign posters were posted everywhere, this was the only one of its kind that could be located. In this particular image, the ANC appears to be recognising the value of individualism which is significant as it suggests there is a potential identity shift happening between generations and especially among those with access to university education. However, on other occasions the ANC has shown disdain towards individualist values, such as freedom of speech. It has been seen to hold up a strong hierarchical form of social organisation that speaks to collectivism and an interconnected worldview (see Chapters 5 and 6). Nonetheless, the emphasis this poster gives to individuality indicates a move among students towards Western liberalism. Yet, and in contrast, on the same campuses there are protests articulating the need to assert an African identity (which challenges Western individualism) through the removal of statues from the colonial era. These examples are good illustrations of how worldviews can overlap and social changes can affect identity.

In conclusion, this section shows the tremendous impact transitional policies have had on reshaping 'black' identities. It raises important considerations for transitional justice when thinking about redress for past grievances. While transitional policies have been instrumental in contributing to the growth of the 'black' middle class they have also contributed to new divisions within 'black' identity that reflect a growing class-based society. Therefore, as well as providing the possibility of justice for victims, they have created the space in which new identity struggles are being fought. It also raises the question as to whether class-based divisions are perceived to be more acceptable than race-based divisions in deeply divided societies.

7.2 Equal Opportunities: Unequal and Hardened Intergroup Relations

In addition to transitional policies (especially BEE) contributing to a changing social landscape, they were also seen by the respondents in the study to promote both equality and inequality between race groups and harden intergroup boundaries. Those who perceived the policies to be promoting equality (as there are supposedly intended to do) were mostly 'black' participants. This was experienced through the opportunity for equal employment and appropriate remuneration. Further to this, the equality people were talking about also referred to rebuilding the image of 'black' South Africans as capable and able to engage at the highest level. This is important given that Apartheid was not only about economic exclusion but psychological exclusion, i.e. 'blacks' were perceived as inferior, incompetent and unable to manage and lead. Thus, the policies were seen to challenge such prejudices forcing people to see 'black' South Africans as people who could make a positive contribution to society.

In stark contrast to the positive policy outcomes, they are also seen to have reinforced racial stereotypes, perpetuated racism and hardened intergroup boundaries. Informing many of the negative perceptions that participants held towards the transitional policies was the view that they have caused a drop in the standard of service delivery across the nation. Contributing to this is the belief that it forces businesses to employ people based on race and not their skills set. As already alluded to, it validates a view that 'black' South Africans are incompetent. Observing the impact of these policies facilitates justifying 'white' superiority without being racist. It also validates 'white' identity, which continues to be based on notions of superiority (Steyn 2001; Steyn and Foster 2008; Botha 2009; Verwey and Quayle 2012). By using the perceived impact of these policies to justify pre-existing racist views, it entrenches intergroup boundaries keeping groups polarised.

From a worldview perspective, these perceptions raise a number of analytical challenges. As discussed in previous chapters, the normative response in South Africa is to apply a racial framework when interpreting conflict. However, such interpretations pose a problem as they can perpetuate the cycle of racism. Part of the purpose of this research is to challenge this narrative and inquire whether or not there are deeper hidden values and worldviews contributing to these interpretations. The difficulty with this is some people might argue it is another means of legitimising racism. However, there are several reasons why a worldview analysis is useful here. Firstly, as stereotypes are often the outcome of one culture not understanding the logic or rules of the 'other', it requires interrogating whether the hardening of stereotypes points to competing worldviews. Therefore, the persistent use of stereotypes could point to a lack of understanding of the 'other's' way of being in the world. The following interview excerpt is a good illustration of how competing worldviews might be contributing to hardening of racial stereotypes:

> But there's this mind-set that we can get a grant from the government if we have another child, or if we have someone in the family who is handicapped in some way or another, or if we have a pensioner. So, there's that mind-set that, and I said before that there's this inherent *laziness*. So there's this mind-set of 'let's just get what's coming to us and we don't have to then', *they're not driven*. Our domestic, who we don't have anymore, but she still works for a friend I know, I said to her, 'The guy that does the unemployment is walking around the estate now. I need to register you for unemployment otherwise I'm going to get into trouble'. I said, 'Do you want to be registered for unemployment?' She said, 'No I can't be'. I said, 'But why wouldn't you want to be?' She said, 'No, because I am registered as a pensioner'. And I looked at her and I said to Bernadette,[1] 'You can't be much older than me'. She just laughed. She says, 'No, I'm not but my ID [identity document] book say's I'm a pensioner'. I said, 'No, but then you must go and *have it corrected*.' She said, 'No, no, no. I'm getting a pension grant every month'. So there's this 'I'll take what I can get and I'll help myself that way. *I won't help myself through hard work or diligence*'. So, it's about what I can get. And maybe that comes from a place of 'I'm so desperate,' you know. (Respondent 51, English-speaking white, emphasis mine)

A review of the interview excerpt shows the respondent using words such as 'driven' and 'hardworking' which are indicators of an individualised and future-orientated worldview. The reference to correct the error in the ID book also suggests the respondent is functioning with a rule priority. Significantly, there is also a depiction of the 'other' as lazy and lacking personal responsibility. From a worldview perspective, it could be argued the respondent reaches this conclusion by interpreting the 'other's' actions through her framework of meaning-making. This would

---

[1] Not her real name.

result in a failure to understand the rules that govern the behaviour of the 'other' and points to different ways of being in the world. Without this understanding, and due to the way racism is deeply embedded within the society, it follows that the conclusions the respondent draws will reinforce existing racist stereotypes and reinforce the perception of 'white' superiority. However, what this indicates is a deep lack of understanding of the 'other'. Coupled with the loss of an exclusive, dominant identity and prevailing racist attitudes, this becomes a potent mix for exacerbating intergroup conflict in a multicultural and divided society.

Secondly, the extract also raises the question of the extent to which this interpretation is race-based or class-based. Indeed, one could imagine the same narrative between poor and rich English residents. In this instance, it may be that race and class are operating together. Given that both are rooted in worldview, if it were class based, it would still point to different ways of being in the world. Speaking to a constructivist's definition of identity, this demonstrates how experience and social context influence worldview and is not fixed to race.

Overall, this section shows that transitional policies have contributed to promoting equality and equal opportunities for those who were oppressed under Apartheid. This underscores the value of redress as a structural pillar for building a sustainable peace. However, the impact of the policies on intergroup relations undermines the relational pillars in that they are not seen promote reconciliation and positive intergroup relations. They are even seen to introduce new divisions and exacerbate inequality and exclusion. Using race as a determinant of advantage or disadvantage speaks to a fixed notion of identity that will reinforce a society based on race. It also shows an overgeneralisation of the society, i.e. in as much as there are rich 'blacks' there are also poor 'whites'. In this way, these policies are contributing to a new kind of inequality (*The Economist* 2010). When thinking about transitions in culturally plural societies, it requires consideration of how mechanisms intended to promote peace may also reinforce and restructure news lines of division. It also raises the question of how peace-building and transitional justice interprets equality. Consideration needs to be given to questions such as equality for whom, equality at what cost, and equality for what purposes.

7.3 Fixing of Identities

A third finding emerging from the research relates to the influence transitional policies have had on fixing identities. While these policies are seen to be providing equal opportunities for 'black' South Africans, they are also seen to be contributing to a strong sense of exclusion, rejection, discrimination and marginalisation among other groups. Many participants expressed a sense of losing their value within the society. As a result, the policies are seen to be making the society more race conscious (and racist) despite most people recognising the importance of redressing the inequalities of the past. One of the goals of peace-building and transitional justice is to promote reconciliation and a peace that can be sustained. In South Africa, this encompassed building a multicultural, equal and inclusive society under the rubric of the Rainbow Nation. However, it is antithetical to the nation-building project if the policies that are implemented are causing identities to become fixed and inter-group boundaries to become hardened. This could be interpreted in several ways:

At one level, the experience of rejection and marginalisation could be interpreted as a reaction by 'whites' to the loss of exclusive power and a challenge to their beliefs in superiority. However, at another level, it also relates to one's experience and interpretation of citizenship and belonging. This is reminiscent of the theme 'national unity' that was identified as a requisite for building a sustainable peace in which civic responsibility was expressed differently across groups (see Chapter 6). This theme resonated with an individualised worldview which speaks to an identity and sense of well-being in the world based on personal achievements, the ability to advance and contribute to the future. Bearing in mind that individualism, as a worldview attribute, was particularly strong among 'white' participants (see Chapter 5) suggests that a sense of threat and insecurity at the deepest level of meaning-making could be experienced if the former avenues for expressing these values are removed, e.g. through the loss of exclusive power or opportunities for advancing in one's career. This does not mean that with an alternative worldview one would be more content with exclusion or that one would necessarily see loss differently. Rather, it is about understanding how the loss impacts upon the sense of belonging in the world and the reaction to it. For 'white' South Africans living in a fundamentally changed society requires finding a new way of being in the world. This includes understanding how to relate to the collective while holding an individualist worldview.

Transitional policies were also seen to be shaping the conversation about who can claim to be a South African. There was general consensus among the participants that anybody born in the country is a South African which reveals a civic construction of identity. What is significant for this study is that loyalty to the country emerged as an inclusion criterion for South Africanness. This was mostly expressed by the 'black' and, to a lesser extent, Afrikaans respondents. Other groups did not link South African identity to loyalty to the country in the same way. Nonetheless, the emphasis given to loyalty indicates a more communal formulation of identity. It also points to a collective worldview and a relationship priority in which loyalty as a value is prioritised. This demonstrates an overlap of worldviews between 'black' South Africans and Afrikaners.

This discussion raises the question why 'whites' are critiqued for not embracing their South Africanness as suggested by the former politician and anti-Apartheid activist, Mamphela Ramphele, in her statement: 'White people need to stop thinking of themselves as white and start thinking of themselves as South Africans' (John 2013). Contrary to this assertion, many 'white' respondents did indicate a strong desire and expression of being 'South African' and wanting to be part of the country. This brings into question whether or not Ramphele was interpreting 'white' engagement through the lens of loyalty to the collective. Pointing to a perceived lack of loyalty, her interpretation could also be compounded by the links many English-speaking 'white' South Africans have maintained with their European heritage which gives them the option to emigrate (Lambert 2009; Bornman 2010, 2011; Andrucki 2010). While this contributes to the perception of 'white' privilege, it also raises the question of how groups interpret and experience loyalty. For example, it would be less likely that someone with an individual worldview would express their loyalty by participating in mass rallies than it might be for someone with a collective worldview. It also shows how a specific manifestation of worldview can be linked to the context, i.e. most 'whites' are nationalists and have a strong South African identity at the same time as expressing values relating to individualism. Nonetheless, this tension points to different understandings of the nation, i.e. one that is built on a mechanical construction of community and promotes the individual, and the other that stems from an interconnected worldview, is more organic and speaks to collectivism (see also Chapter 4). A worldview interpretation of nation-building can help promote understanding how different groups experience belonging and, in turn, this can contribute to building positive intergroup relations.

Despite most of the respondents seeking to assert their South African identity they explained how, due to the transitional policies, especially BEE, they felt they had no choice but to categorise themselves based on their 'race'. This is suggested in the following interview extracts:

> You don't run away from the fact that you're Indian or you're white or you're coloured. You can't. (Respondent 37, Indian)

> I am a white South African. That's who I am. That informs you. I don't know that in South Africa we can let go of that yet. It would like letting go of the fact that I'm female. It's who I am. It doesn't make it wrong. (Respondent 5, English-speaking white)

> If you are black you are black, finished and *klaar*.[2] Even the Queen can put a sword on your head, we are still black, it won't change. (Respondent 15, Xhosa)

As indicated by the above respondents, there is a perception that BEE policies and transitional policies, more generally, are 'forcing' people to maintain their race-based identity. In doing so, race-based notions of identity are being fixed and entrenched within the psyche of the society. This is seen to be making South Africans more race conscious and contributing to more rigid intergroup boundaries. In efforts to redress the past, transitional policies in South Africa are, by definition, designed around race-based identities which reflect a primordial interpretation

[2]The Afrikaans word for 'finished'.

of identity in which identity is interpreted as a fixed and unchanging entity (Arthur 2011). This raises an important challenge for societies in transition: how does one employ a constructivist understanding of identity which allows identities to shift, change and develop while still addressing the inequalities of the past. Can a society become more inclusive and move beyond its historical lines of division if its policies are built on primordial interpretations of identity? This is an important consideration for post-conflict societies such as Northern Ireland whose policies aimed at promoting reconciliation and an inclusive society continue to use the language of two fixed communities, i.e. Catholic and Protestant (Office of the First Minister and Deputy First Minister 2013). Consideration also needs to be given to the extent to which contradictions in how, for example, belonging is experienced arises from the failure to understand and share in a joint worldview. Should culturally diverse societies create an expectation of merging worldviews?

7.4 Gendered Identities

The fourth influence transitional policies have had on identity relates to their influence on shaping gendered identities. This suggests transitional policies may be contributing to a greater awareness of gender in the society, as has been found in other research (see Hamber et al. 2006). Interestingly, the majority of respondents who referred to their gender were women suggesting that women are perhaps more conscious than men of their gender identity. For women, this was usually included in their primary self-definition and referred to in positive terms. For previously disadvantaged groups, the transitional policies were seen to have a positive impact on opening spaces and creating equal opportunities for women. As one respondent noted, it has opened an industry to her which was previously associated with males. From the perspective of human rights and gender equality, this is a positive outcome.

However, this has not been without a perceived cost. The view among many of the male respondents, especially 'white' males, was that gender-based transitional policies resulted in the loss of job opportunities. In contrast to women, on the occasions men referred to their gender identity it was usually in the context of felt exclusion and hardship. This suggests transitional policies not only challenge race-based power relations but also gender-based power relations which may exacerbate a sense of exclusion and marginalisation. If this is true, then it may strengthen the belief that one is a victim, which Eidelson and Eidelson (2003) argue is integral to intergroup conflict. It would also partly account for why 'whites' are perceived by others to be the most resistant to these policies.

Notwithstanding the positive outcomes these policies have had on gender equality, among several respondents there was a view that they have placed an unwanted financial burden on women for the upkeep of the family and home. As a result, these policies are seen to have destabilised masculine identities. It has also has contributed to a perception across the race groups in South Africa that these policies are causing increased violence against women and illustrates some of the kickback against women and the new forms of insecurity these policies, aimed at equality, are seen to have introduced (Hamber et al. 2006; Hamber 2010).

Given the focus of this book, how gender is interpreted in the context of human rights compared to an African traditional system needs consideration. The new spaces that transitional policies are opening for women speak to a lateral form of social organisation. This can present new challenges as illustrated by the following respondent working in a hierarchical society:

> I think people within the church, they take their own cultural background and they come with it in the church. Even when it comes to minor things like greeting in my culture, my Zulu culture, being a minister, a female, young, most times you are not greeted. For instance, when you stand and greet the people and observe all the protocols; we greet the fathers, ministers, the fathers, already what are you? (Respondent 17, Zulu)

In this example, the respondent is explaining that in her profession she is not given the same recognition as the men and those who are older than her are given. This is denoted by the phrase 'already what are you?'

Not only does this illustrate how worldviews within a group can shift, given that the respondent locates herself within the culture she is critiquing, but it also raises the question of how authority is interpreted. For example, while equality policies may have opened the space for Lindiwe Mazibuko to act as DA parliamentary leader, her authority in Parliament was undermined based on her age and gender by those with a hierarchical form of social organisation (see Chapter 5). Jacob Zuma's polygamous marriages also exemplify the challenge that worldview can present as it stands in opposition to the human rights dialogue and an individualised understanding of gender equality.

Further illustrating the challenges different systems of meaning-making present on promoting gender equality is the surprising support by the ANC Women's League (ANCWL) for Jacob Zuma during the legal trial in which he was accused of raping a woman (*Sowetan Live* 2007). From a Western liberal and human rights perspective, one would assume the ANCWL would have condemned the behaviour that led to such an accusation. However, as discussed in Chapter 6, this requires understanding the influence of worldview in how the women's group interpreted their response to the situation. While transitions need to do more to address the security concerns of women (Hamber et al. 2006), they also need to engage with how gender is interpreted in culturally diverse societies.

7.5 The Influence of Transitional Policies on Identity and Intergroup Relations

This chapter examined how transitional policies impact on identity and intergroup relations. As a means of redressing the past, they were instrumental in promoting equality and challenging power relations across race, class and gender lines. By creating opportunities for formerly oppressed groups to participate in the economic and political life of the country, they are also forcing 'whites' who were more open to these policies to see the value and skills that 'blacks' can contribute. Consequently, transitional policies are seen to be contributing to both an economic equality and a psychological equality among South Africans. This is important as it speaks to the need for cultural equality 'black' South Africans see as necessary for building sustainable peace (see Chapter 6).

Responsible for a growing 'black' middle class alongside persisting levels of poverty, transitional policies have also introduced new forms of inequality and insecurity into the society leading to the emergence of new hybrid identities as Western liberal attributes, such as individualism, are incorporated into an African identity (Durrheim et al. 2011; Mpama 2007; Seekings 2008). This suggests that worldviews between generations are shifting. It also highlights the relationship between context and worldview, and the influence transitions in culturally plural societies can have on shaping identities. It also brings into question whether there is a hierarchy of inequality within peace-building theory as new forms of inequality such as classism appear to be more acceptable than racism and sexism.

This analysis also suggests that transitional policies are entrenching fixed notions of identity based on race. This is due to the policies being designed around a primordial and fixed interpretation of identity which acts to confirm long-held stereotypes of the 'other'. Consequently, perceptions of 'white' privilege and superiority and inherent 'black' inferiority and incompetence are maintained (Steyn and Foster 2008; Verwey and Quayle 2012). Indeed, inequality between 'black' and 'white' South Africans continues to persist. However, while 'white' identity continues to be rooted in a sense of superiority and entitlement that supports racism, a worldview that prioritises material success is also a driving factor (Andrucki 2010). This does not suggest that other groups do not strive to achieve. Rather, viewed through a racial framework it reinforces race-based interpretations when there are deeper contributory values.

A race-based interpretative framework also contributes to the perpetuation of negative stereotypes integral to maintaining intergroup boundaries—as theorised in Social Identity Theory (Tajfel and Turner 1986; Ashmore et al. 2001). Using a worldview framework was useful for understanding the deeper hidden values that were at play and for understanding the way some people reacted to these policies. Indeed, different systems of meaning-making functioning within the same space can result in a failure to the grasp the worldview of others. Together with the findings of Chapters 5 and 6, this raises the question as to whether or not people have an expectation that others understand or even adopt their worldview. Perhaps transitions and the goal of sustainable peace create this expectation.

These policies, in conjunction with fixed notions of identity, have also had a part to play in intergroup conflict. While some studies have suggested that intergroup relations and attitudes were generally improving (Bornman 2011; Durrheim et al. 2011; Gibson and Claassen 2010; Schlemmer 2001) this research shows there are significant challenges that remain. The findings show transitional measures implemented to promote equality do not necessarily result in positive intergroup relations and a more peaceful society as most participants who expressed a strong sense of marginalisation and exclusion largely attributed this to exclusion from the benefits of BEE policies (see also Bornman 2011; Horowitz 1991). Significantly, this was also true for migrants who argued that the policies were largely to blame for the xenophobia directed towards them (Misgun 2007; Rogerson 1997; Reilly 2001). Indeed, a primordial interpretation of identity, which these policies are build on, is associated with racism and xenophobia.

In seeking to address the past, these policies have had significant implications on identity formation to which transitional justice must pay attention. While transitional policies have contributed positively to the reshaping of society, they have also been counterproductive to the goals of sustainable peace at an intergroup level. South Africa continues to be a landscape in a struggle over identity and belonging. Despite the desire of most respondents wanting to be identified as South African, 'race' continues to be a marker of identity (Seekings and Nattrass 2005; Seekings 2008; Isaacs-Martin 2012; Ansell 2004). This chapter demonstrates the need for a deeper and more complex understanding of identity and culture to accompany the implementation of transitional policies in multicultural and deeply divided societies, i.e. peace-building and transitional interventions need to be culturally attuned (Merry 2006; Kelsall 2009; Sriram 2007; Krog 2008, 2015).

References

Adhikari, Mohamed. 2005. *Not white enough, not black enough: Racial identity in the South African coloured community*. Cape Town: Double Storey Books.

Andrucki, Max J. 2010. The visa whiteness machine: Transnational motility in post-Apartheid South Africa. *Ethnicities* 10 (3): 358–370.

Ansell, Amy. 2004. Two nations of discourse: Mapping racial ideologies in post-Apartheid South Africa. *Politikon* 31 (1): 3–26.

Arthur, Paige. 2011. *Identities in transition: Challenges for transitional justice in divided societies*. New York: Cambridge University Press.

Ashmore, Richard D., Lee Jussim, and David Wilder. 2001. *Social identity, intergroup conflict, and conflict reduction*. New York: Oxford University Press.

Bangeni, Bongi, and Rochelle Kapp. 2007. Shifting language attitudes in a linguistically diverse learning environment in South Africa. *Journal of Multilingual and Multicultural Development* 28 (4): 253–269.

Bornman, Elirea. 2010. Emerging patterns of social identification in post-Apartheid South Africa. *Journal of Social Issues* 66 (2): 237–254.

Bornman, Elirea. 2011. Patterns of intergroup attitudes in South Africa after 1994. *International Journal of Intercultural Relations* 35: 729–748.

Botha, Liz Johanson. 2009. 'Them and us': Constructions of identity in the life history of a trilingual white South African. *African Identities* 7 (4): 463–476.

Business Tech. 2015. How big is South Africa's black middle class? *Business Tech*, August 4. http://businesstech.co.za/news/wealth/94987/how-big-is-south-africas-black-middle-class/. Accessed 5 September 2018.

Colpo, Rienzo. 2013. Is South Africa 'really an angry nation'? *News24*, March 26. http://www.news24.com/MyNews24/Is-South-Africa-Really-an-Angry-Nation-20130326. Accessed 5 September 2018.

Davies, Rebecca. 2009. *Afrikaners in the new South Africa: Identity politics in a globalised economy*. London: I.B. Tauris.

Dürr, Benjamin. 2013. A toast to South Africa's black middle class. *Africa Renewal Online*, December. http://www.un.org/africarenewal/magazine/december-2013/toast-south-africas-black-middle-class. Accessed 5 September 2018.

Durrheim, Kevin, Colin Tredoux, Don Foster, and John Dixon. 2011. Historical trends in South African race attitudes. *South African Journal of Psychology* 41 (3): 263–278.

Durrheim, Kevin, John Dixon, Colin Tredoux, Liberty Eaton, Michael Quayle, and Beverley Clack. 2011. Predicting support for racial transformation policies:

Intergroup threat, racial prejudice, sense of group entitlement and strength of identification. *European Journal of Social Psychology* 41 (12-08): 23–41.

Eidelson, Roy J., and Judy Eidelson. 2003. Dangerous ideas: Five beliefs that propel groups toward conflict. *American Psychologist* 58 (3): 182–192.

Erasmus, Zimitri. 2001. *Coloured by history, shaped by place: New perspectives on coloured identities in Cape Town*. Cape Town: Kwela Books.

Gibson, James L., and Christopher Claassen. 2010. Racial reconciliation in South Africa: Interracial contact and changes over time. *Journal of Social Issues* 66 (2): 255–272.

Glaser, Daryl. 2010. Class as a normative category: Egalitarian reasons to take it seriously (with a South African case study). *Politics and Society* 38: 287–309.

Hamber, Brandon. 2010. Masculinity and transition: Crisis or confusion in South Africa. *Journal of Peacebuilding and Development* 5 (3): 75–88.

Hamber, Brandon, Paddy Hillyard, Amy Maguire, Monica McWilliams, Gillian Robinson, and David Russell. 2006. Discourses in transition: Re-imagining women's security. *International Relations* 20 (4): 487–502.

Hammett, Daniel. 2010. Ongoing contestations: The use of racial signifiers in post-Apartheid South Africa. *Social Identities* 16 (2): 247–260.

Horowitz, Donald L. 1991. *A democratic South Africa? Constitutional engineering in a divided society, perspectives on southern Africa*. Berkeley: University of California Press.

IOL News. 2014. We are a broken nation—Lapsley. *IOL News*, August 15. http://www.iol.co.za/news/south-africa/gauteng/we-are-a-broken-nation-lapsley-1.1736065#.VnGis9KLTcs. Accessed 4 September 2018.

Isaacs-Martin, Wendy. 2012. National identity and distinctiveness: Developing a common identity in a nation state (with reference to South Africa). *Africa Insight* 42 (2): 169–170.

Jeffery, Anthea. 2014. *BEE: Helping or hurting?* Cape Town: Tafelberg Publishers.

John, Victoria. 2013. Agang SA's Ramphele: White people, be more active citizens. *Mail & Guardian Online*, October 2013. http://mg.co.za/article/2013-10-31-agang-sas-ramphele-white-people-be-more-active-citizens. Accessed 6 September 2018.

Kelsall, Tim. 2009. *Culture under cross-examination: International justice and the special court for Sierra Leone*. New York: Cambridge University Press.

Krog, Antjie. 2008. '…if it means he gets his humanity back…': The worldview underpinning the South African Truth and Reconciliation Commission. *Journal of Multicultural Discourses* 3 (3): 204–220.

Krog, Antjie. 2015. Research into reconciliation and forgiveness at the South African Truth and Reconciliation Commission and Homi Bhabha's architecture of the new. *Canadian Journal of Law and Society* 30 (2): 203–217.

Lambert, John. 2009. 'An unknown people': Reconstructing British South African identity. *The Journal of Imperial and Commonwealth History* 37 (4): 599–617.

Maimane, Musi. 2014. On being African. *Twitter*, May 3. https://twitter.com/MmusiMaimane. Accessed 17 December 2015.

McKinney, Carolyn. 2007. 'If I speak English, does it make me less black anyway?': Race and English in South African desegregated schools. *English Academy Review* 24 (2): 6–24.

Merry, Sally Engle. 2006. *Human rights and gender violence: Translating international law into local justice*. Chicago and London: University of Chicago Press.

Misgun, Biniam. 2007. Foreign migrants in the inner city of Durban. In *Undressing Durban: Beyond the tourist gaze*, ed. Rob Pattman and Sultan Khan, 92–100. Durban: Madiba Publishers.

Mpama, Sibusiso. 2007. Black solidarity and black divisions. In *Undressing Durban: Behind the tourist glaze*, ed. Rob Pattman and Sultan Khan, 332–333. Durban: Madiba Publishers.

Office of the First Minister and Deputy First Minister. 2013. *Together: Building a United Community*. https://www.executiveoffice-ni.gov.uk/sites/default/files/publications/ofmdfm_dev/together-building-a-united-community-strategy.pdf. Accessed 6 September 2018.

Ramsamy, Edward. 2007. Between non-racialism and multiculturalism: Indian identity and nation building in South Africa. *Tijdschrift Voor Economische en Sociale Geografie* 98 (4): 468–481.

Reilly, Janet E. 2001. Nation building and the construction of identity: Xenophobia in South Africa. *Refuge* 19 (6): 4–11.

Rogerson, C. 1997. *International migration, immigrant entrepreneurs and South Africa's small enterprise economy*. Cape Town: Institute for Democracy in South Africa.

Rudwick, Stephanie. 2008. 'Coconuts' and 'oreos': English-speaking Zulu people in a South African township. *World Englishers* 27 (1): 101–116.

Schlemmer, Lawrence. 2001. *Race relations and racism in everyday life*. Johannesburg: Institute for Race Relations.

Seekings, Jeremy. 2008. The continuing saliency of race: Discrimination and diversity in South Africa. *Journal of Contemporary African Studies* 26 (1): 1–25.

Seekings, Jeremy, and Nicoli Nattrass. 2005. *Class, race and inequality in South Africa*. New Haven, NJ: Yale University Press.

Southall, Roger. 2007. Ten propositions about black economic empowerment in South Africa. *Review of African Political Economy* 34 (111): 67–84.

Sowetan Live. 2007. Why ANC women's league backed Zuma. *Sowetan Live*, November 28. http://www.sowetanlive.co.za/sowetan/archive/2007/11/28/why-anc-women_s-league-backed-zuma. Accessed 25 February 2016.

Sriram, Chandra Lekha. 2007. Justice as peace? liberal peacebuilding and strategies of transitional justice. *Global Society* 21 (4): 579–591.

Steyn, Melissa. 2001. *'Whiteness just isn't what it used to be': White identity in a changing South Africa*. Albany, NY: State University of New York Press.

Steyn, Melissa, and Don Foster. 2008. Repertoires for talking white: Resistant whiteness in post-Apartheid South Africa. *Ethnic and Racial Studies* 31 (1): 25–51.

Tajfel, Henri, and John C. Turner. 1986. The social identity theory of intergroup behaviour. In *Psychology of intergroup relations*, ed. Stephen Worchel and William G. Austin, 33–48. Chicago: Nelson-Hall.

The Economist. 2010. A new kind of inequality: Black economic empowerment has had unintended consequences. *The Economist*, June 3. http://www.economist.com/node/16248651. Accessed 6 September 2018.

The South African Depression and Anxiety Group. n.d. Why are South Africans so angry? http://www.sadag.org/index.php?option=com_content&view=article&id=585:why-are-south-africans-so-angry&catid=78&Itemid=161. Accessed 4 September 2018.

Vahed, Goolam, and Ashwin Desai. 2010. Identity and belonging in post-Apartheid South Africa: The case of Indian South Africans. *Journal of Social Science* 25 (1–3): 1–12.

Verwey, Cornel, and Michael Quayle. 2012. Whiteness, racism, and Afrikaner identity in post-Apartheid South Africa. *African Affairs* 111 (445): 551–575.

8

Contributions and Recommendations: A Worldview Perspective for Peace-Building and Reconciliation in South Africa and Beyond

In 2015, there was an outbreak of xenophobic violence in South Africa (Wicks 2015; Haffejee 2015; BBC News 2015). This started when the Zulu king, King Goodwill Zwelithini, in a public speech, allegedly blamed 'black' migrants for many of the country's social ills and called for their removal from the country (Letsoalo 2015). In response to this Max du Preez, a 'white' South African author and public commentator, criticised the King for his remarks and called for him to 'face the consequences of his actions' as he was 'not above the law or the constitution' (du Preez 2015). However, this was strongly rebutted by Edward Zuma, the son of the former President Jacob Zuma, who accused him of being racist and 'disrespecting the Zulu king and our culture'; a reflection of the importance attached to the role of elder (Khoza 2015).

It is fascinating to consider these two positions from a worldview perspective. Zuma and du Preez's remarks illustrate the significance of competing worldviews, i.e. a relationship priority compared to a rule priority and a collectivist approach set against individualism, on building a sustainable peace. By arguing that action should be taken against the King for breaching the law and the Constitution through incitement to violence du Preez appears to be invoking a rule-based priority

C. Bollaert, *Reconciliation and Building a Sustainable Peace*,
Palgrave Studies in Compromise after Conflict,
https://doi.org/10.1007/978-3-030-03655-3_8

to support his position. The value he places on the King's personal responsibility for his speech also suggests he is approaching this matter from an individualistic perspective. Within this worldview, expressing open and direct condemnation of a King, also an elder, for inciting violence would be seen by Western individualists as not only acceptable and legitimate but also as crucial to condemning violence and the violation of human rights. However, in doing so, he is perceived by African collectivists to be attacking the core of Zulu identity and, with South Africa's history, the cry of racism is quick to follow. Was du Preez being racist or was he simply being true to his worldview, as communicated through his values?

In contrast to du Preez, Zuma's response centres on defending the honour and respect of the King and Zulu culture which draws on social rules of collectivism and a relationship priority. Being reminded that in a collectivist culture a threat to the head of the collective is effectively a threat to its survival and that of the identity of each individual within it, it follows the honour of the King must be vehemently protected. In all probability, Zuma's reaction is exacerbated by South Africa's Apartheid past and the current struggle for identity in the society. This interpretation would also account, in part, for the violent threats directed to the Durban Branch of the South African Human Rights Commission as a result of its investigation into the Zulu King's words (City Press 2015). It also asks the question as to whether Zuma was using du Preez's challenge as a smokescreen to defend the King and his incitement to violence or, like du Preez, was acting within his cultural rules and worldview.

One of the consequences of the exchange between du Preez and Zuma is that it moves the issue from one of accountability and protection of human rights to one about racism. Bearing in mind South Africa's history of Apartheid, a race-based interpretation of the issue stands to reason but is insufficient as it leaves the debate in a deadlock. Interpreting it from a worldview perspective provides insight into the values and identity each party is defending. However, the difficulty with this approach is it could be seen to undermine human rights in South Africa. Significantly, this illustrates the challenges surrounding the intersection between identity, culture, worldview and building a sustainable peace.

8.1 Contributions and Recommendations to Peace-Building Theory and Practice

Recognising that approaches to reconciliation need to be considered in conjunction with other factors such as histories of oppression, power and persisting poverty and inequality, this book has shone a spotlight on the issue of worldview as an under theorised area of study in relation to building a peace that can be sustained. Although several scholars recognise the relevance of different systems of rationality in peace-building and transitional justice, the field as a whole has not. Thanks to an interrogation of worldview, the analysis in this book raises important considerations for peace-building approaches that engage with Western and non-Western ontological assumptions and systems of meaning-making.

Firstly, the ontology peace-building theory is built on, which is largely underpinned by a Western liberal worldview, needs to be considered. This suggests peace-building theory speaks to objectivist ontology based on a scientific worldview; the result of the Enlightenment which separated the physical and spiritual realms of reasoning (see Chapters 3 and 4). Central to this system of meaning-making is the question 'what', 'how' and 'why' which seeks to find the 'scientific' causes behind, for example, poverty, conflict and conflict escalation. Consequently, peace-building interventions tend to address the structural pillars of building a sustainable peace, such as institutional reform, the rule of law, the need for accountability, the promotion of human rights and socio-economic transformation. In the context of the Truth and Reconciliation Commission (TRC), the study found that approaching it from a Western worldview contributed to many of the criticisms (and misunderstandings) levelled at it, including how the process interpreted concepts such as reconciliation, nation-building, forgiveness and accountability.

In contrast to the 'what-how-why' approach taken by objectivists is the interpretative question of motive and 'who' is behind the causes of hardship and suffering within an interconnected worldview (see Chapter 4). For example, for with an interconnected worldview, Apartheid was interpreted as an evil that needed to be exorcised from the land (Tutu 2008). By failing to engage and develop a theory of peace-building around the question of 'who', Ashforth (2005) argues the TRC failed to receive full confessions from the perpetrators of violence during Apartheid and uncover the source of evil (which remains hidden and powerful) and which is seen to account for the persisting mistrust, suspicion and inequality between groups.

The importance of competing ontologies is seen in the events surrounding the 'Rhodes Must Fall' campaign. The campaign called for the removal of the statue of Cecil John Rhodes, a symbol of British colonialism, at the University of Cape Town (Boroughs 2015). It would be easy to interpret this call by students to reorder the country's symbolic landscape as a means of asserting an African identity and of addressing the legacy of racism (Rhodes Must Fall, n.d.; Schutte 2015). While this holds true, a worldview approach raises the question as to whether or not this movement was also a means of exorcising the evil in the country. It requires asking if the removal of this statue is about removing the symbolic representation of the colonialists' ancestors? Is the statue an affront to the ancestors of the various 'black' groups or a link that 'whites' have with their forbearers that might be perceived to provide the strength that permits them to maintain their hegemony? Is the removal of the statue perceived as reducing the strength of 'whites' in the past and present? If so, these are understandings that are not communicated but are essential to recognise for building a peace that can be sustained. Nonetheless, it provides further evidence surrounding the importance of a worldview approach in peace-building and the need to contextualise interventions.

The question of ontological differences also suggests further comparative research is required for understanding how they shape core concepts in peace-building and transitional justice. For example, how are reconciliation, nation-building and accountability interpreted from a Western liberal perspective compared to an interconnected perspective? How are these notions prioritised, if at all, across groups? How do competing interpretations influence the goal of reconciliation and building a sustainable peace in societies emerging from conflict? Particular consideration needs to be given to how worldview impacts on protecting human rights in societies that may not share the same value system as those underpinning the human rights discourse dominant in Western societies. While it is important for peace-building and transitional justice to protect victims of gross human rights violations, it also needs to consider how its approach impacts on the identity and dignity of victims who may hold different worldviews and prioritise different values. The importance of this is illustrated in the breakdown in relationship between the International Criminal Court (ICC) and the African Union (AU) which is seeking immunity for African heads of state and which resulted in the failure of South Africa to arrest al-Bashir, the president of Sudan who was wanted by the ICC for crimes against humanity.

Secondly, the worldview model developed in this book requires the interrogation of the values underpinning transitional policies. Do transitional policies speak to individualist societies with values that tend to prioritise the structural pillars of sustainable peace? If so, what are the implications for how transitional policies are implemented in collective societies which have different forms of social organisation and may prioritise different values? Does this account, at least in part, for some of the challenges and frustrations experienced across the groups relating to these policies? For example, while people's experience of Apartheid could certainly be seen to inform how transitional policies were interpreted, the research found that this was also informed by values such as individualism and achievement. These values are not inherently racist but when coupled with South Africa's Apartheid past and prevailing attitudes of superiority among 'white' South African people's reaction to the policies can be perceived as racist, when in fact there is more at play. Similarly, the way in which access to land ownership is interpreted is central to the current controversy surrounding land redistribution and land ownership in South Africa. Indeed, the research uncovered different notions of land ownership which, in the context of an unequal past, contributed to hardening intergroup relations. The worldview model developed in this book raises the question as to the extent to which intergroup relations assume that the deeper processes of meaning-making across groups are shared and understood by the 'other' or that one's worldview must be adopted by others. Therefore, approaching intergroup relations from a worldview perspective is essential for understanding the hidden transcripts that shape societies. This requires thinking about the historical context of each group, the worldview its culture and symbolic landscape communicates, and the values that are prioritised.

Thirdly, peace-building and transitional justice tend to focus on political and economic transformation. However, the worldview model presented in this book raises the question of cultural transformation and whether or not this is something that needs to be addressed within peace-building theory. The challenge with this question is it raises the issue of cultural relativism. Does promoting cultural equality promote cultural relativism? If so, does this risk condoning the abuse of human rights in non-Western societies, as suggested in the above example with King Zwelithini? However, cultural equality does not mean condoning the abuse of human rights. Rather, it means engaging with the 'other' and addressing human rights in a language that speaks to the cultural values of the society and practice in question. For example, one could argue that former President Thabo Mbeki's strategy of 'quiet diplomacy', which received severe criticism, was a culturally appropriate mechanism for addressing the political turmoil that was taking place in Zimbabwe at the time (Adelmann 2004). By engaging him 'quietly', Mbeki was affording Mugabe culturally appropriate forms of respect necessary for any potential positive outcome towards ending the political violence in Zimbabwe. Furthermore, this book shows that by failing to treat cultures equally, issues such as accountability in the protection of human rights can quickly move to an issue of racism. This is also exemplified in the case of al-Bashir (and the failure by South Africa to arrest him) and how the ICC in Africa is perceived as a neo-colonial construct. Consequently, if peace-building and transitional justice can inculcate worldview and cultural equality into its theory and practice, it will contribute to promoting the dignity of victims and those functioning outside the Western liberal worldview which is integral to the human rights agenda. Nonetheless, when considering the dynamics of post-conflict transformation, the importance of promoting cultural transformation in conjunction with political and economic transformation needs to be considered.

Fourthly, the way in which transitional policies in this study were seen to impact intergroup relations raises several issues for peace-building and transitional justice theory. In many instances, the policies contributed to hardening of intergroup boundaries and entrenched fixed notions of identity. This was partly due to the way the policies are based on fixed notions of identity. Furthermore, the study found that transitional policies were also influential in shaping new identities. It found that as the context changes and as people interact with others with systems of meaning-making different to their own, worldviews can change, fuse, compete and contradict each other. While this makes it difficult to research and write about identities in a way that contributes to the theory and practice of the discipline without essentialising identities, it makes the task even more vital. It also underscores the chasm that exists between policymaking (which tends to draw on fixed notions of identity) and academic thought (which tries to promote constructivist interpretations of identity). This highlights the need for further research on the complexities surrounding identities and the schools of thought peace-building policies are built on.

Recognising the importance of worldview in building a sustainable peace, there is a need to develop cultural or worldview principles for dealing with the past (as gender specialists in transitional justice have begun to do) (see Legacy Gender Integration Group 2015). Principles could include the need to value and incorporate cultural expertise and the need to be inclusive of different cultural perspectives. They would need to accommodate the complexity of identities and try to understand how worldviews shape political and social processes. While there is growing sensitivity surrounding identity and culture, I am suggesting there is a need to go deeper still to understand the hidden transcripts shaping societies.

To inculcate worldview principles into peace-building practice would require people who can act as what Docherty (2001) refers to as 'worldview translators'. As has been shown, the need for understanding the deeper process of meaning-making and how this is communicated through culture is crucial to building positive intergroup relations and a peace that can be sustained. However, this requires practitioners to have a good understanding of their own worldview and that of others, which most people do not have. Furthermore, it requires challenging the reticence to engage in a discussion surrounding the issues of culture and race for fear of appearing racist or xenophobic. This is partly due to the move towards political correctness and way culture has been historically abused to justify colonialism and other forms of oppression. However, it underscores the challenge of political correctness in researching divided societies and engaging with sensitive issues in a way that does not prevent research on crucial issues being carried out or compromise its rigour. Nonetheless, worldview translators can assist with understanding how key concepts in peace-building are interpreted across groups. This is a particularly important consideration if a hybrid model for peace-building that functions at the intersection of Western liberal and indigenous, grassroots approaches to peace-building is to be developed.

8.2 Competing Worldviews Beyond South Africa

If a worldview approach to peace-building and transitional justice can make a difference in South Africa, and if proper attention is paid to the historical context of a society, it can enhance the possibility of making a difference in other divided societies. It requires asking if the seemingly intractable nature of conflict in societies such as Israel/Palestine, Northern Ireland and Colombia, and the growth of violent extremism is a massive failure to contextualise peace-building? Indeed, the last-minute inclusion of the 'Ethnic Chapter' in the Colombian peace-agreement recognised the importance of acknowledging and engaging with different systems of meaning-making for implementing a peace that can be sustained (Sánchez-Garzoli 2017). Moreover, there is increasing recognition among international relations experts of the need for a deeper understanding of culture to mitigate security concerns European and other Western societies are currently facing (Nicholson 2015). This requires asking if the right questions are being asked in these situations?

In thinking about Northern Ireland, a worldview approach could be useful for addressing the ongoing challenges surrounding its fragile peace. Central to this is the Constitutional question (the elephant in the room) of whether to remain in the UK or be united with the Republic of Ireland, which has been forced into the open through

Brexit. A worldview approach requires asking whether the two opposing nationalisms and understandings of community are interpreted in the same way across the Protestant-Unionist-Loyalist and Catholic-Nationalist-Republican divide. Given that Unionism is traditionally rooted in Protestantism, which speaks to an individualist worldview, and Republicanism is traditionally rooted in Catholicism, which supports a more collective worldview, suggests a worldview analysis could be useful for finding solutions to a seemingly intractable conflict (despite the presence of a relative peace). The conflict between the communities is now taking the form over the meaning of particular cultural symbols such as the displaying of flags, murals and memorials (Bryan 2000, 2006; Bryan and Stevenson 2009; Bryan and Connolly 2009). A worldview analysis could also be useful for understanding the system of meaning-making underlying these symbols that continues to keep the society polarised. Such an analysis can also be extended to uncover the hidden transcripts and sacred values expressed through political slogans, such as 'for God and for Ulster' and 'our day will come', and the sectarian theologies that act as the powerhouse driving and giving justification to the conflict (see also Liechty and Clegg 2000). Within this context, a worldview analysis can be used to challenge the intolerance between groups at the deepest level of meaning-making which is further complicated with the arrival of new migrants which Morrow (2016) argues has challenged historical narratives of tolerance relating to sectarianism to include a wider intolerance of 'otherness'.

While not dismissing the complexity of the political, social, historical and economic factors that converge in the Israeli/Palestinian conflict, a worldview analysis could be useful to uncover the worldviews and belief systems that justify the conflict. In protracted conflicts such as this, normative solutions based on Western liberal approaches alone may be inadequate. It requires uncovering the sacred values that are often rooted in religion and inextricably intertwined with people's identity which is integral to a society's desire and ability to survive (Clark 1989; Docherty 2001; Atran 2010). This requires asking what sacred symbols and values are being defended within Judaism, Zionism and Islam and which provide the impetus for violence? It also requires exploring how the value that is attached to land is interpreted and whether there are competing worldviews contributing to the way in which access to land is violently disputed.

A worldview model requires asking if different systems of meaning-making are contributing to the growth of (in)security in Europe. Can it help in understanding the seemingly incomprehensible behaviour of suicide bombers? For example, the consequences of competing worldviews can be seen in the lethal violence that ensued following the printing of cartoons depicting the Prophet Mohammed by the French magazine, Charlie Hebdo. From one perspective, the cartoons are perceived as providing legitimate political commentary and can be defended within the right to the freedom of speech, a key value within Western democracies. For others, the cartoons were interpreted as deeply offensive and disrespectful of the Islamic community which, as ISIS declared, needed to be avenged. This illustrates how competing worldviews (one that is rooted in a Western, secular worldview which values the freedom of speech; and one that is rooted in a religion in which the honour of the group is prioritised) can contribute to lethal violence.

The increase in violent extremism has led to the burgeoning field of combatting violent extremism (CVE). A recent consultation relating to this discourse recognises CVE is rooted and supported by Western states (Peace Direct 2017). If this is the case, it raises the question as to the extent CVE employs approaches rooted a Western way of being in the world? Unless, these approaches resonate with non-Western ways of being in the world they carry the risk of exacerbating the problem. Moreover, if they are built on fixed understandings of identity, they carry the risk of fuelling racism and, in the case of ISIS and other extremist Islamic groups, Islamophobia. In seeking to prevent violent extremism, it is also important to consider the need for identity and belonging; people need their identities (integral to worldview) to be acknowledged. The significance of this is echoed in the call by 'black' South Africans for cultural equality and respect. Further to this, the rise of Islamic extremism underscores the influence of religion in conflict. Indeed, conflicts such as those in Northern Ireland, Israel/Palestine, Nigeria and Sri Lanka all have a religious dimension to them. A worldview model can help provide a deeper understanding of how this influences conflict and in finding more culturally relevant and sustainable solutions.

The centrality of culture and worldview is also evident in the growing sense of insecurity and intergroup conflict between local and migrant communities in Europe. In France, the 'burkini' (a symbol of religious conviction) was seen as a threat to secularism which resulted in efforts to have it banned from being worn on public beaches. In Switzerland, the refusal of Muslim school boys to shake the hand of female teachers due to their cultural and religious beliefs was seen as an affront to Swiss culture, in which shaking the hand of one's teachers is a cultural norm and a sign of mutual respect. This has resulted in the potential for monetary fines to be imposed on those who fail to do so. The significance of culture is also echoed in the voices of immigrants in Europe whose lack of understanding of European social rules has led them to fear talking in public spaces and integrating into local society. In efforts to mitigate growing intergroup tensions, the approach Switzerland has taken is to encourage migrant groups 'to show greater awareness of the practices of the Swiss life and everyday rules' (Lettau 2015: 10). In other words, the Swiss government has recognised that different ways of being in the world carry with them different cultural rules which are contributing to intergroup conflict and which need to be understood.

Further to this, the attacks on women in Cologne, Germany, were seen as challenging a Western cultural understanding of gender equality (Breedon 2016). This is fuelling tensions between refugees, who are mostly Muslim, and the European host societies who perceive their values for freedom and gender equality are being infringed (*The Economist* 2016). Recognising the impact of culture, the mayor of Cologne responded by saying: 'We will explain our Carnival much better to people who come from other cultures so there won't be any confusion about what constitutes celebratory behaviour in Cologne, which has nothing to do with a sexual frankness' (Eddy 2016). Significantly, this statement acknowledges the consequences of competing systems of meaning-making and the need for a deeper understanding of cultural rules (which are informed by worldview). Moreover, the Cologne incident speaks to a broader issue about how the role of women in society is perceived across different cultures. Significantly, there is growing recognition among practitioners about how competing worldviews lie at the heart of interventions aimed at promoting the rights of women in society (Baumann 2018).

This book has shown that a failure to understand the values and worldview of the 'other' contributed to the fixing of race-based identities, the hardening of intergroup boundaries, and the perceived growth in racism and xenophobia in South Africa. The growth in right-wing politics (and extremism) in Europe and the USA with its accompanying hostility towards migrants suggests that similar dynamics may be at play. The arrival of new communities and new forms of 'otherness' can present a perceived threat to American and European values which could account for the rise in intolerance and the hate of 'otherness', the rise in anti-immigration policies, racist ideologies and the growth in violent extremism. This could also partly account for the failure of many European societies to respond to their moral and humanitarian obligations surrounding the migration crisis. A failure to understand the worldview of the 'other' could also be contributing to new forms of nationalism which is exemplified by Britain's decision to regain its sovereignty by leaving the European Union.

8.3 Conclusion

The worldview model developed in this book is captured in the words of the novelist Anaïs Nin (1961) 'We don't see things as they are; we see them as we are'. To build a peace that can be sustained, societies in transition will have to find ways of accommodating different belief systems. Acknowledging one's way of being in the world is fundamental to a person's sense of dignity, which conflict and histories of oppression seek to strip away, and, therefore, to promoting healing among victims and formerly oppressed groups. To foster reconciliation requires engaging with how Western liberal values which largely underpin current approaches to peace-building can be translated into societies with fundamentally different systems of meaning-making. It also requires asking to what extent peace-building assumes that the deeper processes of meaning-making across groups are shared and understood by the 'other'. All this moves beyond what Huntington calls 'a clash of civilisations' (Huntington 1993, 1996), a theory which has been critiqued for overgeneralising rendering societies as culturally homogenous (Sen 1999; Said 2001; Fox 2005).

I am talking about something much deeper and more profound; about the essence of meaning-making and its impact on peace and reconciliation.

References

Adelmann, Martin. 2004. Quiet diplomacy: The reasons behind Mbeki's Zimbabwe policy. *Africa Spectrum* 39 (2): 249–276.

Ashforth, Adam. 2005. *Witchcraft, violence, and democracy in South Africa*. Chicago: The University of Chicago Press.

Atran, Scott. 2010. *Talking to the enemy: Violent extremism, sacred values, and what it means to be human*. Great Britain: Allen Lane; USA: HarperCollins.

Baumann, Jonas. 2018. Reflection by practitioners: Worldview conflicts about the role of women in society: Dilemmas for Third Parties. *Center for Security Studies*, July 25.

BBC News. 2015. Xenophobic violence: South Africa's identity crisis. *BBC*, May 7. http://www.bbc.co.uk/news/world-africa-32580807. Accessed 6 September 2018.

Boroughs, Don. 2015. Why South African students say the statue of Rhodes must fall. *National Public Radio*, March 28. http://www.npr.org/sections/goatsandsoda/2015/03/28/395608605/why-south-african-students-say-the-statue-of-rhodes-must-fall. Accessed 30 August 2018.

Breedon, Jennifer R. 2016. Culture clash: When violence against women is accepted, lawful and expected. *Huffington Post*, February 8. http://www.huffingtonpost.com/jennifer-r-breedon/culture-clash-when-violen_b_11234168.html. Accessed 6 September 2018.

Bryan, Dominic. 2000. *Orange Parades: The politics of ritual, tradition and control*. London: Pluto Press.

Bryan, Dominic. 2006. The anthropology of ritual: Monitoring and stewarding demonstrations in Northern Ireland. *Anthropology in Action* 13 (1–2): 22–31.

Bryan, Dominic, and Clifford Stevenson. 2009. Struggles over symbolic landscape and the new Northern Ireland. In *Culture and belonging in divided societies: Contestation and symbolic landscapes*, ed. Marc Howard Ross, 68–84. Philadelphia: University of Philadelphia Press.

Bryan, Dominic, and Sean Connolly. 2009. Identity, social action and public space: Defining civic space in Belfast. In *Theorizing identities and social action*, ed. Margaret Wetherell, 220–237. Basingstoke: Palgrave Macmillan.

City Press. 2015. Xenophobic thugs: 'We'll burn you alive'. *News24*, April 26. http://m.news24.com/news24/SouthAfrica/News/Xenophobic-thugs-Well-burn-you-alive-20150426. Accessed 6 September 2018.

Clark, Mary E. 1989. *Ariandne's thread: The search for new modes of thinking*. Hampshire and London: Macmillan.

Docherty, Jayne Seminare. 2001. *Learning lessons from Waco: When the parties bring their gods to the negotiation table*. Syracuse: Syracuse University Press.

du Preez, Max. 2015. Zwelithini should face the consequences. *News24*, April 21. http://www.news24.com/Columnists/MaxduPreez/Zwelithini-should-face-the-consequences-of-his-actions-20150421. Accessed 6 September 2018.

Eddy, Melissa. 2016. Reports of attacks on women in Germany heighten tension over migrants. *The New York Times*, January 5. https://www.nytimes.com/2016/01/06/world/europe/coordinated-attacks-on-women-in-cologne-were-unprecedented-germany-says.html. Accessed 6 September 2018.

Fox, Jonathan. 2005. Paradigm lost: Huntington's unfulfilled clash of civilizations prediction into the 21st century. *International Politics* 42: 428–457.

Haffejee, Ihsaan. 2015. Xenophobia in South Africa. *Al Jazeera*, May 3. http://www.aljazeera.com/indepth/inpictures/2015/05/xenophobia-south-africa-150501090636029.html. Accessed 6 September 2018.

Huntington, Samuel P. 1993. The clash of civilizations. *Foreign Affairs* 72 (3): 22–49.

Huntington, Samuel P. 1996. *The clash of civilizations and the remaking of world order*. New York, London, Toronto, and Sydney: Simon & Schuster Paperbacks.

Khoza, Amanda. 2015. Zuma's son hits back at Max du Preez. *News24*, April 24. http://m.news24.com/news24/SouthAfrica/News/Zumas-son-hits-back-at-Max-Du-Preez-20150424. Accessed 6 September 2018.

Legacy Gender Integration Group. 2015. *Gender principles for dealing with the legacy of the past*. Belfast: Legacy Gender Integration Group.

Letsoalo, Matuma. 2015. King Zwelithini blames 'third force' for violence. *Mail & Guardian Online*, April 21. http://mg.co.za/article/2015-04-21-king-zwelithini-blames-third-force-for-violence. Accessed 6 September 2018.

Lettau, M. 2015. A look at the major issue of integration. *Swiss Review* 3: 8–11.

Liechty, Joseph, and Cecelia Clegg. 2000. *Moving beyond sectarianism: Religion, conflict and reconciliation in Northern Ireland*. Dublin: Columba Press.

Morrow, Duncan. 2016. Acknowledging religious and cultural diversity in an antagonistic society: The challenge of Northern Ireland. In *Tolerance and diversity in Ireland, North and South*, ed. Iseult Honohan and Nathalie Rougier, 211–231. Manchester: Manchester University Press.

Nicholson, Craig. 2015. Decline in cultural research undermines security, says report. *Research Professional*, May 21.

Nin, Anaïs. 1961. *Seduction of the minotaur*. Chicago, IL: The Swallow Press.

Peace Direct. 2017. Peacebuilding and violent extremism: Key insights and lessons from a global consultation convened by Peace Direct. https://www.peacedirect.org/wp-content/uploads/2017/09/Peacebuilding-low-res.pdf. Accessed 6 September 2018.

Said, Edward W. 2001. The clash of ignorance. *The Nation*, October 4. http://www.thenation.com/article/clash-ignorance/. Accessed 6 September 2018.

Sánchez-Garzoli, Gimena. 2017. Colombia's peace implementation will only succeed with an ethnic perspective. *WOLA*, August 18. https://www.wola.org/analysis/colombias-peace-implementation-will-succeed-ethnic-perspective/. Accessed 3 September 2018.

Schutte, Gillian. 2015. White privilege carved in stone. *Sunday Independent*, March 29. https://www.iol.co.za/sundayindependent/white-privilege-carved-in-stone-1838405. Last accessed 19 November 2018.

Sen, Amartya. 1999. Democracy as a universal value. *Journal of Democracy* 10 (3): 3–17.

The Economist. 2016. Migrant men and European women. *The Economist*, January 16. http://www.economist.com/news/leaders/21688397-absorb-newcomers-peacefully-europe-must-insist-they-respect-values-such-tolerance-and. Accessed 6 September 2018.

Tutu, Desmond. 2008. *Interview in: Truth, justice, memory: South Africa's truth and reconciliation process*. Cape Town: Institute of Justice and Reconciliation.

Wicks, Jeff. 2015. Several dead as xenophobic violence boils over in Durban. *Mail & Guardian Online*, April 14. http://mg.co.za/article/2015-04-14-several-dead-as-xenophobic-violence-boils-over-in-durban. Accessed 23 August 2018.

Index

C. Bollaert, *Reconciliation and Building a Sustainable Peace*, Palgrave Studies in Compromise after Conflict, https://doi.org/10.1007/978-3-030-03655-3

The manufacturer's authorised representative in the EU is Springer Nature Customer Service Centre GmbH, Europaplatz 3, 69115 Heidelberg, Germany. If you have any concerns regarding our products, please contact ProductSafety@springernature.com

Printed and bound by CPI Group (UK) Ltd, Croydon, CR0 4YY
30/09/2026
02225442-0007